HALLS OF JADE   WALLS OF STONE

STACEY PECK

HALLS OF JADE, WALLS OF STONE

WOMEN IN CHINA TODAY

Franklin Watts 1985 *New York Toronto*

A GROLIER COMPANY

ALL PHOTOGRAPHS BY BUFF AARON
(except photographs of Xia Juhua
and of Talitha Gerlach)

Library of Congress Cataloging in Publication Data

Main entry under title:

Halls of jade, walls of stone.

Bibliography: p.
Includes index.
1. Women—China—Bibliography—Addresses, essays,
lectures.   2. China—Bibliography—Addresses, essays,
lectures.   3. China—Social life and customs—
1976–   —Addresses, essays, lectures.
4. Peck, Stacey.   I. Peck, Stacey.
CT3710.H34   1985   920.72'0951 [B]   85-3268
ISBN 0-531-09790-0

CONTENTS

Like most writers on contemporary China,
I have used the modern pinyin system of
romanizing Chinese proper names and places.
The older Wade-Giles romanization system
has been retained for names such as Peking,
Mao Tse-tung, and Chou En-lai, which were
familiar to Westerners long before the new
system was adopted. The pronunciation of
almost all words can be determined phonetically
by English-speakers, except for letters such as
x, pronounced approximately like *sh* (as in *shade*);
c, like *ts* (as in *its*); q, like *ch* (as in *chair*);
and *zh*, like *j* (as in *jam*).

ACKNOWLEDGMENTS

I would like to express my gratitude to all
the people who helped make this book possible:

The people of the *Guangming Daily*—
Deputy Editor-in-Chief Lu Zhun, Foreign Affairs
Director Zhang Qiliang, and reporter Ding Ke
—for their kindness, patience, and great efforts
in arranging the interviews. Also the
representatives of China's provincial newspapers
for their cooperation and warm hospitality.

The people whose advice and support made my
China journey possible—Sidney Rittenberg,
Mme. Sylvia Wu, Beverly Polokoff, Linda Mathews,
Harry Bernstein, Dr. Bernice Ennis, Sue Fan,
Lucy Hirata Chen, Dr. Otto Schnep, Mme. Xie Heng,
Wang Ji-kong, and Kang Keqing.

To Roby Eunson, who transcribed most of the
interviews with great accuracy and constant
words of encouragement, and who is herself the
author of two books on China, special thanks.
Also thanks to Tan Shih Ying, the young woman
who patiently audited all of the interview tapes
to ensure their accuracy; and to my editor,
Ellen Joseph, for her invaluable assistance.

And, of course, thanks and best wishes to the
government of the People's Republic of China, and
to all the Chinese and Western women who gave
their time, warmth, and hospitality. Without them
this book could not have been written.

To my husband Jim,
the source

HALLS OF JADE   WALLS OF STONE

They are admirable, infuriating,
humorous, priggish, modest, overweaning,
mendacious, loyal, mercenary, ethereal,
sadistic, and tender.
They are quite unlike anybody else.
They are the Chinese.

David Bonavia
The Chinese

INTRODUCTION

When I conceived the idea of this book, I began to read everything I could find on contemporary China—newspapers, magazine articles, and books. Except for scholarly works, most of these materials were either personal accounts published in China and written by Westerners whose interest was accompanied by an ideological commitment to the Chinese regime, or by correspondents whose assignments had included the China beat.

The former were invariably uncritical of life in their adopted country; their reports were glowing, to say the least. Most of the correspondents, on the other hand, painted a picture so bleak as to make the reader question whether anything at all had been done to benefit the Chinese people since the Communists took control in 1949. Since reality seldom fits nicely into such self-assured and uncompromising descriptions, I decided to suspend judgment and see for myself. This book is the result.

The People's Republic of China is a communist totalitarian state. Most of the freedoms guaranteed Americans under our Constitution and, indeed, many of those guaranteed the Chinese under their own Constitution, simply do not exist there. Further, as I discovered long before I left home, the surly monsters of bureaucracy and xenophobia stalk the land of dragons. It took eight months of letter writing, phoning, and pleading for recommendations from people considered influential with the People's Republic of China before my request to visit was approved. Bureaucracy aside, I am convinced the delay can be attributed partially to the very real Chinese paranoia about "unfriendly" American writers.

To some extent this paranoia is understandable. Political scientist Peter Van Ness, in his article "The Mosher Affair" (*The Wilson Quarterly*, New Year's, 1984), describes "an American compulsion to paint China in either black or white colors." Discussing the controversial case of Steven W. Mosher, a graduate student who was expelled from Stanford University's anthropology department for engaging in "illegal and seriously unethical conduct while in the People's Republic of China," Van Ness labels Mosher's subsequent book, *Broken Earth: The Rural Chinese*, as "another in the current 'China stinks' genre of books by Americans who have recently lived and worked in China. His bias is transparent." Van Ness continues, "Everything is wrong and nothing is right in the People's Republic."

The same charge might be leveled against such books as *From the Center of the Earth*, by Richard Bernstein, China correspondent for *Time*, and *China: Alive in the Bitter Sea*, by Fox Butterfield, first Peking bureau chief of *The New York Times*. Both present highly literate and fascinating accounts of their experiences in China, but both also paint an almost totally "black" picture.

The best available statistics show that the Chinese are much better off economically than they were before the Communists took power in 1949; that the wealth of the country is much more equitably distributed; that by 1979 the average life expectancy in China had risen from thirty-five to sixty-four years (well above the average of sixty-one reported in most developed countries, according to the World Health Organization); and that with the passage of the 1950 Marriage Law, Chinese women moved almost overnight from the status of mere chattels to one of near equality with men. The truth, it seems, is often a rather unsensational shade of gray.

On October 7, 1983, my photographer, Buff Aaron, and I boarded a CAAC (Civil Aviation Administration of China) flight from Hong Kong to Peking. Since it is literally impossible for a writer to travel in the People's Republic of China without official sponsorship, we were fortunate that the *Guangming* (Enlightenment) *Daily*, a prestigious national newspaper with bureaus in major cities throughout the world, was assigned as our host. *Guangming's* staff arranged our itinerary, accommodations, transportation, interpreter, and—working from lengthy lists and descriptions I had sent them well in advance—the interviews with Chinese women that were the object of the journey. We paid a prearranged price for the entire trip and were thus blessedly relieved of the confusing and wearisome details of the strange, two-tiered (native vs. foreign) monetary system.

That first flight on China's national airline, from Hong Kong to Peking, included an incident both hilarious and revealing. Only a half-hour into our scheduled four-hour flight, we found ourselves making a surprise landing at a city we later learned was Hangzhou. The flight attendants spoke no English, but a Chinese-American couple seated near us clued us in: Two pieces of luggage had been put aboard by mistake and were to be returned to Hong Kong. Instead of waiting for our first scheduled stop, the pilot landed at the first opportunity. We waited an hour while the plane's entire cargo of luggage was unloaded on the steaming tarmac. Then it was our turn; every passenger disembarked and selected his or her luggage from the huge pile, thereby creating a new one. With this lengthy but undeniably logical process completed, we and our luggage were reloaded and the flight, two hours late by then, continued. The vagrant bags presumably went back to their rightful owners.

I learned a valuable lesson: Don't attempt to apply Western logic to Chinese.

Over the next two months, traveling with our female interpreter, Zhao Yaqing, I interviewed some forty-five women in eleven cities and villages of this incredibly large and crowded country.

China is the oldest civilization in the world, with a recorded history spanning more than 3,700 years. Ravaged by natural disaster and disease, raped by invaders, oppressed by its own elite, it has not only survived, it is more powerful today, and more crucial in its global importance than at any time in its past. It would be both absurd and arrogant to pretend that I understand China's *half-billion* women. The "women of China" comprise at least fifty-five distinct and disparate nationalities. Their languages, their life-styles, their cultural glosses, their prejudices, their goals, and even their physiognomies differ to degrees that stretch credibility. But they all have one important thing in common—their lives, and the lives of their children, are being drastically changed by the policies of Peking.

The tiers of government in China—national, provincial (state), municipal, and district—are very similar to those in the United States, with one very important difference. Each district is further divided into neighborhoods with neighborhood committees. Usually composed of eight to ten retired workers appointed by the district government and paid small salaries, these committee members provide important welfare services such as caring for the sick, organizing activities for the aged and nursery schools, funding small, cooperative businesses for the unemployed, and mediating disputes within and among families. But they also provide a means by which government surveillance can be extended into the lives of every individual in a nation with a population over one billion.

Authoritarian governments are not famous for their eagerness to expose their failures to foreign eyes. The People's Republic is no exception. The women I interviewed made very few negative statements about life under the current Deng Xiaoping regime. In general I found that their willingness to be even mildly critical was in direct proportion to their rank, and I am sure that many personal convictions were left unspoken for fear of retribution. Although token "opposition" parties are maintained (for cosmetic reasons, I assume), dissent, as we know it, is nonexistent. Yet much of what these women *did* say has the hard ring of truth.

Two other groups of interviews are included: Western women who have given up lives of comparative luxury to live in China and devote themselves to the "new China," and Chinese women who are now living in the United States and thus, presumably, have no fears about expressing their opinions about life in the People's Republic of China. (One of the latter requested anonymity, and in her case I used a pseudonym.)

I recorded all the interviews as they took place. After returning home I had them all audited by a Chinese woman who has no ties to the People's Republic of China. She found a few minor errors, evidently due to misunderstanding rather than any attempt at censorship, as well as a number of "party-line" phrases added to the answers by the interpreter, presumably for their propaganda value.

Because almost all Chinese women today are workers, and because the Chinese are very reticent about discussing their personal lives, the chapters have been divided by areas of occupation. Almost everyone suffered to some extent during the ten years (roughly 1965–1976) of the Cultural Revolution. Many had their schooling or work interrupted for three to ten years, when they were sent to the countryside to do farm labor. Others were imprisoned and beaten; many had relatives who committed suicide or were murdered. Yet I found only one woman, now living in the United States, who was obviously bitter about those years and spoke in detail about the terrible tortures she and her family endured. The attitudes of the other women I spoke to, both in China and the United States, seemed to be that although those were terrible years, it was best to forget them and to go on.

The significant number of books now available in every Chinese bookstore on the excesses of the Cultural Revolution, and the reports in newspapers and magazines on current Communist Party efforts to punish those who perpetrated those excesses, make it evident that public discussion is now permitted. Part of the explanation for the reluctance to do so is the Chinese characteristic of privacy concerning personal matters—and also a fear that new repressions may occur, bringing harsh ex-post-facto punishment for statements made in the past.

Another possible reason may be the centuries-old teaching of Confucius that one should accept one's lot in life without complaint. Perhaps that also helps explain the ability of the world's oldest civilization to endure.

Here they are, then, the women of China. I make no attempt to disguise my admiration and affection for them, nor my deep respect for what they have been able to accomplish.

CHAPTER

COMING
INTO
THE
TWENTIETH
CENTURY

*Women are indeed human beings,
but they are of a lower state
than men and can never attain to
full equality with them.*

Confucius
(Fifth Century B.C.)

There is no doubt that for thousands of years the women of China were the most repressed segment of a predominantly repressed and exploited society. Treated as possessions, first by their own families and then by their husbands' families, throughout most of China's history they suffered under a moral code promulgated by Confucius. In essence, he described a virtuous woman as compliant, humble, and submissive; her role was to serve others.

Women were believed to possess inferior intellects. They were sold as prostitutes, concubines, servants, and child-brides, and in times of economic hardship female infanticide was common. The crippling and painful practice of footbinding, considered a sign of gentility and beauty, was widespread. Suicide at the death of a fiancé or husband, though not mandatory, met with approval. Women had no right to select their own marriage partners, no right to divorce, and no right to own property. What amounted to an obsession with the protection of women's chastity resulted in their being almost totally confined within the home and segregated from all contact with men except for their husbands. In the compounds of the wealthy, women had their own apartments; in poorer homes they cleaned, cooked, and served but did not sit with males. Thus, under the guise of being protected, women were virtually enslaved.

The first challenge to this ideology occurred after the 1840 Opium War, when the Ching dynasty (China's last) failed to repel the British in their effort to obtain commercial access to China. Under the ensuing peace treaty, several trade ports were opened to Western nations, bringing in American and European residents. Missionaries in particular were horrified by Chinese attitudes toward women and, in an attempt to remedy the situation, began to open schools for girls. The first was established in Shanghai in 1849, and over the next few years others were opened in Canton, Fuzhou, Tianjin, and Peking. But they were largely unsuccessful because of strong opposition from Chinese families. Their few pupils were mainly foundlings, beggar girls taken from the streets, and daughters of the very poor, whose families were enticed by bribes of cash and free food and clothing.

The women's liberation movement in China began in earnest at the end of the nineteenth century. By then many intellectuals had lost confidence in the old institutions and viewed their country as a backward and decaying nation. With the goal of restoring China's old greatness and bringing it into the modern age, they began to study Western political and social philosophies, and realized that women were an undeveloped resource. Anti-footbinding societies were established in major cities, and by 1902 they had received the sanction of the Empress Dowager, who instituted a system of fines to be levied against anyone practicing the custom. During that same period, education for girls became more acceptable among the wealthier families, and mission schools finally began to flourish.

A BEGINNING IN
THE SCHOOLS

In 1897 the first Chinese school for girls was established in Shanghai under the sponsorship of wealthy merchants, government officials, and intellectuals. Others soon followed in Shanghai, as well as in other cities, but the students' families approved of women's liberation only in terms of literacy and unbound feet. The teachers, however, were women, and because many of them opposed all repressive practices and attitudes against women, female students were encouraged to rebel against many of the old strictures and to seek to become doctors, teachers, nurses, and other professionals.

The status of women had begun to change by the end of the nineteenth century, but only among the urban elite who were influenced by Western attitudes. Educated women began to enter new political groups and professions in which roles had not yet been defined by gender. Thus, although the entire women's movement before the 1911 Revolution was elitist, it was the first challenge to Confucian doctrines.

Because the women's movement in China has closely paralleled political events, it is useful to present the progression in women's status against a background of major political changes from 1911 on.

In her book *Feminism and Socialism in China*, Elisabeth Croll describes how "each national crisis precipitated a wave of patriotic activity among women. . . . An issue which aroused strong national interest was the smoking of opium which, introduced into China by foreign powers, was not unnaturally a nationalist issue. Numbers of mass meetings for women were held to discuss this subject and various petitions in opposition to the practice were circulated. . . . There were no separate women's political organizations but women joined revolutionary societies such as the Society for the Revival of China, the Restoration League and the China Revival League which later merged into the Revolutionary Alliance associated with Sun Yat-sen. . . . Women played a limited but conspicuous role in the events of 1911 to overthrow the Manchu [Ching] dynasty. They went to the front as nurses, conveyed messages and smuggled arms and ammunition and some even donned military uniforms and organized themselves into small fighting companies. . . ."

From the 1911 Revolution on, the country was in a state of turmoil and disunity, with a series of corrupt central government leaders and warlords in control of various areas. But once the republic was established, women again became primarily interested only in feminist issues such as the right to vote and representation at the national and provisional assemblies. They formed suffragette societies, wrote newspaper and magazine articles, and mounted demonstrations, but their numbers were still small and confined to the intellectual and wealthy classes: women who had the education and personal funds that enabled them to be independent of their families.

On May 4, 1919, thousands of students marched through the streets of Peking protesting the decision of the major world powers to sign a treaty at Versailles that supported the demands of the Japanese to continue the occupation of Shandong province, and also to have a major voice in Chinese government affairs. Student demonstrations spread throughout the nation, and merchants and consumers joined in a boycott of Japanese goods. The result was the dismissal of pro-Japanese officials from government and the refusal of China to sign the Versailles treaty.

The May Fourth movement marked the beginning of modern Chinese nationalism. For the first time the entire country had been unified by a common cause.

HIS—BUT NOT HERS

But the women's movement was at a standstill. Women were still not allowed to vote and were, for the most part, regarded as inferior. Some occupied themselves with social reforms like improved housing and working conditions for women in factories. Others searched for alternative political action groups, and many of those joined the recently formed Chinese Communist Party. The CCP rejected not only Western imperialism but existing social structures as well, and from its beginnings committed itself to equal rights for women.

A women's section was established in 1923 to work independently in the revolutionary movement, and that same year the Kuomintang (KMT), under the leadership of Sun Yat-sen, allied itself with the new Communist Party under the banner of the Nationalist Party. Both agreed that the priority was to achieve national unity and independence. At the First National Party Congress in 1924, a manifesto was issued: "In law, in commerce, in education and in society, the principle of equality between the sexes shall be recognized." Two women, one of whom was Sun Yat-sen's wife, Soong Ching-ling, became members of the KMT Central Executive Committee.

As the KMT took on a more radical hue through its alliance with the CCP, Chiang Kai-shek, one of Sun's most trusted lieutenants, was directing officer training at the Whampoa Military Academy—established with Soviet money in 1924 near Canton. The academy attracted young men from all over the country, who saw in Chiang—though he was rapidly moving toward the right politically—the embodiment of Sun's ideas to liberate China from the warlords and unify the country under democratic ideals. They developed an almost blind loyalty to Chiang, and the academy soon became the center of anti-Communist influence within the KMT.

Women from the CCP and KMT worked together for revolution and women's equality. They organized a school where recruits were trained in propaganda techniques and sent to other districts to teach women about their rights and to urge them to organize into unions. March 8 was declared Women's Day, in observance of the emancipation of women.

In July 1925 Chiang and his Whampoa cadets, with significant help from peasants organized by the Communists, succeeded in smashing the ruling government in southeast China and establishing the Nationalist government in Canton. But the death of Sun in March of that year accelerated the deterioration of KMT-CCP cooperation and marked the beginning of Chiang's spectacular rise to power. Communist activity among the workers and peasants was alarming to the rightist elements of the KMT; they feared a buildup of Communist strength. Rather than break with the CCP, however, Chiang agreed to maintain peace if they would help him launch his Northern Expedition to destroy the power of the warlords and to unify central and north China under the Nationalist flag.

The successful march of Chiang's armies from Canton to the central valley of the Yangtze River in 1926 was greatly aided by the newly organized workers and peasants. Female propaganda teams, trained by the Communists, traveled with the armies and in their wake, educating workers and peasants on the objectives of the Nationalist movement. They also organized women into unions to promote equality.

OFF WITH
BOBBED HEADS

In 1927 Chiang decided to destroy the CCP and almost succeeded. One result of the purge was that the women's department of the KMT was closed down, and the network of women's unions throughout the country was labeled Red and disbanded. Anyone suspected of being a Communist, especially women with bobbed hair (the telltale sign to KMT soldiers), was arrested and often tortured and executed. Thousands of men and women activists died during the bloodbath, which lasted until 1930.

With the country more unified and a strong central government established in Nanking, the foreign powers recognized the KMT under Chiang as the legitimate government of China. In 1928, still under pressure to fulfill its promise to emancipate women, the new government issued an order providing for the free choice of husbands, the right to divorce, the right to inherit property, the right to monogamy, and the right to equal pay for equal work. Men, however, retained the right to rule the household. But because there was very little attempt to publicize and enforce the law, especially among the illiterate, few women were aware of their rights.

Mayling, Chiang's wife and a sister of Soong Ching-ling, also set about establishing a women's movement, but its emphasis was again on domesticity. Called the New Life Movement, it urged women to stay at home and tend to their husbands and children. It even supported legislation guaranteeing husbands the right to demand that wives be dismissed if their jobs interfered with domestic tranquility. Thus, whatever other political implications one may read into the ideological battle between Chiang's Nationalist Party and Mao's Communist Party, the issue of women's rights was by that time clearly defined at least in terms of stated policy. The KMT's policy was husband, children, and home; the CCP's was full equality.

Mme. Chiang traveled throughout the nation to spread the gospel of her New Life Movement, urging women to form new chapters and teach the virtues of home life and helping others. Young girls were trained (somewhat like American Girl Scouts) to help strangers on the street, and to go into homes and teach the principles of frugality, orderliness, and cleanliness. Very little, however, was taught about the new laws concerning women's rights. In 1928 there was even a movement to end coeducational schools, on the premise that the flirtatious behavior of girl students was hindering boys in their studies. But the return-to-the-home movement had little effect on educated women who had already tasted the heady wine of independence, and their numbers increased considerably in the major cities.

DO AS I SAY

Mme. Chiang's position—essentially that a woman's place is in the home—was rather ironic in light of her own considerable political involvement. During the KMT war with the Communists and later with the Japanese, she traveled throughout the world enlisting support for the Nationalist cause and eventually even assumed command of China's air force, an unprecedented position for a woman.

In 1931 the Japanese again invaded China, and the failure of the government to repel them, combined with high unemployment and inflation, created another period of crisis. Chiang, more concerned with his obsession to eliminate the CCP than with the nation's problems, pursued the Communists with his armies until they were driven into the mountains and then out of south China entirely. In 1931, at the first All China Congress of Soviets in Juichin, the young peasant revolutionary Mao Tsetung was elected chairman of the Soviet Republic, and the now-legendary general Chu Teh was confirmed as commander in chief of the First Red Army.

From 1930 to 1933 the KMT launched four different offensives against the Communists. Finally, with a half-million troops and the aid of American air power, the Nationalists succeeded in encircling the Juichin Communist area, cutting off supplies to the Red Army.

At the end of 1934, after a year of resistance, the Communist forces broke through the blockade and began their historic Long March. It took a year, and of the 90,000 men and fifty women who set out on that 6,000-mile journey through some of the most rugged terrain in China, only 20,000 reached their destination—Yenan, in the north, the last remaining Soviet haven. Joining the few other surviving Communist units there, they consolidated their position, increasing their strength by recruiting the peasant populations in the surrounding areas. Despite its policy providing for a separate women's movement, the CCP delayed implementing that goal for the next three years in favor of the wider revolutionary movement.

By 1937 the areas under Communist control (generally referred to as the liberated areas) had increased considerably, and thousands of peasants, including women, had been recruited to their cause. During a period of relative stability, women leaders, with the full support of the party, set about creating a new women's movement, but this time its backbone was peasant women rather than the city elite. The movement was slow because of the difficulty in overcoming traditions that had been inculcated for thousands of years among both men and women. But slowly, by living with the peasants and helping them with their household and farm chores, the CCP women were able to ingratiate themselves and finally win their confidence. Gradually, women were persuaded to gather together in the evenings and talk about their lives. In "speak bitterness" meetings, many recounted humiliations and degrading experiences they had suffered, and eventually some became convinced that the only way to change and improve their situation was by organizing women's associations, the forerunners of today's All China Women's Federation.

Still occupied with war against the KMT and the Japanese, the Communist government in the liberated areas did not institute any land-reform policies. Instead, it alleviated economic hardship somewhat by reducing rents. Women's reforms were also limited to taking part in farm production, the war effort, and political activities. Classes, held by the women's associations, taught women plowing, spinning and weaving skills in the belief that participation in production was vital to their social and economic emancipation.

IN WAR, EQUALITY

In the war effort, many women served as guerrilla fighters; others joined the Red Army women's militia and engaged in combat; some became spies; and thousands worked behind the lines, nursing the wounded, making clothing and shoes for army personnel, and supplying food.

During those years, the Japanese continued to occupy large areas of China, mainly through diplomatic treaties with Chiang. When they attempted to take Shanghai, however, they met surprising resistance from a coalition of students, merchants, and the Nationalist 19th Route Army, whose leader, despite Chiang's disapproval, held the city for thirty-four days. The Japanese bombing of civilians and regular use of prisoners for bayonet practice unleashed such powerful hatred that Chiang was forced to send reinforcements. But an even stronger Japanese troop buildup finally resulted in a humiliating Chinese surrender.

Despite the continued Japanese inroads and mounting pressure from the population to organize a united front against the invaders, Chiang continued to devote most of his resources to wiping out the Communists. In December 1936 he flew to Xian to find out why his generals were not launching an offensive against the Soviet-held areas. The result was the famous Xian Incident. Chiang was held prisoner for fourteen days by his own officers while they attempted to convince him to abandon his anti-Communist crusade and instead form an alliance with them to fight the Japanese. Chou En-lai, a former colleague of Chiang's at Whampoa, flew to Xian to add his entreaties. But Chiang remained unconvinced until his wife arrived, and it was made clear that he would not leave Xian alive unless he agreed. He signed a document pledging to recognize the CCP army and their control of the liberated areas, and to unite with them in the war against Japan.

WORLD AT WAR

In 1937 the Nationalist government formally declared war on Japan. Shortly after, Chiang signed a nonaggression pact with Russia, resulting in Russia's commitment of the equivalent of $250 million plus air power to the KMT. The United States and Britain remained apathetic until 1939, when World War II began. Then, acknowledging the Japanese threat, they too extended help.

The Eighth Red Army, lead by Chu Teh, fought the Japanese in the north, and the New Fourth Army, under Mao, fought them in central China's Yangtze River valley. Using the guerrilla tactics developed by Mao years before in his battles against the KMT, both armies fought successfully while Chiang diluted his war efforts by fighting two enemies, the Japanese and the Communists.

As historian George Mosely points out, "while continuing to stand on the defensive vis-à-vis the Japanese, he now tried to neutralize Yenan and paralyze its military operations by means of a blockade. Meanwhile such war matériel as the Soviet Union and the United States would send him was husbanded for the civil war which Chiang knew would follow Japan's defeat by the Allies."

By October 1938 the Japanese had occupied north China, the Yangtze River valley, Peking, Tianjin, Canton, and all major ports along the east coast, thereby effectively blockading supplies to China. When Nanking was taken, the Nationalist capital was moved to Hankow (Hangzhou) and when that city fell, it was established in Chungking (Chongqing).

That same year, however, through the almost superhuman efforts of a million Chinese workers using only their hands and primitive tools, the Burma Road was completed. A back door was opened and supplies began arriving from the southwest. Then, in 1940, the Japanese succeeded in blocking all land routes including the Burma Road, leaving China's only contact with the rest of the world by air, over the "Hump" (the mountains) from India.

After war against Japan was officially declared, Mme. Chiang organized the women of her New Life Movement into two separate groups, the Women's Association for War Relief and the Association for Care and Education of War Orphans. The first raised funds and provided clothing and medical supplies to the army. The second established orphanages for the children of war casualties. The thousands of women mobilized for the war effort also served as drivers, nurses, and propagandists.

THE SMOKE CLEARS

In 1945, with the defeat of the Japanese and the end of World War II, the Red armies were a force of one million and the Communist-controlled areas had increased to include some 100 million people.

Chiang and his Nationalists, on the other hand, had suffered a decline in power, and despite the continued support of the United States, they never regained their hold on China. At the end of World War II, the Nationalist government was bankrupt and Chiang, by then allied with the most reactionary elements of his party, had lost most of his popular support. His government was crippled by corruption, inflation was soaring, and the peasant population, mobilized by the Communists, seemed determined never again to return to the old order. Chiang's police-terror tactics again resulted in student demonstrations throughout the country, and by the time the KMT fled from the mainland to Taiwan in 1949, its support from all classes—merchant, intellectual, working, and peasant—was virtually gone.

On October 1, 1949, Mao Tse-tung climbed the stairs to a high podium erected in Peking's beautiful Tiananmen Square and proclaimed the establishment of the People's Republic of China. Just a few months later, on May 1, 1950, the new Marriage Law was enacted. Legally, at least, it gave the women of China equal rights with men.

The opening principles state: "The feudal marriage system based on arbitrary and compulsory arrangements and the supremacy of man over woman, and in disregard of the interests of the children, is abolished.

"The New-Democratic marriage system, which is based on the free choice of partners, on monogamy, on equal rights for both sexes, and on the protection of the lawful interests of women and children, is put into effect."

The Marriage Law guaranteed women the right to divorce, to child support, to inherit property, to equal status in the home and at the workplace, and to use their own surnames.

It prohibited bigamy, concubinage, the interference of fam-

ilies and exchange of money in connection with marriage, infanticide, and discrimination against children born out of wed-
lock. In short, the new Marriage Law codifed equal rights and
protection for women and children, and for the first time, a
government program to implement the law was created.

This task was delegated to the new All China Women's
Federation, established at the First National Women's Congress
held in April 1949, shortly before the liberation. It became the
national umbrella for the network of local women's organizations that had proliferated in the liberated areas and already
claimed a membership of seven million. There still remained
the enormous task of educating and organizing millions more,
especially in the southern and central areas that had been controlled for so many years by the KMT or the Japanese.

Passing laws can be relatively simple, but changing ideas that
have been ingrained for centuries in the minds of a population
numbering hundreds of millions is another matter. As the central government went about the business of socializing the country
through measures such as land reform, collective farming, and
nationalized business and industry, the women's federation worked
for women's equality. Federation representatives spread into every
village, township, county, and city neighborhood, holding con-
sciousness-raising meetings, publicizing the new Marriage Law,
and conducting literacy and job training classes.

Interestingly, land reform, which gave both husbands and
wives deeds to land plots, brought one immediate result that
surprised even the government and created a good deal of anger
among the population. So many women demanded divorces that
party leaders became concerned that the socialist revolution's battle
between the classes would take second place to a battle between
the sexes. A directive issued by the central government in 1953
accused women's rights workers of moving too quickly and using the Marriage Law as a means of oppressing men. The wom-
en's federation was instructed to work more slowly, using education among men and women rather than militancy. The
government also felt that women's liberation would automati-
cally follow the entry of women into the work force.

Much has already been written about the turbulent years in

China under the leadership of Mao Tse-tung. When he died in 1976 at the age of 82, most objective observers agreed that his ideas had resulted in great benefits for the people as well as incredible hardships and injustices. Epidemic disease was eradicated, health care and education were made available to all, the wealth of the country was more widely distributed, and equality for women was actively promoted. On the other hand, his obsession with the evil of foreign influences, his belief in his own omnipotence, and his absolute trust in the peasants—coupled with an almost paranoid distrust of intellectuals—led to the formation of a total police state and a series of disastrous campaigns like the Hundred Flowers, the Great Leap Forward, and worst of all, the Cultural Revolution, which began in 1965 and lasted over ten years. That countless thousands were tortured, imprisoned, and murdered is horrifying in itself, but the loss to the country in terms of economic, scientific, and industrial development is also tragic. The result was that China lost a decade in its desperate struggle to take its place among the modern nations of the world.

BLIND
TO THE EXPLOSION

Perhaps one of Mao's most serious errors was his refusal to listen to his own experts, who advised him as early as the 1950s to institute population control measures. His blindness on the subject resulted in China's most difficult problem today—more than one billion people, a population so huge it exacerbates every other problem. Since the late 1970s, under the leadership of Deng Xiaoping, China has been striving to compensate for those lost years of the Cultural Revolution through a set of goals called the Four Modernizations—the modernization of agriculture, industry, science and technology, and national defense—by the year 2000. But the enormous task of feeding and housing over a billion people alone makes those goals difficult to achieve.

However, except for the Cultural Revolution years when Jiang Qing, Mao's wife and leader of the Gang of Four, disbanded the women's federation, political events in China since 1949 have affected men and women equally. Today, the All China Women's Federation still works to promote equality for women. And though obvious progress has been made, as the ensuing dialogues will reveal, the major problem remains the same: Large numbers of people, especially among the peasant population, still retain the old feudal ideas. That is a problem to which the women of Western countries can relate very well.

CHAPTER

WOMEN
AT
THE TOP

*Chinese women have come a long way
but they still don't own half the sky.*

Lei Jieqiong, chairperson
All China Women's Federation
China Daily
August 23, 1983

Lei, seventy-eight, and one of China's leading feminists, in the preceding quote was paraphrasing a speech by Mao Tse-tung in the early years of the Communist movement. Emphasizing the importance of women in the revolution, he said, "women hold up half the sky."

Lei's article went on to attack the old feudal ideas in China that discriminate against women. She decried the demand for betrothal gifts as a disguised way of selling girls, literary works that suggest women should set aside their own careers in favor of supporting those of their husbands, criticism of women who divorce, and the lingering double standards for men and women.

Admitting that women have made considerable gains, she claimed that there are now 5.35 million women leaders, thirteen times more than in 1951, and there are 39.35 million urban women workers, sixty times more than in 1951. On the other hand, she cited figures showing that while women make up 31.6 percent of the scientists and technicians in China, only 2 percent have senior ranking, and that of the 235.8 million illiterates in China, 70 percent are women.

During my stay in China, newspapers ran a number of articles describing various types of prejudice against women, including discrimination in hiring and promotion, the rise in female infanticide because of preference for male children (partly a result of the government drive to limit each family to one child), bride sales, businesses forcing pregnant women to take unpaid leave, and an increase in the beating and rape of women.

At the Fifth National Women's Congress held in Peking just a month before I arrived in China, Kang Keqing, president of the All China Women's Federation and a veteran of the 1934 Long March, gave a lengthy report on the achievements of women over the past five years and the work remaining to be done. Pointing out that China has 200 million able-bodied women, she claimed that the implementation of Deng's "responsibility system" (allowing each family to farm its own plot, and encouraging sideline or private industries) has provided more opportunities for peasant women and improved their economic and social status.

Educational levels have also risen, she said, especially in the cities. In 1982 statistics showed that 60 to 70 percent of urban working women were graduates of junior or senior high school, and that one-fourth of the nation's children could attend nursery school and kindergarten due to the increase in facilities.

Affirming the rights of women to full social and economic equality, Kang pledged that the federation would continue to pursue those goals. Equal status for women, she said, still depended on the need to "mitigate the conflict between job and household responsibilities" through increased production of labor-saving appliances and through the sharing of household and child-care responsibilites with men. "The women's federation will carry out ideological education among the people and track down and punish those who discriminate against, mistreat, humiliate or persecute women," she promised.

Banned by the 1950 Marriage Law, but still common in Chinese society, are arranged marriages. According to a report in a September 1983 issue of the *China Daily*, a survey of 462 couples in Tianjin's Hexi district showed that "only 8.4 percent married partners of their choice, more than 80 percent married following various kinds of recommendations, while parents arranged the remaining 10 percent."

Also, the lack of adequate housing—while affecting both sexes—is particularly hard on women who must live with their husbands' parents. The result is not only a lack of privacy, but a position of subservience to mothers-in-law. Throughout my trip, conversations at every level led me to believe that China's women perceive the mother-in-law to be one of the most despotic institutions in the society.

Jay and Linda Mathews, former Peking bureau chiefs for *The Washington Post* and *The Los Angeles Times* respectively, wrote in their recent book, *One Billion: A China Chronicle*, that there is a long waiting list for apartments and that many couples have to live with relatives. A few years prior to 1983, they said, the average floor space per person was less than twenty square feet and is now probably about half that because the population increase has been double the amount of space provided by the massive building program.

In discussing how a neighborhood committee in Peking helps to settle problems created when mothers and daughters-in-law must live together, the *China Daily* reported that "106 of the 530 households in the neighborhood are shared; 80 with married sons, 26 with married daughters. It is an unwritten rule that sons have priority if there are any extra rooms for married children."

While we were in China, we saw a number of apartments, both old and new. The new ones, which we were told were a great improvement for those fortunate enough to have them, were very small and all of the same uninspired design. We visited one on the seventh floor of an eight-story building. Because of the power shortage, the elevators ran for only short periods in the morning, around noon, and in the evening. Fortunately, we arrived at noon and were received by a retired couple who lived with their two grown sons in three tiny rooms—a living room, bedroom, and kitchen, adjoining a rather primitive bathroom with only a stoop toilet (a plumbed hole in the cement floor) and a sink, no bathtub or shower. Because of an injured leg the husband could walk only with the aid of crutches, making him virtually a prisoner in his own home during the hours when the elevator was inoperative. Though it was hard to visualize any more people living in that small space, the wife said that if one of her sons married, his bride would probably move in with them.

Reports from both inside and outside China are almost unanimous that the "old feudal ideas" concerning women are still prevalent in the rural areas. According to the Mathewses, "the traditional adage, 'a daughter is like spilled water,' still holds for many Chinese. Once married, young women usually move off to live with their in-laws, depriving their families of the harvest share they earn in the fields. Young men, however, will usually settle near their parents. They earn larger shares than their sisters, anyway, and have the obligation of supporting their parents in their old age. The government has only enough money for social security in the cities, and no matter what it says about guarantees for the elderly, it counts on rural sons to observe the ancient Confucian custom of filial devotion. So the old bias in favor of boys lives on."

In Peking, I interviewed two high-ranking women in government: Huang Ganying, vice president of the All China Women's Federation, and Qian Zhenying, minister of water resources and electric power.

HUANG GANYING

All China Women's Federation

The offices of China's guardian of women's rights, the All China Women's Federation, are housed in an old gray stone building in the heart of the city. Our driver deposited my photographer Buff Aaron, my interpreter Zhao Yaqing, and me at the entrance, where a young woman greeted us. We were led up three flights of stairs and ushered into a large reception room about thirty feet long and fifteen feet wide, which was almost a duplicate of those in just about every office building, factory, university, and farm meeting hall we visited in China. The furniture was an assortment of overstuffed, vinyl-upholstered chairs and straight chairs, slipcovered in cotton with pleated ruffles, lined up against the walls. After seating ourselves, we were served hot green tea—the leaves floating at the top—in handleless china cups with lids. This ritual took place everywhere. Within a few minutes, Huang Ganying, sixty-two, vice president of the federation, entered the room, followed by an entourage of four federation officials plus her own interpreter—all women. Though small, Huang exuded an air of quiet authority. Her husband is vice minister of education and they are the parents of four children.

Teenage Revolutionary

There were four children in my family: myself, an elder brother and sister, and a younger brother. Our parents died when I was ten and my elder brother took care of us because my grandparents had also died by then. In fact, I still look upon my elder brother and his wife as my parents.

After I graduated from senior middle school [high school] in 1938, I went to join the Communist revolutionary forces in the liberated areas of the north. It was during the Japanese War and I helped in the fight against the Japanese imperialists, and later against the Kuomintang, until the whole country was liberated in 1949. Then I came to Peking and have lived here ever since.

I have believed in the revolution ever since I was very young. The reason was simple, and it was a common attitude among many young people in those years. China was being invaded by imperialist powers, and we did not want our country to fall into the hands of foreigners. I joined many patriotic organizations, and it was through those activities that I arrived at the understanding that China was a semifeudal and semicolonial country. So in order to liberate the entire nation, we had to fight, not only imperialism and bureaucratic capitalism, but also feudalism. Then we had to support the socialist movement until we reached our final goal, Communism. That was the only way to bring about the liberation of the nation and its people, particularly women.

I have been working with the women's federation ever since its founding at the First National Women's Congress in April of 1949. When Beijing [Peking] was liberated, there were still some areas in China occupied by the Kuomintang, but we had representatives to the congress from those areas too. You see, during the war years, we had set up women's organizations in both the liberated and the occupied areas, so a network was already established. After the liberation, it became obvious that all the women's organizations should join together and form one national organization.

We played quite an active role in the formulation of the Marriage Law that was passed in 1950. The new government attached great importance to promoting equality for women and also to protecting the legitimate rights of women and children. So when they were about to formulate the new Marriage Law, they first sought the suggestions and opinions of the women's federation. It was the first law issued after the liberation, and all

*Huang Ganying, vice president,
All China Women's Federation*

the federation representatives were very satisfied with it. In old China, it was totally impossible to have any government protection of the rights of women and children in terms of marriage, morality, and family responsibilities.

I have been interested in women's equality most of my life because I always believed it was impossible to liberate the Chinese people without liberating women; we comprise half the population. I also felt that without the participation of women, the revolution against the Kuomintang would not be successful. Actually, I myself did not suffer very much in terms of discrimination because I joined the revolution at a very young age, sixteen or seventeen. But I knew quite a bit about the suffering of my mother's generation. As you probably know, in the old society, men could have concubines and they could abandon their wives whenever they wanted to. All this brought great suffering to wives. Of course, we revolutionaries could not put up with all that discrimination and inequality. We thought and thought and finally came to the realization that if we relied on women's strength alone to gain equality for ourselves, it would be impossible. We felt that women had to fight along with men for the liberation of our country and ourselves, and that was another motive for my joining the revolutionary movement.

The new Marriage Law has done a great deal for the fight for equality, but in reality some people have not done a good job in implementing the law. For instance, when a male and female with the same academic background and qualifications apply for a job, the people in authority at that work unit often prefer the male. They think women are more troublesome because they get pregnant and afterward have all the burdens of rearing the children, so they take more time off. I understand that women in the United States have the same problem. We know something about your situation and the Equal Rights Amendment.

Last September [1983] we convened our Fifth National Women's Congress, and at that meeting our president gave a report on the goals or tasks of the federation. The first was to call on women throughout China to improve their qualifications so they could be more competitive. In other words, they should work harder to upgrade themselves on cultural, scientific, academic, and professional levels in order to make greater contributions to the socialist spiritual and material civilization.

Women should also give top priority to the education and rearing of the younger generation. We have about 300 million children in China under the age of fourteen, and because we see that generation as the future of our country, we consider their all-around development to be an important task for women.

Another important goal is to fight any kind of discrimination against women. If a woman feels that she is being discriminated against, she can come to the women's federation for help. We have special offices in every area of the country that handle the complaints or grievances brought to our attention through letters or personal visits. Recently, we also formed a legal advisory office that helps women to find lawyers and handles the papers involved in bringing legal actions. Beijing is the national headquarters of the federation, but we also have many provincial and municipal branches. So, though the government supports us, the women's federation is considered a grass-roots organization.

There are cases of female infanticide, but the main reason for that is that old feudal ideas are very hard to change. Some people still believe that only baby boys will carry on the family line. They feel that when sons marry, they will bring their wives home to produce babies for the family, while daughters are bound to live with their husbands' families.

I wouldn't say that this is caused by the government decreeing that there should be only one child per couple, because in the old society there were many more cases of female infanticide than now. It was common practice, but no one paid any attention to it so it was never publicized in the newspapers. In new China, that kind of practice is against the law, and we have been reporting it in the press in order to bring it to the attention of the entire nation and mobilize public opinion against it.

Many people still cling to the old feudal ideas, so we still need a great deal of re-education in our country. And I have to say that the chaotic years of the Cultural Revolution brought a lot of confusion to the people, especially young people. The Cultural Revolution was a great disaster for everybody. That whole period was counterproductive to life, to study, to education, and to every field of development. They pitted production against the revolution; those who did not do a good job at their work were considered revolutionaries, and those who performed well were referred to as counter-revolutionaries. They turned all the values around, so some of the young people became very loose.

In the education field, they cited someone who failed an examination as a hero because he was rebelling against the educational and entrance-examination system. So during those years, young people didn't learn much and now we have many people over twenty years old who are illiterate. Even in areas like courtship, marriage, and family, many of the old feudal ideas made their way back. For instance, practices like arranged marriages have reappeared.

We also have some capitalistic trends in the society due to the opening of our doors to the Western world in recent years. Chinese people have a long history of traditional moral standards, and under the socialist system we have legalized what we call socialistic morality and responsibility to family. We advocate respect for the old and love of the young. But during the ten chaotic years, Western influence caused some of our young people to change their thinking and behavior. Many are not acting well toward the elderly; they are very rash in their marriages and are not behaving responsibly in the family. Many also pursue materialistic goals. For example, when some girls get married they expect all kinds of gifts from the betrothed, like a whole new set of chairs. That is a very old practice. So all of these things have aroused our attention in recent years. But we think it is quite natural for young people to be influenced by bad ideas, and we have a re-education program going on throughout the country. There are special columns in newspapers and magazines where these issues are discussed and advice is given. So I can say that things are better now than they were a few years ago.

QIAN ZHENGYING

*Minister, Water Resources
and Electric Power*

Qian, sixty-one, was appointed minister of water resources and electric power in 1975 and is one of only three women of the thirty-four ministers in the central government. (The others are Chen Muhua, minister of foreign and economic relations, and Wu Wenying, minister of the textile industry.) Considered one of the most powerful women in government, she has a reputation for being a very capable technologist and not at all pretentious. She greeted us with warmth as we seated ourselves at a long conference table in the center of the room, and she served the inevitable tea herself.

A spontaneous and open woman, Qian spoke frankly about her own life. Though dressed in the usual drab pantsuit, her mobile and expressive face, with its strong features, provided the color. She told her story with humor and apparent honesty, laughing often—and sometimes at herself.

A Family of Achievers

My parents were both educated people who believed that girls as well as boys should have an education. My father received his master's degree in hydraulic engineering at Cornell University in the United States, and my mother, though she was a housewife, had studied Chinese classical literature.

There were six children in our family, and we were all educated. My elder brother is a professor of English at a university in Shanghai, my elder sister is a foreign-trade expert, one of my younger brothers is a doctor, another is an engineer, and the youngest is a mathematician. I studied civil engineering at a private university in Shanghai because in those days most universities did not allow women students to enroll. Actually, I never finished. I was supposed to graduate in the spring of 1943, but

*Qian Zhengying, minister of water resources
and electric power*

in the winter of 1942 the Japanese captured Shanghai and I had to leave school.

I joined the People's Liberation Army in the Communist areas in the north and fought against the Japanese and the Kuomintang. I also worked with the army on flood-control projects. In 1944 I was responsible for controlling the Huai River [a branch of the Yellow River] in the liberated area, and later I worked on the construction of roads and bridges. Then, in 1947, I left the army and went to Shandong province to work on the Yellow River flood-control project. Our main job was to build up the embankments along the river, using natural materials from the land. In 1950 I was appointed vice minister of water conservancy of the East China Military Commission, which was both a military and civilian commission.

I was married in 1951 and a year later, after giving birth to my first child, was appointed vice minister of water resources and electric power of the central [national] government. In 1975 I became minister. My experience during the Cultural Revolution was the same as that of many other cadres. I was sent off to the countryside to do farm work, but I was able to return to my regular work much earlier than most intellectuals because a major power station broke down. Premier Chou En-lai, who was an old friend, was able to convince the government leaders that I was needed and I was brought back. So I was much more fortunate than most of the others who were persecuted.

My husband is now minister of education, so we are on the same level in government. We have three children, one boy and two girls. That number is not the party policy now, so before I can request anyone to obey the new birth-control requirements, I must practice some self-criticism. [Early on the Communist regime established the policy that workplaces hold regular meetings where workers could criticize their colleagues if they had any grievances; they were also encouraged to criticize themselves. This practice was carried to an extreme during the Cultural Revolution.]

In the liberated areas, there was not much difficulty for women in upper levels of work. In fact, women were given priority and that is true even now. The new government has always made it a point to select and promote women for leadership positions in order to bring them up to the level of men. But I must admit that in the whole society, there are still some views that are not good for women. I will tell you two stories.

One took place during the anti-Japanese war in a rural liberated area. At the time I was responsible for the Huai River flood-control project, and we were building a gate on the river embankment. One day, when I was walking around giving instructions to the workers, my landlady told me she was going somewhere. I suggested she go through the new gate because it was a shortcut, but she said she had to go the long way because women were not allowed to go through the gate. When I pointed out that I went that way every day, she said, "You are responsible for building that gate and that is why we pay respect to you. You deserve a special honor." In other words, I was different.

My second story took place in 1945, just before the end of the war against Japan. I had designed a memorial tower to the martyrs who lost their lives during the war, and we employed some old workers to build it. At the ceremony for the laying of the base stone, the foreman, who was a very old worker, came and spoke to me me very hesitatingly, but I got his meaning. He was trying to tell me that women were not supposed to be in the building area, especially at the base-stone ceremony, because it was bad luck and an accident would surely happen. Of course, he didn't have the right to send me away, but out of respect for him, I made an excuse and left, and I stayed away while they were building. But I had designed the monument with a round top, and the workers were having difficulty because they had no experience with that kind of structure, so they had to ask me to come back. One day I had to go to the top of the monument, but first I asked the same old worker if there was anything wrong with my doing that. He said, "It doesn't matter, you will bring us luck." He saw that they needed me.

What I'm really talking about is the old feudal ideas about women in the Chinese society. As I mentioned earlier, some of the universities didn't allow women students. My father received his undergraduate education at an old transportation university in Shanghai, and they did not allow girls to enter. And it was difficult for those women who did go to college to find jobs after they graduated. But I have to admit that even today there is still prejudice against women. For instance, if a girl baby is born, some parents are unhappy because they still believe they need a son to take care of them in their old age.

According to the Chinese tradition, there is no doubt that children should take care of their parents, but my husband and I don't feel we will need them. We have our own plans for retirement, so we don't have to be dependent on our children. Actually, when they grow old, parents prefer daughters because they would rather live with a daughter and son-in-law than a son and daughter-in-law. It's easier to have a good relationship with a son-in-law than a daughter-in-law. I'm sure your mother would rather live with you than with your brothers.

I think women themselves should work and study hard so they can compete with men for equal positions. In other words, they should get those positions through their own capabilities. Even in this new society, some women still have feudal ideas; they are prejudiced against themselves and they should try to liberate themselves from those restrictions. Women should not feel dependent on men. They should not stop working after marriage or after their children are born. On the other hand, according to law, men and women are supposed to have equal opportunities to compete for jobs, but that is not always true in actual practice. Because of the old feudal ideas, there are still cases where women are discriminated against. So women have two tasks: They must work hard and improve themselves, and they must fight against the prejudiced ideas that are still in the society. As I said, parents are not happy if their only child is a girl, which means that girl didn't even have a right to be born. So she will have to fight for her position because from the very beginning of her life, her family will give her the idea that she is not as good as a boy. That's why we have a national women's federation, trying to re-educate people. We don't have any men's federations in the world because they don't need them.

I'll tell you another story. I got pregnant with my first child in the spring of 1952. At the time I was working at the Huai River flood-control site. The project had started in 1951, so you can imagine how busy we were by the following year. I was vice minister of the engineering department of the Huai River Control Committee, so I had a great responsibility and the pregnancy was very inconvenient; I wanted an abortion.

I went to the president of the committee, who was a very good comrade, and he advised me. He said, "My wife has had many children, so I've had a good deal of experience with these things. I can tell you how to manage this matter, and you will have no problem. After the delivery, you don't have to feed the baby—you can find a wet nurse. But if you have an abortion, it will not be good for your personal health." Though he did not approve my application for an abortion, I was quite moved by his concern. I kept on working until just before the delivery and was able to go back soon after. My mother-in-law took care of my child, and later on I hired a nanny who took care of all three of my children. So I was a lucky woman, and now we have more and more lucky women. Women do have to work harder for what they want, but their hard work will improve their capabilities.

CHAPTER

THE
SPORTS
LIFE

Aside from its top-ranking political leaders, to Westerners, China's best-known personalities are its athletes—especially since their outstanding performance at the 1984 Summer Olympics in Los Angeles, where they won fifteen gold medals. It was the first Summer Olympics for China since they withdrew from the games in 1956 to protest participation by Taiwan.

Many Americans also recall the nationally televised "Ping-Pong diplomacy" of the early 1970s, soon after which Richard Nixon—the first American president ever to visit China—was hosted by Mao Tse-tung in Peking. The Chinese table-tennis champions, who subsequently toured the United States, enthralled millions as they played exhibition matches with their American counterparts. These matches may have contributed more to thawing relations between the two countries than any other event in contemporary history.

As well as being a great source of national pride, sports are a very significant means of establishing international friendship and goodwill for the People's Republic outside the realm of politics. This has become especially important to the current regime. Since taking power after the regressive years of the Cultural Revolution, Deng Xiaoping seems determined to move China as quickly as possible into the modern age in terms of industry, technology, agriculture, and the military. And, since much of Deng's modernization program is dependent on investment capital and expertise from foreign countries, the goodwill engendered by athletes is money in the bank.

Though paid the same low, government-set salaries as other workers, sports stars often receive cash bonuses and enjoy special privileges unavailable to the average Chinese. But they pay an even greater price in terms of personal freedom. During my stay in China, I interviewed two outstanding woman athletes: Zheng Minzhi, a former world champion and a member of the table-tennis team that visited the United States in 1972, and Sun Jinfang, captain of the volleyball team that won the world championship in 1982. Though Sun retired soon after, her team went on to capture a gold medal at the 1984 Summer Olympics.

After my return to America, I interviewed Hu Na, China's leading woman tennis player until July 1982 when she made world headlines by defecting to the United States during the Federation Cup tournament in Santa Clara, California. The defection of the then nineteen-year-old athlete caused a serious rift in United States–China relations that took almost a year to heal.

ZHENG MINZHI

Table-Tennis Champion

Americans who watched the Chinese table-tennis champions in 1972 were enchanted by the speed, agility, and grace of a pretty young woman who darted like a hummingbird about the table.

I met Zheng Minzhi one sunny afternoon at the Peking Sports Research Institute, a very large complex in the center of the city that resembled a midwestern American college campus. The old stone and brick buildings were set among large expanses of patchy lawn and numerous huge old trees, their leaves stained the fall colors of yellow and red. At thirty-eight Zheng did not appear to have aged much since I had seen her on television twelve years earlier. With her short hair curled and worn in bangs, and trimly dressed in a blue-and-white jogging suit, except for her traditional black cloth Chinese shoes, she was a picture of sports chic.

Zheng has an impressive record. In 1965 her team won the world championship matches in Yugoslavia, and she took first place in the women's doubles. Competition was banned for four years during the Cultural Revolution, but in 1971 Zheng's team took second place in the world championship games in Japan, and again she won the women's doubles. Now a coach and referee, her work still enables her to travel extensively. She has visited more than thirty countries throughout the world, an experience enjoyed by very few Chinese citizens.

Table-Tennis Diplomacy

I began playing table tennis at the age of twelve. It was a very popular sport even in those days, and because my father was a great fan, he always took me to see the competitions and encouraged me to play. One of my three sisters is also a very good player, though not a champion.

China has many special schools for youngsters who show outstanding ability in sports. When I was fourteen I was selected to attend a local sports school and then, a few years later, a national sports institute. Most of my time was spent practicing table tennis but I studied other subjects too and also competed in many tournaments, so I was very busy. Because I lived at the school, I did not have time to see my former friends very often, though I did go home once a week.

I enjoyed the school very much; the living conditions were very good, and it was a great opportunity for me. I feel that because our government supports athletes, we receive better training than the athletes in other countries, though I understand that the United States has the best cricket [baseball] and basketball players in the world.

I visited the United States in 1972 when the doors had just been opened for our two countries to re-establish relations. For almost twenty years there had been no contact between China and the United States, and the political atmosphere was being defrosted. It was a great honor and pleasure for me to visit at that time, though at first I was a little bit timid. But after I had some contact with the American people, I felt relaxed because they were very warm and hospitable. Americans are more open and frank than other people, and they made every effort to make us feel comfortable. Before our team left China, we met with Premier Chou En-lai, who was still quite healthy at that time. He told us to go to the United States and meet the American

Zheng Minzhi, former table-tennis champion

people with friendship and understanding, and that made a deep impression on me.

Table tennis is not as popular in the United States as it is in China, so the level of American skill is not as high as ours. For instance, this year at the world championship games in Japan, the American men's team came in thirteenth and the women's team twentieth. But I did meet a few American players who could compete quite well with our players.

When players score well, especially in world championship games, they are given rewards by the government. They try to provide better living conditions for extremely talented players. That's a little hard to do because our living standards in general are behind the Western countries, and with over a billion population it's difficult to offer all the players better housing conditions. But they do give bonuses. If a player scores well in championship competition, he or she can receive from 1,000 to 3,000 yuan [in 1983 one yuan was equal to slightly over half an American dollar]. That may not be a lot in comparison to the United States, but in China it's quite impressive. We treasure all genius in our country.

My husband and I met when we were teenagers attending the same sports school in Shanghai. His specialty is Japanese-style chess, and he's now vice chairman of the Chess Association. When we were older and courting, we were both traveling a lot, so we had some understanding of the life of athletes, which made it easier. He supports my work, and although we are separated quite often, we cherish the time we have together even more. Actually, before our marriage it was simpler, because now we have a five-year-old son and when we travel I must send him to my mother in Shanghai, so she can take care of him.

Of course, it's natural for young people to have personal problems, but Chinese men and women are very serious about marriage. We select our partners very cautiously and by the time we decide to get married, we know each other very well. So we have fewer problems in comparison to couples in other countries. When a Chinese girl decides to marry a gentleman, she thinks in terms of living her whole life with him. That's why we have fewer divorces than in other countries. The Chinese also put work before their personal lives, which keeps our marriages stronger.

We live nearby in housing provided for people who work at this sports research institute. In China the government generally provides housing for people near their workplace. We have a two-room apartment with a kitchen and a toilet. Right now only my husband and I are living there, because I'm going to Japan soon for a competition and my son is in Shanghai with his grand-mother. But I want him home soon, otherwise he will stop call-ing us mother and father.

During the Cultural Revolution I could not participate in competitions, and we had to stop training for a short time. It was not correct. The only reason we were allowed to go to the United States during that time was because table-tennis diplo-macy was a national strategy at the time. Also, the visit was sponsored by Premier Chou, who was still powerful. [Chou En-lai's power decreased in direct proportion to the ascent of the Gang of Four.] He felt that it was quite important to establish relations between our two countries, and the other leaders agreed with him. Of course, the Gang of Four did not want the ath-letes to make contact with foreigners, but Premier Chou told us again and again that the American people would welcome us and to just go. Competition was stopped for about four years during the Cultural Revolution, so we missed the 1967 and 1969 world championship tournaments. They also banned all train-ing, but I used to practice secretly on my own.

SUN JINFANG

Volleyball champion

Sun retired from play soon after her team won the women's vol-leyball world championship in 1982 and finally married her fi-ancé, an army engineer, after a four-year courtship. The Sports Physical Institute, where we met, is in a lovely country area a few miles outside the city of Nanking, a well-known educational and cultural center. The city itself is quite beautiful, with its broad

Sun Jinfang, former captain,
world championship volleyball team

tree-lined streets, well-kept parks, and many waterways. One may visit a number of attractions, including the magnificent Sun Yat-sen Mausoleum, built on the lower slope of the Purple Mountain in the eastern suburb.

On a mild, sunny day, we found the twenty-eight-year-old champion out on a playing field, tossing a volleyball around with several students. She led us into a nearby building and, as we settled down with our tea in the ground-floor reception area, promptly informed me that because of her world championship status, she is always being pursued by journalists from all over the world. She complained that interviews consume too much of her time. After the interview, she charged that when she was in the United States for a competition soon after her team won the world championship, she was approached by two members of the American women's team. They proposed that the Chinese team deliberately lose to the Americans because it would mean a great deal of money to them, which they would be willing to share. When I questioned her further about specifics such as names and places, she quickly dropped the subject, leaving me more than a little skeptical.

National Honor First

There were four children in my family, two boys and two girls. My father was a railway official and my mother a worker on the railway. As a young girl I was not very active in sports, but because I was quite tall, I was asked to join the volleyball team in senior middle school [high school] and I became very skilled. After I graduated in 1971, I was selected to go to this sports institute and eventually I became a member of the team that won the world championship.

At the institute we spent most of our time on athletics—volleyball, swimming, running, and jumping—but we also studied subjects like Chinese literature, history, and geography. Whenever an important competition was coming up, however, we concentrated only on training for quite a long period of time, and then afterward we returned to our school work. But by the time I trained for the world championship competition in 1982, I had already finished with school, so I was only practicing and playing. During my career, I played in almost 170 competitions throughout the world; I have been in so many countries I can't remember all of them, but I'll tell you just a few. I've been to America twice, Russia once, Japan five times, and I've also gone to India, Thailand, Bulgaria, Korea, Peru, and West Germany—all over the past five or six years. Then in February of this year, I retired and got married.

At first I was not used to the life of an athlete. I was always traveling, and I missed my family very much. But the institute and the leaders of the volleyball team always taught us to put national honor before our personal lives, and gradually I became used to it. When I was traveling I wrote often and made phone calls to my family and my boyfriend, so I knew they were all right. At first my boyfriend was upset about my being away so much, but I kept telling him about the value to China of what I was doing, and gradually he understood and became very supportive.

I never worried about losing him because I believed in him and loved him so much, I knew he would never be unfaithful or change his mind. You see, the custom in China is that if a girl doesn't trust the boy she has fallen in love with, she will not accept him as a fiancé. I did not marry him before I retired because it's quite important that athletes concentrate on their work and on winning championships for the motherland. If the women on my team got married, they would have a lot of household chores to do and couldn't concentrate all their energy and strength on playing. So none of us married while we were playing.

At foreign competitions it was quite difficult to contact athletes from other countries because our time was always so limited and we concentrated on practicing for the competition. The only chances we had to make acquaintances and exchange views were the short periods of time we spent waiting for a bus to take us to the stadium, or when we were traveling. But I did notice that their attitudes and life-styles are very different from ours. For instance, when they are not actually competing, the girls can do as they like; they have that freedom. They would go out on dates or go to bars together for an evening. Chinese girls could not do that and, in my opinion, that kind of behavior is immoral. I suppose if a girl feels it's all right, she should do it, but I'm against it. The Chinese government and the Communist Party ask very seriously that we behave ourselves honorably.

Sometimes, when we are all together for two months of concentrated training, we never see our boyfriends or families the whole time. But we feel that is quite natural, and our duty to our country, so we have no complaints. I think if other countries were as strict as ours, it would cause a lot of trouble among their athletes. In the very beginning, I felt that my trainer was very cruel because he was so strict with us. But after my team won the world championship, I felt differently; he was quite right.

Because I played on the team for many years and attended so many competitions, I have a lot of experience. Now my task is to write about my experiences so that others can learn from them. If we want to keep the women's volleyball championship in China, the younger generation must learn from the older; that is our duty. So I will be giving the benefit of my experience to the new players coming up. After I finish my book, I hope to become a trainer at this sports institute. Right now, I'm taking the opportunity to relax for a while. I've been so busy, the government wants me to rest and recover my strength. I would like to take a real vacation, but I can't because I have so many social obligations. If you don't mind, I would like to say a few words about journalists like you. So many foreign journalists request interviews that I am kept quite busy with them almost every day and I have no time to rest, not to mention take a vacation. They occupy almost two-thirds of my time and I can't get used to that kind of life. Sometimes it makes my head ache.

Fame has raised my political status. When I came back to Nanjing [Nanking] after the world championship games, I was named chairman of the Fourth Institute of Nanjing and awarded the titles of Best World Sportswoman, Model Woman, and New Long March Pacesetter, which mean that I am a woman who is breaking the road toward modernization. [These are some of the many titles conferred by the government on individuals who have excelled.]

But I don't like being such a famous person because it causes me a lot of trouble. I can hardly go into a store to shop because everyone recognizes me from watching me on television, and they want to talk to me. And I hardly have any private time with my husband, so there is almost no freedom or privacy. Since our marriage, my husband has done almost all the shopping; I have done almost nothing because I don't want to go out. I'm also so busy with my studies and social life that my husband does most of the household chores, though sometimes, if I have a little free time, we share them. But my husband is very nice about that; he never complains. He does all the cooking, cleaning, and shopping because he loves me and realizes I don't have the time. He feels that the household chores are his duty because I have dedicated my body, my life, and my health to the honor of China.

HU NA

Tennis Star

Sometime after midnight on July 21, 1982, Hu Na, the Chinese tennis star, walked out of a hotel in Santa Clara, California, taking with her only the clothes she was wearing. Nothing was heard until a week later, when—in an action that made world headlines—a San Francisco lawyer, Edward C. Y. Lau, known to have Taiwan connections, filed a statement on Hu's behalf with the United States Immigration and Naturalization Service, asking for political asylum.

The attractive nineteen-year-old, who ranked third on China's national tennis team, had disappeared during the Federation Cup tennis tournament, an international women's competition equivalent to the men's Davis Cup. Over the next eight months, while the American government debated whether to grant Hu's request, a furor raged that threatened seriously to set back United States–Chinese relations so carefully nurtured over the preceding ten years. When it was finally announced on April 4 that asylum had been granted, the Chinese angrily charged that

Hu's defection had been orchestrated by agents of the Nationalist government on Taiwan, who had enticed her; that there was no reason to grant political asylum, because she had been happy in China, and that the Reagan administration had acted in collusion with the Taiwanese in an effort to embarrass the Communists.

According to a report from Peking Los Angeles Times *correspondent Michael Parks, the Chinese contended that "Hu was a politically naive girl assiduously wooed by Nationalist agents promising her a big professional career and minimizing the effects of defection on her family, friends and even herself. . . . Their evidence is largely circumstantial but not unpersuasive: How could a 19-year-old of limited education, with no knowledge of English, no relatives in the United States and no knowledge of the workings of the U.S. government decide to defect, find a safe haven for a week and hire a lawyer to represent her, all within a few hours of her disappearance from a Santa Clara hotel in the middle of the night?"*

In retaliation, the Chinese canceled all official athletic and cultural exchanges with the United States for the rest of 1983. These included already-scheduled art and film exhibits, tours by performing artists, and Chinese participation in ten athletic events, most of them warm-ups for the 1984 Olympic Games in Los Angeles. Not affected were the games themselves, science and technology exchanges, or the upcoming visit by President and Mrs. Reagan to China. Apparently, the Deng Xiaoping regime was determined not to allow Hu's defection to interfere with goals that include maintaining good relations with a country necessary to China's modernization efforts.

In newspaper reports Hu explained that her reason for requesting political asylum was the constant pressure from local Communist officials in her native Sichuan province to join the party, a move she had been resisting for a long time. Citing the fate of her grandfather, a tennis coach who had been forced to give up his career when he found himself on the losing side of a party power play, Hu said she wanted to remain apolitical because she did not want to become caught up in interparty factionalism. Though she had been able to hold out, she feared that if she returned to China, the pressures would be greater than she could withstand.

With the prohibition that I would not ask questions about her defection, I interviewed Hu at the home of the Taiwanese-American family with whom she was living. Located in La Jolla, one of Southern California's most elegant and scenic areas, one might have expected to find a young woman reveling in that luxurious setting. Instead, I found a very unhappy girl, homesick for her family and working desperately to live up to the expectations of a group of Taiwanese-American patrons who hoped she would become the first Chinese professional world champion.

Although she had been taking English lessons and had learned a good deal by then, Hu preferred to have the interview conducted through translation by her host.

The Lonely Champion

I have an older sister who was a champion motorcycle racer and a younger brother who is also talented in tennis. My father is a basketball coach and my grandfather was a tennis coach, so you see I come from an athletic family. As a small child, I used to watch my grandfather play, and when I was eight I picked up a racquet and began to play myself.

In 1977, when I was fourteen and had just graduated from junior middle school [junior high school], I was selected to go to the sports camp in Chengdu. I lived there for the next four years and studied nothing but tennis and politics. In 1982 they began giving me courses in Chinese language and Communist literature, but before that I had no real academic education—only tennis, physical exercises, and political training in what the government wanted young people to know about the social system of China. There were about 200 boys and girls at the camp who were talented in tennis, basketball, volleyball, and chess.

My family first lived in Chongqing [Chunking], and then my father, who is a basketball coach in the military, was sent to Chengdu, and it was three years before we could join him. He visited us only on weekends, so during that period, my mother

*Hu Na, tennis star who defected
to the United States in 1982*

took care of us. After we moved to Chengdu in 1971, she worked as a teacher for a few years and then became an administrator at the athletic association. But I remember my mother as always taking care of the family; she did everything for us and made most of the household decisions except for the very important ones, which were made by my father.

My father is especially fond of boys. When mother delivered me, father was out of town. He came back expecting to see a baby boy and when grandmother told him I was a girl, it was very rough. Then, because she wanted to please him, she said I was a very tall girl and would be an athlete. He felt better, but he really wanted a boy. I think Chinese fathers still have a preference for sons. That's very traditional.

They pushed my brother harder to study than they did my sister and me, but I think that was because we always did very well in school anyway.

Actually, in China, sports are not really held in such high esteem. But in those years, after graduating from senior middle school, young people were supposed to go to the countryside and do farm labor. It was part of Chairman Mao's rustification [farm work] program. Life is very tough there and once you're sent away, you don't know when you'll be able to come back to the city and your family. But if you were selected to go to the sports camp, you didn't have to go to the countryside, so that was my incentive to work hard at being a good tennis player. Also, I was from an athletic family and they encouraged me. In 1978 Deng came into power and stopped the rustification program, but I had already been selected. Though I lived at the camp, I could see my family every day, but I stopped seeing my former school friends. My friends became the other girls at the camp. There was very little social life—no music, no dancing parties, and we could not even go to the movies very often because we had to practice sports even on weekends. Our entertainment was mainly just talking with friends.

During my first year there I competed in only one tennis tournament and that was in Sichuan province, but by the following year, I was playing all over China, and in 1979, I became the national women's junior champion. That's when I was allowed to go out of the country for the first time, and I saw the differences between us and foreign athletes.

It was difficult to talk to players from other countries because I didn't know the language and we were closely watched by our team leader. But we were shocked when we noticed how differently athletes from other countries were treated. We talked about it privately among ourselves and complained that we had no freedom at all compared to them. I never had a date. I couldn't even be friendly with boys. If a girl was caught just having a conversation with a boy, the leader would tell her not to, and we were always watched. It was better for the boys. They were able to date girls outside the camp, so we were really not treated equally. There were a few women, already twenty-seven or twenty-eight, who had managed to find men they wanted to marry, but the leaders would not allow it. They said that for the party and for the people, they had to postpone marriage until they were of no use to the country as athletes anymore. If a girl really wanted to get married, she purposely played rotten tennis so they would let her go. I knew some people who did that.

We had hardly any chance to meet outside men. Our only opportunity was to make friends with the men in the camp— basketball, tennis, or volleyball players. And we married them. Also, if you were a good player but did not believe in Communism, the leaders tried to establish a Red [strongly Communistic] image for you. Then, if you started seeing a young man, they tried to make sure he was Red too, so that the match would be correct. They did that to earn credit for themselves. They could say that a girl played well because she thought correctly and played for the glory of the party. But if a girl started seeing a man whose thinking patterns or qualifications were considered undesirable, he was categorized as a bad member, and the girl was simply told to stop seeing him.

I was a champion player, but that was not enough. There are two requirements: You must be a champion and you must also have a strong commitment to the Communist Party. Even though I was considered very talented, they felt I was not committed, not very Red. They tried to convince me that the reason I played so well was because the party had cultivated me, so I should appreciate it and become a party member. Otherwise I would be criticized. When any boy payed attention to me, they always tried to find out if he was committed to the party. Then, when I was old enough and if the boy was Red enough, I might have been allowed to see him, but not marry him.

You said you interviewed a champion woman volleyball player when you were in China, and she told you she did not want to marry her boyfriend until she had retired. I'm sure that's not true. They just wouldn't let her, but she would not dare to tell you that.

When athletes become too old to compete, only the very good ones can stay in sports, because the government will not invest a lot of money in those who prove to be only average. After two or three years, those kinds of players are usually assigned to low-level jobs in hotels or factories because they have no training for any other type of work. That happened to my sister who was a motorcycle racer, one of the best. When she retired from racing, she was assigned to work as a maid in a hostel. It was one of the places where cadres and army officers go for vacation. When I became a leading tennis player, I was able to use my influence to get her a better job in an office.

Only the very talented players can become coaches or teachers. Those who are not as talented have no place to go, and they really suffer. In fact, you didn't have any choice in the matter even if you were a top player. If I didn't want to be a coach after I was too old to play, I would have had to anyway if that's what they wanted. The same thing is true for male players.

Right now I'm very worried about my brother. He is fifteen and was at the sports camp because he is also a very good tennis player. But I'm afraid they will not allow him to play anymore and will send him to a factory because I decided not to go back to China.

Compared to the Chinese, American women are in a much better position. In China, especially in lower-class families, women are not treated equally. They have no status and are only meant to work and clean, nothing else. Men also usually get better work opportunities. In the factories the high positions and light clerical jobs are given to people who have influence and can use the "back door" [the use of influential connections rather than normal channels]. The other jobs usually take a great deal of strength and are given to men. So women rarely get good jobs.

But the back-door policy applies equally to men and women, all those who came from influential families. It's really a question of class status; upper-class people have more opportunities. I held a few very important positions; I was vice chairman of the Chengdu Youth Association, vice president of the Sichuan province branch of the All China Women's Federation, a New Long March Pacesetter, and a Model Woman, but except for helping my sister, I never used my influence. My conscience always made me feel it was wrong.

The best thing about the United States is that there is no pressure being imposed on me by a leader anymore. I do not have to be a model, and I'm free to do as I please. Being a model was always a big burden. Since I've been in America, I've really been concentrating on tennis; that's most important to me now. I'm playing professional tennis, and since my case had such an impact on my family in China, I feel a great responsibility to do well. There's a big difference between professional and amateur tennis. Amateurs are in competition only three or four times a year, but professionals compete all the time. Professional tennis is also much more aggressive; there's really a lot of difference, so I have to work very, very hard because it's up to me to prove myself.

And I feel a great responsibility to the Chinese families here who are helping me. So far, I am one of only two Chinese players in the top fifty, and the other woman is not a star. The Chinese community would really like me to succeed as a champion as they have not had one yet. They keep asking whether I feel confident about making it to the top, so that is a great pressure and I must work very hard. For example, this morning I got up at 6:30 and from 7:30 to 9 I had an automobile driving lesson. I'm almost ready to get my driver's license because last week I passed the written examination. Then, I practiced with my trainer until my appointment with you. At 2:30 I work out with the San Diego tennis team, and after that I will just exercise for another hour to keep myself in condition.

Financially, I have nothing to worry about because the Chinese community has been so wonderful to me. But I miss my family very much. Since I've been here, I've written about twenty letters to them but there has been no response. I worry and think about them all the time and I have lots of dreams about them. I had one again last night.

I'm also taking piano, English, and history lessons. I learned nothing about the history of my country at the sports camp, and I'm very surprised about what I'm finding out. But even though I know I made the right decision when I decided to stay in America, it's hard to enjoy myself when I miss my family so much.

CHAPTER

WOMEN
AND SCIENCE

AN ASSUMED
DISABILITY

I n conversations with a number of educated Chinese women, I was amazed to find that many still feel males are inherently more intelligent, especially in the area of science and technology. For example, during an interview at Wuhan University, Huang Ling, a young woman from the school's foreign affairs office and a graduate of Peking University, said she believed men were biologically smarter than women in the sciences because they have different chromosomes. She cited articles in *Reader's Digest* and other magazines, both Chinese and American, as the basis for her belief. As Lei Jieqiong, chairperson of the All China Women's Federation, pointed out in the *China Daily* interview, "while women make up 31.6 percent of scientists and technicians, only 2 percent have senior ranking." She, however, attributed the disparity primarily to the traditional ideas about women still prevalent in the society.

It seems that American women are in the same boat. In March 1984 *Los Angeles Times* science writer Lee Dembart interviewed a number of scientists and sociologists who maintained that women have attained places in law, medicine, and business in much closer proportion to their numbers in the total population than they have in the sciences, particularly engineering and physics. Of some two million American engineers, he discovered, only 3.5 percent are women. One explanation is that many girls are advised at an early age that science and engineering are not appropriate careers for them. The result in most cases is that a large percentage of female students have what educators call an assumed disability in subjects like mathematics, chemistry, and physics; they feel they cannot do well in those courses and are afraid even to try.

Another problem that seems common to both Chinese and

American women is that many husbands still do not share household and child-care duties with working wives. Though males in both countries are being educated to the idea that it's only fair to share those chores, the majority either refuse to cooperate or perform in a manner so unsatisfactory that women complain it's easier to "do it myself." The result is that most working women carry a double load, which makes career success much more difficult. This is especially true in the sciences, which require continuing study in order to keep up with rapid advances.

Yet we live in a world where science and technology have become more important than ever before to the economic, environmental, and political survival of nations, a fact well recognized by China's current leadership. In May 1983 Michael Parks reported that despite sharp political differences, China signed a pact with the United States to cooperate on joint research projects in aeronautics, ground transportation, nuclear physics, and biomedical sciences.

China now welcomes with open arms experts from all over the world, especially in the areas of science and technology, and each year sends thousands of Chinese experts and students, women as well as men, to other countries as part of its constantly expanding scientific exchange programs.

While in China, I interviewed three high-ranking women scientists: Li Bing, an epidemiologist and director of the Cancer Institute of the Chinese Academy of Medical Sciences; Wei Yu, an associate professor of physics at the Nanking Institute of Technology; and Wu Xi-Jun, senior chemical engineer and chairman of the Science Committee at the Jiangsu Province Scientific Academy.

For other points of view, I interviewed three China-born scientists in the United States: Wang Li-Jean, a research scientist at the University of Southern California, now living permanently in the United States; Yen Junling, who is studying for her doctorate in chemistry at the University of California at Los Angeles; and Jennifer Yang, also a permanent resident of the United States and working in computer sciences at the University of Southern California.

LI BING

Director, Cancer Institute
Chinese Academy of Medical Sciences

It was a cold and rainy afternoon in October when we drove into the large parking area of Peking's major cancer center. At the fourth-floor reception room, we were greeted cordially by Li, sixty-three, a short, plump woman with a quick wit and a ready smile.

Her father, Li Pe Hua Konung, was a member of the Communist underground as early as 1926, when Li was five or six years old, and she, too, became committed to the revolution at a very early age. Later her father rose to the rank of general in the People's Liberation Army, and when the Communists came to power in 1949, he was named assistant minister of foreign affairs and head of the nation's security police apparatus. He died in 1962.

Li herself rose quickly in the party and in September 1983 was appointed an alternate member of the Party Central Committee, China's most powerful political group. She is considered one of the new leaders.

A doctor by apprenticeship rather than formal schooling, Li is best known for a ten-year survey she conducted, using an incredible network of 640,000 investigators, to gather statistics on the incidence of cancer throughout China. Her work gained worldwide recognition from cancer specialists, and Li has traveled to many countries to present her findings. Though deeply committed to the Communist philosophy, she seemed quite open and forthright in discussing her nation's shortcomings, often using the rudimentary English she had taught herself by listening to radio and television. Most of the interview, however, was conducted through my translator.

When we were finished, Li insisted on walking us to our car and, along the way, showed us the new wing that was being added to the cancer center. Complaining about the length of time it was taking to complete, she placed the blame on the lack of incentive among workers due to China's "iron rice bowl" policy [a lifetime job guarantee regardless of performance]. She said the

government had recently initiated work incentives through a sys-
tem of bonuses based on performance, but because of the lack of
administrative skills and often sheer laziness on the part of man-
agers, almost everyone was receiving a bonus, so the system was
not working. She emphasized that if her country was to achieve
its goals for scientific and economic development, something had
to be done to provide real incentive.

Born a Red

When I was a small child, my parents were both members of
the Communist Party in Shanghai. My father worked for the
Kuomintang, which controlled the city in 1926, but actually he
was a member of the underground that supplied information to
the Communists. When the KMT forces pushed the Communists out of the area, my father was among those who made the
Long March to the liberated area in Yenan, and later my mother
joined him there. My sister and brothers and I went to live with
my grandparents and we heard nothing from my parents for ten
years until the Xian Incident in 1936. My father was there with
Chou En-lai during the negotiations with Chiang Kai-shek.

So I was aware of the Communist Party from the time I was
very young, and my family was made to suffer a great deal because of my parents' connection with the party. The KMT
searched our home and confiscated our property.

Because my father was fighting with the People's Liberation
Army and not earning any money to support his children, we
were very poor. I went to school in my hometown in Anhui
province and after finishing middle school I studied nursing at
the Anhui nursing school, which had been established by an
American Christian church. But by the time I graduated in 1940,
Anhui was occupied by the Japanese. When they discovered that
my parents were with the PLA, they were going to arrest me,
but some members of the party underground helped me escape
to Shanghai. From there I wanted to go to Yenan, but that was
impossible, so they sent me to Hong Kong. I finally made my
way to Yenan with a group of other young people, but it took

us almost two years, because we had to find ways of getting through the Japanese- and KMT-occupied territories.

When I arrived, they sent me to medical college. It was not a real one—the quality and the conditions were poor—but they called it a college. They wanted us to become surgeons, and we worked on wounded soldiers even though most of us had no real training in surgery. After Japan surrendered in 1946, some Chinese, Russian, and American doctors came to Yenan, and I learned a great deal from working with them. We had very few medical books, only a few from Russia, so we learned mainly by doing. I suppose I can compare it to my English, which I learned myself just from listening to radio and TV.

In 1947 KMT troops attacked Yenan. I was a surgeon with the militia for three years, following the troops and attending to the wounded, so I was always close to the front and often under fire. In March 1949 I was with the PLA when we liberated Peking, and it was a very thrilling experience. Then, after all of China was liberated a few months later, I moved to Peking permanently because my parents were here, and I continued to practice medicine.

Many women like me became doctors during the revolutionary years, but after liberation that gradually changed. Compared to men, few women continued in medical work. You see, when the new government was established, they needed cadres [leaders] from the Communist Party who could teach people how the new society functioned, and many women were chosen to do that. The medicine they had learned in Yenan was not sufficient to handle normal hospital work; they had been doing that only because of the emergency situation and they didn't have adequate training. Also, after liberation the new government had access to all the doctors in China.

I didn't give up medicine because I loved it so much, even though I never really attended a medical school. After liberation I sometimes took some courses in medicine, and in 1957 I began to specialize in cancer. Before the new government was established, cancer work was not very widespread in China because we had to contend with so many chronic or infectious diseases like cholera, typhoid fever, and malaria. But by 1958

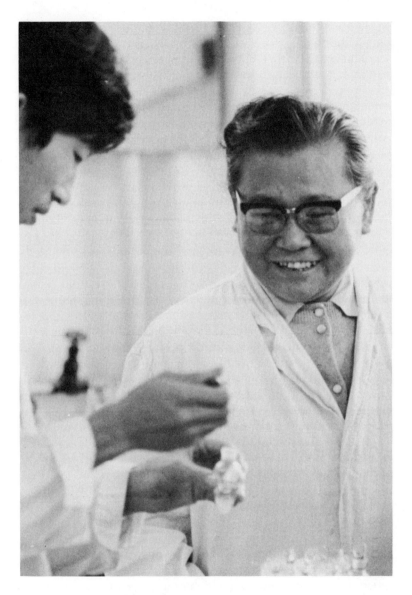

Li Bing, director, Cancer Institute,
Chinese Academy of Medical Sciences

we had controlled most of those diseases, and cancer became one of the major causes of death.

That year, with the support of Premier Chou En-lai, this national cancer center was built, the first in China. Previously, all cancer treatment was done at general hospitals. When the center opened, I was assigned by the minister of public health to do cancer research, and I've been in charge of the cancer control office ever since. Eventually I became deputy director of the center, and last year I was appointed director. I'm also secretary of the Communist Party Committee here.

Though heart disease is the leading cause of death in China now, cancer is the second and our government is very interested in controlling it. I had a lot of encouragement from Premier Chou. One day he criticized me. He said, "Cancer is the enemy, and you must organize an army to defeat the enemy. Study the methods used in foreign countries and learn how to solve this problem in China." That was in 1970, when we really started to investigate cancer; we spent ten years surveying the entire country. At that time, according to official reports, the population of China was 950 million. With a staff of 640,000 investigators, we interviewed 850 million people, family by family, in every village, town, city, and county throughout the nation. It was a massive job, but when our work was completed, we understood much more clearly what the cancer picture was in China. Now we have maps showing where the highest incidences of the various kinds of cancer are.

And because China is such a big country, many foreign scientists have become interested in our work. We have one-fourth of the world's population, many different environments, and with fifty-six national minority groups, a great variety of life-styles. We feel those factors have an effect on the incidence of cancer. For instance, ithe most common type in both men and women in China is gastrointestinal. For men, the second most common is cancer of the esophagus, and for women, uterine/cervical.

But in the mountain areas of Hebei, Shaanxi, and Henan, cancer of the esophagus is the highest for everyone. So we study such factors as eating habits and the environment to see if there is any relationship to the causes. Now uterine/cervical cancer is going down, perhaps due to better feminine hygiene and educating women on the need to have regular Pap smears. In the factories they have clinics where they give women workers Pap smears every six months. That way we can detect cervical cancer early, and the five-year survival rate has now risen to 92 percent. In the rural areas we use the barefoot doctors [peasants who are trained for three to six months at hospitals or clinics and then return to their villages to practice simple medical procedures]. It's very easy for them to take a Pap smear and send it to the hospital. So we are really beginning to control cancer in China now, but we have a long way to go in prevention, early detection, and cures.

Recently we signed a joint contract with the United States National Cancer Institutes to implement a three-year cancer control program. In China, because most people spend their lives in one place, it's easier to study life-styles and their relationship to various kinds of cancer.

Half of the students in our medical schools are now women. They are much more accepted in medicine than they were before liberation. But, of course, there are problems. Women get pregnant, which makes it hard for them to pay attention to their work. But we are trying to solve those kinds of problems.

Of the 300 members of the Party Central Committee, about 50 are women, and of the 125 medical subcommittee members, only 3 are women. However, I feel women enjoy equality with men and sometimes even surpass men. For instance, I am a leader in the medical field, and a lot of men respect my opinions and obey my instructions. Legally, men and women are quite equal, though of course in some jobs or professions, women are less equal than men. But you can't look at things only from that angle. In rural areas and villages there are more men in the labor force because women have so much housework to do. Historically, China was a feudal society and, especially in the rural areas, there are still a lot of ideas held over from the past. But women do want equal opportunities and rights and, compared with old China, they are doing well.

I think that, even in years to come, we still won't see as many women as men holding high positions. Yet I feel strongly that women will enjoy more and more equality in various fields. Our party and our government put special emphasis on the rights of women, and they continue to place them in leading positions.

I married late, at age thirty, because I was so busy making revolution. My husband was also very busy. He's a social scientist. So when we had children, we hired a housekeeper. She was an older woman who could not work at anything else, and she cooked, cleaned, washed clothes, and took care of the children until they were grown. Now my daughter is a doctor, one son is in the army, and the youngest son is studying foreign language at the university. During the Cultural Revolution we were labeled Capitalist Roaders, along with most of the intellectuals in China. I worked in a laundry, washing clothes for two years, but then Premier Chou liberated me and my family. All the universities and institutes were closed, so many scientists who wanted to work organized themselves and went to the countryside to work with patients and conduct scientific investigations. I was able to travel around a lot, and I didn't lose too much time away from my work. I also escaped criticism and self-criticism sessions with the Red Guards because I was working with the peasants.

But China lost a whole generation of progress. My daughter graduated from middle school in 1966, and my sons graduated in 1968 and 1969, all during the Cultural Revolution. They were also sent to the countryside, but I asked them to study on their own so that after the downfall of the Gang of Four they could continue their education. And that's what they did.

I don't think a Cultural Revolution could ever happen again in China. I'm a member of the party and when it began, I thought it might be a good thing and that I should follow the instructions of Chairman Mao, so I went along with it. But after two years, I was against it. When I was a very young girl I joined the revolution, but now I'm anti-revolution, and many other people think the same way since the "correcting the wrong and making it right movement" [the Cultural Revolution]. They pushed me the wrong way, so I turned to the right. In the old days, we had a very fine tradition of criticizing and helping each other. When I did something wrong, everybody criticized me and I listened carefully to their opinions. The idea was to help and serve the people, but during the Cultural Revolution, no one could do that for fear of being called a counter-revolutionary. Now we have gone back to that fine tradition. Otherwise we couldn't have recovered in such a short time. I feel if the tradition of freedom to criticize is preserved, a Cultural Revolution could never happen again.

We have learned from the past, but our leaders must set a good example. They must behave themselves like common people and not decide anymore that they should have things like fine houses. And we must have free speech and discipline.

DR. WEI YU

Physics Professor

The Institute of the University of Technology is about a twenty-minute drive from the city of Nanking along a pleasant tree-lined country road. Covering about four acres of land, the institute is hidden behind an old brick wall. As one enters by a long drive-way, a number of weathered brick buildings come into view. Surrounded by trees, flowering shrubs, and grass, and connected by winding pathways, they present a serene and attractive picture.

When we arrived at the building that housed her laboratory, Dr. Wei was waiting at the entrance. A short, pleasant-looking woman, her face suddenly became quite lovely when she smiled. Although she spoke English, it was with a thick German accent that was surprising, somehow, coming from a Chinese—but understandable when I learned she had spent a number of years in West Germany, studying for her doctorate in physics. I was told she was the first woman in China to obtain a Ph.D. since the Cultural Revolution. At the time of our visit, the forty-three-year-old scientist was working on the development of an ultrasonic device for the early detection of breast cancer.

Dr. Wei Yu, *associate professor of physics,*
Institute of the University of Technology

Afraid to Try

My parents were both teachers. Father taught in a middle school and mother in a primary school. I was born in Guilin, a very beautiful city in southern China, in 1940, just nine years before liberation.

Though my parents were not party members, they supported the Communist Party's ideas. So when liberation came, they were very happy because life was improved for all the Chinese people. I was the eldest of nine children, six girls and three boys. Because my parents were very advanced, they encouraged their daughters as well as their sons to become educated. Even before liberation, things were changing for women in the big cities. In the countryside people were not educated at all, especially women, but in the cities a few women were even going to college. But not many women in China had the chance to go to school, and life was very difficult for them. My mother had two sisters, but she was the only one who had any education. She left home when she was eighteen and went off to do something for herself. She was a very courageous woman, and she succeeded in going through middle school.

In my own family all the children had some education, though only four went to university. That was because of the Cultural Revolution, but it did not affect me because I was the oldest and had already graduated by then. Some of my brothers and sisters were able to go after the Cultural Revolution, but not the ones who were ready for university during those ten years when all education came to a halt.

I graduated in 1961 and then went to a postgraduate school for my master's degree. There were no doctoral degrees being given in China at that time. Then, in 1979, when we established diplomatic relations with the United States, our government sent fifty people to study in America and fifty to West Germany. I had studied English, Russian, and German, so I was able to pass a German language examination and was selected to go to a technological university in West Germany. After a year there, I received a grant from the Humboldt Science

Foundation and was able to continue my studies in microwave technology for nearly three more years.

Of the fifty who were sent to Germany, only six were women. In China many more men than women are interested in science. Few women had done the necessary postgraduate work, so not many could compete with men because they were not qualified.

I'm now doing research on ultrasonic medical instruments, specifically high-powered microwave. In Germany I worked with a gyrotron, but I felt that while the work is important, it is not useful for China at this time because it is too expensive. Now I'm working on more practical things.

Some women have less courage than men. They think they can't do certain things, so they don't try. In 1950 the government passed the Marriage Law, giving women full equality with men. But we are equal only in some ways. You must remember that our country was a feudal society for 5,000 years, and there was much discrimination against women. You cannot change that in a short time because the law cannot change people's ideas.

I also think women must have the courage to improve their feelings about themselves. That's the only way women can get as high positions as men. If women don't feel equal, they will not be treated as equals. I don't feel men are smarter, it's just that women don't think of themselves as smart because of the old attitudes. Changing that will take time. I don't know of any case where a man was promoted over a woman at this university because of discrimination against women. In fact, sometimes it's just the opposite. They will promote a woman just to encourage her, even though a man may be a little more qualified.

Of the 1,500 students who enter this university every year, about 30 percent are women, but they are only 5 percent of the graduates. And in the postgraduate school, there are no women. Yet I feel the opportunities are equal. The women just don't try because they are afraid. I always tell my women students, "You can do it. You must try." And some of them do, but not as many as the men. So I really feel that it's the fault of the women themselves that they don't achieve. I'm a lecturer and usually you cannot become a lecturer here until you're a full professor;

I'm only an associate professor. This institute has thirty to forty women associate professors out of 200, and only one female is a full professor. But that's because women don't like the hard work and the responsibility. Most of them have too many household chores. Men and women should share household chores, but women usually do them. For instance, when a baby cries, the father can ignore it, but the mother will jump right up. I think a woman's heart is different.

My husband is also a lecturer at this university and we have two sons, but we also have a *hausfrau* who comes every morning to clean. That is not very usual in China, but she is one of our neighbors and several of us made that arrangement with her. She divides her time among three families. And our sons, who are grown now and studying violin at a music institute in Shanghai, are home only on weekends. So I don't have the problem that most women have of taking time away from my work for house duties.

As I was leaving, Wei's assistant, a young woman, asked to have a few words with me. "I admire Doctor Wei very much," she said. "She has money she could use to buy things like a color TV or a refrigerator for herself. But instead she buys equipment for the university. Many people tell her to use her extra money to send her husband to Germany for his doctorate degree, but she says he must make his own efforts, that she wants to spend her money to buy scientific equipment for the institute and her country."

WU XI-JUN

Chemical Engineer

With its attractive blue tile roofed buildings surrounded by trees, shrubs, and flowers, the Jiangsu Province Scientific Academy, also located in a suburb of Nanking, is a lovely campus similar in appearance to the Institute of Technology. We were met at the entrance to Wu's building by a male aide and taken to a sunny conference room on the third floor, where she was waiting.

Though quite warm and friendly, the fifty-year-old chemical engineer has a no-nonsense manner. The academy's Science and Technology Committee, which she chairs, is very important to China's modernization plans. Its responsibility is finding ways to increase scientific and technological development while holding down costs and maintaining quality. Wu's own research in the fields of chemical engineering and computer science has brought her many honors. A member of both the Scientific Association and the Industrial Institute of China, she is also editor of the industrial institute magazine and has been designated a Model Woman of China.

Her work has enabled her to travel extensively to a number of foreign countries including the United States, and she speaks a fair amount of English.

The Responsibility of Women

My father was a university professor and my mother a middle-school teacher. I have a sister who is a computer engineer, and my brother is a physical science professor at Nanking University, so I came from an educated family. My parents felt it was important that daughters as well as sons be educated, so we were all treated equally. That attitude was not unusual among educated city people even before liberation. The wealthy intellectuals of a certain class did not have the old feudal ideas about women, and my grandfather was very well-to-do, so they could afford education for all the children. My mother's brothers were both educated overseas, one at Harvard in America and the other at Oxford in England.

I went to Shanghai University in 1951, right after liberation. I passed an examination and was accepted. When I was at university, we had no doctoral programs in our country as we do now. And at that time there were only 200 women among 3,000 students. Now, about a third of the students at my university are women. I think the great majority care about equality. The important thing is that they respect themselves and double

Author with Wu Xi-Jun (right), *senior chemical engineer, Jiangsu Province Scientific Academy*

their efforts for the country. And they should not wait for their husbands to make achievements. But of course, there are a few women—not many—who just don't care.

I think too many women in America just want to be housewives. I know the younger generation likes to work and make their contribution, but I would like to see all the women in the world take jobs and develop themselves as people.

At this academy one-third of the cadres are women, which shows that most of my women colleagues think they are as capable as men. Of course, there are always some women here who still prefer to have sons rather than daughters, but very few.

At this university it's the same for women and men. I didn't have to work harder to become a senior engineer here. And we have many women leaders in Jiangsu province. The governor is a woman, and there are about a dozen others—bureau leaders, senior scientists, and vice presidents of various organizations. But considering the fact that women make up over 50 percent of the population, that's still not enough. The reason is that women do more household tasks and take greater responsibility for the children. Although they have the same educational opportunities as men, they don't have as much time to study. That's one of the problems women still have in China.

Secondly, there are physical differences. You must admit men and women have different physical conditions. For instance, heavy labor is simple for men, but not for women. But science and technology take brains, not strength, and I feel there are quite a number of women doctors and scientists, so women are making progress. By law women enjoy equality with men socially, politically, and economically, so that is not the problem. But during the ten-year Cultural Revolution, government control of spiritual re-education was not effectively exercised. Therefore, some of the feudalistic thinking revived and women were held back. I suffered criticism during that time, but I never stopped my research because I had confidence that science would be useful in the future. I also thought the Cultural Revolution was temporary, that it wouldn't last forever. But our laboratories were closed, as were all the others, so most scientists could not work. Science and technology were greatly set back for ten years.

I was able to continue working on my own, but not everyone could do that.

Also, I never married, so I didn't have to worry about taking care of a home and children, and I think that was a big help to my career. Now I make policy on how we are going to develop our science, not only in my own fields, which are chemistry and computer science, but in others, too. The Committee of Science and Technology includes all the sciences. It is mainly an administrative organization and our primary purpose is to increase production and efficiency in Jiangsu province.

We also arrange exchange programs with scientists from other countries. I have been to Canada, West Germany, and America, and I have given lectures in your country. The Chinese have made great contributions to Western countries, mainly in the fields of acupuncture and herbal medicine. We, on the other hand, need Western advanced technology, especially the medical instruments we are now importing.

WANG LI-JEAN

Chemical Engineer

Wang Li-Jean appeared quite Westernized and much younger than her forty-four years when I interviewed her shortly after returning from China. Since emigrating from the People's Republic three years earlier, she had been living with her uncle in a small but pleasant and immaculately maintained 1930s-era bungalow, one of many found in California. This one was on a tree-lined street in a quiet, middle-class neighborhood in Glendale, a small city in Los Angeles County.

A graduate of Peking University, a fact she disclosed with considerable pride, Wang was working as a research chemist at the University of Southern California and studying English at night school. She was able to converse in English with little difficulty and seemed willing to discuss her native country objectively, despite the fact that she was attempting to bring her husband and fifteen-year-old son to the United States.

I directed my questions toward personal life-styles, a subject that had brought little response from the women I interviewed in China. During our stay in the People's Republic, we had read newspaper reports of a new campaign against "ideological contamination," causing many to fear another repressive period like the Cultural Revolution. The October 13, 1983, issue of the China Daily, *in an article headlined "Party Launches Rectification," described a Communist Party Central Committee decision to launch an overall drive to reorganize the party with a goal of "achieving ideological unity. That is to correct all erroneous left and right tendencies that run counter to the four basic principles and to the Party line. . . ."*

Having suffered, along with most other intellectuals, during the Cultural Revolution, Wang was very concerned about these reports. She said she had also heard rumors that there would be a movement to "remove the contamination in people's minds caused by Western influences."

In January 1984, however, Los Angeles Times *correspondent Michael Parks filed a story from Peking, announcing that the party leadership was halting its campaign against ideological contamination "amid signs that they were sorry that it was ever launched."*

What was meant to be a final purge of the radical leftists [those who supported the Gang of Four policies], wrote Parks, was mistaken by local party leaders to include those who wore "mustaches, fashionable clothes, and permanents . . . flower growing, waltzing, abstract art, minority customs and religious beliefs were evidence of 'spiritual pollution' and they took steps to eliminate such 'bourgeois decadence.'" In essence, the whole campaign got out of hand and, again, Deng's pragmatism won out.

A Hard Life

I was only ten years old at the time of the liberation, but I still remember what China was like before. It was terrible. The Japanese had invaded and life was very hard for the people.

My father was a medical doctor. He had gotten his training in America in 1930 and when he came back to China, he served as director of two hospitals, one in Chengdu and another in Chongqing (Chungking). He left China again in 1948, just before the People's Republic was established by the Communists. He had three choices at the time: to remain in Red China, to go to Taiwan with the Kuomintang, or to go back to America. He decided on America because he had been there and liked it and he had a lot of friends there. You see, when he worked in Chongqing as director of the hospital, the Communists and the Kuomintang were cooperating so he served them both. That was in 1945, and he knew a lot of high officials in both parties. But in the end, he chose America.

I really didn't know my father very well because when I was very young, I lived with my mother in our hometown and he lived in Shanghai. I just knew he was a very famous doctor. My mother was a home economics teacher in a senior middle school. She taught cooking and sewing and how to be a good wife. She died when I was fourteen, but my parents were divorced by then and my father had remarried. I have one older sister, who lives in Peking, and two half-brothers, who live in America. They are both medical doctors. When my father returned to America, my stepmother and my half-brothers went with him.

Divorce was unusual at that time, but they had been separated for so long. He worked in Chongqing, Chengdu, and Shanghai, and we lived in Amoy. After they were married, he went to America for eleven years for his medical training. My sister was born before he left and I was born after he came back. Then my mother couldn't move to Chongqing or Shanghai with him because of the war. All of southern China was occupied by the Japanese, so my parents really never saw much of each other. After he left in 1948, he never returned to China. He tried to bring us to America, but my mother didn't want to go and my sister had joined the Red Army. She went to north China before the liberation and became an army nurse. I stayed with my mother in Amoy until 1954, when we found she had cancer and moved to Peking for better medical care. But it was too late; she died that same year.

Wang Li-Jean, research chemist now living in California

I was in my first year of senior middle school and I lived with my sister, who was married by then. In 1956 the government encouraged everyone to write to any overseas Chinese we knew who were experts, because the country needed them. My sister and I wrote to my father and asked him to come back, but he said it would be too difficult. My two half-brothers could not get an education in China because they did not know the language. We continued to write once in a while, and then he passed away just before the United States and China formalized their relationship in 1979. The year before, one of his friends came to China on a visit, and my father asked him to try and find us. But he couldn't because we had changed our name and moved out of Peking. A few months later, he visited again and that time he found me and said he would phone my father from Hong Kong. But when he arrived there, he had a message that my father had died suddenly of a heart attack.

I came to the United States because of my father's friend. When he found me, he asked about my education and experience. I told him I had graduated from Peking University, which is very famous, and I had seventeen years experience in chemistry at a research institute. He then suggested I come to America because most of my relatives were there; my uncle, my six cousins, and my half-brothers. I agreed to try and they sponsored me. I wanted to see how well I could do there and felt it might be good for my advanced studies. When I arrived I had an interview at USC, and they said they were doing a research project and needed people like me to work on it. They asked if I wanted to be a student or work on the project and I said I liked research. They said I could work on my advanced degree anytime in America, because there is no age limitation as there is in China.

But I did get the same education and work opportunities as men, and the same pay too. In my time, it was hard to get into a university, especially a good one, because there was a shortage of places. But they gave women and men the same opportunity. We were chosen according to the grades we received on the examination.

My friends and I, those who graduated from this famous

university, worked with men and we were respected. And if we qualified for a job, we were allowed to apply along with men. When I was very young, even in elementary school, I was the leader of my class. I felt strong all my life, and I never thought anyone looked down on me. But the fact is, the other girls always felt they were looked down on and that they couldn't do as well as the boys. So I did see that attitude in China, and that is what keeps some women from achieving true equality. They don't believe they deserve it.

My work here is much harder than it was in China. There we always worked in groups. I was a group leader and I had at least five or six people working for me. But here I have to work alone. I have only one graduate student and sometimes four work-study students helping me, so it's been harder, especially in the beginning when my English was so poor. I took one year of English as a second language when I was at Peking University. The first was Russian, which was very popular in those years. I also studied English on my own, so I could read and write but not speak it. When I first came to this country, that was a problem. I had to phone people and order things, and I had to communicate with my professors. But I attended the American Language Institute at USC, and I did not have to pay tuition because I'm a university employee.

I think some women in China would have liked to form women's rights organizations, but they don't have the freedom to do that. The government does not allow any organizations that are not under its control. So people can't do what they want or think what they want. We did have freedom in our personal lives, but no choice of jobs. When I graduated from university, they gave us a list that told which institutes needed us. We were told to choose three or four from the list in the order of our preference, but then they decided which one to send us to. I got my second choice, but actually we just had to obey the party. For our first choice, we never wrote any exact job. We just said that we would go where they wanted to send us because we just wanted to serve the country. Sometimes I resented being told where to go and what kind of work I could do, but I accepted it. I had to.

My husband is an electrical engineer. When we were married, we did not have a place to live, so we stayed with his family. Many couples have to wait a long time to get married because they have no place to live. The housing shortage in China is a big problem. When I first moved to Peking in 1954, it was very easy to get housing. You just paid your rent and you could get a house or apartment. But that was before the population explosion after Mao encouraged the people to have as many children as they wanted. That was one of his biggest mistakes. Professor Ma Yinchu was a very famous economist and the president of Peking University. In 1956 he submitted a report to Mao, saying it was a good time to control population and he was right. But Mao said no, the hope of China lies in its people. But if they had controlled population then, China would be all right today. The government has worked hard on the housing problem, but they cannot solve it.

There are two easy ways to find a boyfriend: at school and at work. Some are also introduced to men by friends or relatives. My husband and I knew each other in senior middle school, but at that time we were just friends. We couldn't have dates until I was in my fourth year at university; it was a six-year program. The university leaders told us we couldn't concentrate on our studies if we had a boyfriend. If you dated anyway, they got very tough with you. My husband was also at Peking University, but in a different college, and we began our serious relationship in my fourth year. We met twice a week. On Wednesday evenings he came to my college building or I went to his, and we studied together in the library because we had so much work to do. Then on Saturday evenings we went to a movie on campus. If we had done that before our fourth year, people would have criticized us. In America, I know that sounds strange, but in China it was very common.

Also, sometimes we went out to dinner, but not very often, or we'd visit friends together. You couldn't go to a hotel or motel, no way. If you did, you had to have ID, showing that you were married.

At that time, we all lived at the university and, as I said, after our marriage, we lived with his family. Some of my friends couldn't find any housing, so even after they were married they had to live separately. Each would go back to the parents' home and they just met once a week. It was very hard. My in-laws had three rooms at that time, and they gave us a bedroom, so we had some privacy.

If anyone had an affair, it was a very serious problem. People would criticize you and you had to criticize yourself, too, at workplace meetings. You would also lose all your friends and have to change your job. One of my classmates had that problem. She was a very kind woman, but when she got a job at a research institute, she fell in love with a married man. They loved each other very much and they had sexual relations. People found out and they were criticized a lot. She couldn't stay in China so her family, who lived in Hong Kong, was able to bring her out. But I've heard the situation is much more open now.

Most people just accepted those restrictions because in China girls are very careful. They know that if they lose their virginity before marriage they will probably never find a husband. Husbands are boss and women know it. If they lose their reputation, they have to live a life of shame.

Two years after I was married, I got a small apartment in my work unit. I was working in Peking, and my husband had been sent to another province, so we were separated for four or five years. Separating couples was very common in China. He couldn't get back to Peking, and I didn't want to leave because it's easy to get out but very difficult to get back in. Everyone wants to live in Peking, so he wanted me to stay because he hoped to come back one day, and if I had gone to his province, he might never get the chance. We met every year on our twelve-day vacations and sometimes when he came to Peking on business.

Our son was born two years after our marriage, and my husband was very good to me. He wanted me to develop my career, so during the time we lived together, he did half the housekeeping. And that was true with our friends too. All of us had graduated from university, so we were on the same education level. But women who worked in factories had it much harder at home.

They were not as highly educated and did not receive that kind of help or encouragement from their husbands. They felt their wives should work and still do all the housekeeping. So most Chinese women have two responsibilities, one at their job where they work very hard, and the other at home. They have to pick up the children from kindergarten and do the shopping, washing, and cooking. In China, you know, they work six days a week and they have to wash clothes by hand. There are no modern conveniences like we have here—no refrigerators, no washing machines. It's very hard for a woman unless she has a husband who is willing to help.

But it's almost impossible to change all the men. They have changed a little because in old China men never did any housework. But most of them just come home, sit down, eat the best of the food, read the newspaper, and do nothing.

And usually the men make all the decisions, but that also depends on which level of society you are in. At our level, we made them together. But at the lower levels, especially in the countryside, women have no right to make any decisions. They do the same work in the fields as the men, but they have no rights at home, and that is also hard to change.

Most of the teachers in child-care facilities are not well-trained, just housewives who take in children, and they don't need a license. And the neighborhood committees just set up nursery schools, using neighborhood women as teachers. There are some very good ones, but there is a long waiting list for those, and it's hard to get your child in. I tried very hard and got my son into a good one when he was three years old. We have two kinds: one where you send the child in the morning and pick him up at night, and another where they stay all week. You send them on Monday morning and bring them home on Saturday evening. My son was in a boarding nursery school for two years, and he never liked it. Monday morning was always a bad time for him and I felt bad, too. I wanted him to stay with us, but at that time we had very small living quarters and they were far from work. If you're doing research, you have to study in the evening, so we worked very hard and we had no time to take care of him. I think boarding school damaged the relationship between my son and me and that's why I feel so guilty. Recently, I wrote to him and told him how guilty I feel, but he says he's almost forgotten about it. If I had a child now, I would never do it again. The problem is that most people have no choice. Life is so hard, it's the only way they can survive.

People in China need shorter work hours. Parents have so many things to do, they have no time for their children even on Sundays. And I think the new policy of one child per family is good. In my time, I could have had two or three, but most of our friends had only one, so they could give the child more attention.

Most grandparents will babysit, but that creates another problem. They don't know how to train children. They just give them food and let them do as they please. That's why I didn't send my son to live with his grandparents during the Cultural Revolution.

On Sunday morning we washed the whole week's dirty clothes, which took three or four hours. In the afternoon, we cleaned house. Usually Saturday evening was a social time. We visited our friends or parents, or we invited people to our house to have some food and talk. But not very often because every weekend was so busy with household chores.

Sometimes we went to the park with our child on Sunday, but if we did, we had to work very hard Saturday evening, getting all the housework done. Then we would get up early on Sunday and get on our bicycles—those were our cars.

The younger generation is still responsible for the older, but only if their income is big enough. The family structure has changed a lot. Before, families liked to live together, sometimes five generations in one house. But they had big houses in those days. Now the younger generation usually does not like to stay with their parents or their brother's or sister's family. They want their own place, and I think that's good. When three to five generations live together, they have problems. They quarrel and there is no privacy.

The Cultural Revolution was an even harder time. In 1969

my husband and I were sent to work on a farm in Yenan for one year and we did field work. When the Cultural Revolution began, we thought it was a good thing for the country, but after a few years, we knew something was wrong. Fortunately I was able to go back to Peking after a year, and my husband was allowed to go there too, so we lived together again. I had left my son with a friend in Peking while I was away, and I paid her almost all of my salary to take care of him. We didn't know what the future of our country would be during that time. Everything was in confusion. But after the Gang of Four was arrested, we knew there was hope.

The big lesson we learned from that experience was that you don't believe in only one person anymore. Before that, we believed only in Mao, but after the Cultural Revolution, we knew we had to think for ourselves, though even now people are afraid to speak out against the government. That's because in China people don't like to take risks. Even if they question or are uncomfortable about some things, they keep quiet or just give a gentle suggestion to the authorities. They are never sharp.

Western countries have influenced life-styles in China, especially among the younger generation. They learned some good things like modern technology, but they also learned bad things. The worst was wanting to make their own lives better and not caring about other people. They have become more self-centered and materialistic. They all want television sets, radios, and makeup. When some friends from China visited me recently, they asked me why I didn't wear makeup and fine clothes like the girls in China, so things have changed a lot. When I was a student I never wore makeup or dresses, usually just white shirts and blue pants. But I don't think caring about makeup and clothes is bad. It's just that if young people think only of themselves and always want more material things, they may do something bad to get them. In America if you work hard, you get more income. In China if you work hard, you still get the same income.

I sometimes felt bad when I worked hard and saw others, who did not, receiving the same salary. But I lived with it and still worked hard because I like science. China must do something to give people an incentive to work. In America if you don't do your job well, it's very easy to lose it. But not in China.

In both countries women have job opportunities and equality with men, though in China that's true only in the cities. The countryside is different. There is very little equality for women, and they also have different concepts about obeying their parents. Chinese women are also more socially conservative than American women. They don't like much social activity, while in America women are very open. They can do as they please.

In the home the Chinese woman's burden is much heavier than the American's. Here, I don't need to wash my clothes by hand anymore; we have a washing machine. The only thing I have to do is cook Chinese food, which takes time, but it's fun. But one thing that's better for Chinese women is the "iron rice bowl" policy. It means they can have a job their entire life, so they have more security. In America even the men are not secure. I think the Japanese system, which is in between the Chinese and the American, is good. The Japanese can work for the same company all their lives, and they are given benefits that make them feel secure. It's something like China, but it's different because they have incentive. If they work hard, they can be promoted and have more income. They also have the chance to go to America for further study. We have many Japanese engineers and scientists at USC on one-year study programs, and their companies pay for everything. The Chinese have foreign study programs, too, but when they go back to China, they receive almost the same income as before. In Japan study enables people to move higher up the ladder. I hope that will happen in China someday—work harder, more income.

American women have much more freedom and I think that's better. They can even break with their families, which is very important. Most Chinese women keep their family relationships out of a sense of responsibility, not always because of love, and they are very unhappy.

I like living in the United States, though sometimes I feel my job is not secure and I'm not used to that. But I know I will be much happier when my husband and child are with me.

YEN JUNLING

Ph.D. Student in Chemistry

The setting was a two-bedroom apartment in an off-campus University of California at Los Angeles housing unit for students with families. In comparison to most West Los Angeles apartments, it was modest—the rooms small and the furnishings plain and strictly functional. But compared to the housing its occupants were used to in China, it was a palace.

I interviewed Yen Junling, who was then in her third year of a doctoral program in chemistry at UCLA, shortly before I left for China. She and her husband, who was in the same program, were living with their ten-year-old son as well as Yen's sister, a graduate student in music at the University of Southern California.

Yen, thirty-seven, is very vivacious, smiling often and gesticulating frequently to emphasize her points. Yet her anger, especially about the time lost from her work as a research scientist when she was sent to work on a farm during the Cultural Revolution, is very obvious. She feels she is now too old to make any important scientific contributions, concentrating her hopes for the future instead on her child. And though she insisted they had not yet made up their minds about whether they would return to China when their studies were completed, I had a strong impression that they intended to remain in the United States.

After the interview her husband served a bowl of watermelon cubes mixed with lichees. As we sat around the dining room table eating and chatting, my photographer and I were amused to see that while we used the chopsticks he provided, the Chinese family used forks.

Women: The Old and the New

I was born in Suzhou during the Second World War. My father got his Ph.D. in agrobiology in 1937 at the University of Minnesota, and when he returned to China he became a university professor. My mother also had a high-level education. She graduated from a university in China as an economics major. In fact, she was my father's student. That's how they met. But my father died at an early age; I was only seven at the time.

It was unusual in those days for women to go to university, but both of my parents had unusual backgrounds. My father came from a rich and well-known family in Suzhou, which is in central China close to Shanghai. It's a very famous garden city, beautiful and modern, and most of the people there knew the family. My grandfather had five brothers, and my father had five brothers and four sisters. It was a really big family. But even though they were rich, the girls didn't get any education. They just stayed home and learned how to sew, cook, and keep house. They could not even decide who they wanted to marry. The parents decided, so the daughters were not very happy. The eldest was lucky. Her husband was very nice to her, but he died at an early age and my auntie had to take care of their four children. But her husband's family was also rich, so it was not too bad.

The marriage arranged for the second sister was very bad. After they were married, her husband treated her cruelly. He liked to go outside the home and play. He didn't do any work and he also used opium. In those days the British were pushing opium in China, and he became an addict. He spent all of his money on it and his wife's, too. Then he died, and in those days, widows could not remarry, so my aunt had to just stay at home and take care of her child. She lived with her parents-in-law, who were very nice to her, but they were so unhappy about their son that they died soon after he did, and all their money was gone. My aunt went back to her childhood home and lived with her brother, but a woman in that situation has a very low status in the family. She was treated like a maid and had to do everything for everybody.

The husband they chose for the third sister contracted a lung disease before the marriage, but the agreement had already been made so she had to go ahead with it. In old China they believed that if a man became seriously ill he would get well if he mar-

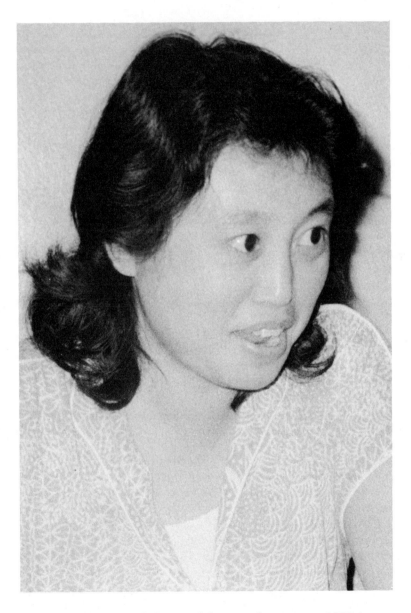

Yen Junling, Ph.D. candidate in chemistry at UCLA

ried, but this man died a short time later. And, because she was so unhappy, she died at an early age, too. Her life was hopeless.

The fourth sister was very lucky. She got a nice husband, and after they were married they found they really loved each other. His family was rich, but she didn't love him because of that, it was because his only wish was to see her happy. So of all the sisters on my father's side, she was the luckiest. But none of them could choose the kind of life they wanted; the family decided everything. In old China a woman had to obey her parents, then her husband. If her husband died, she had to obey her son, and if she had no son, it was her daughter. So, throughout her whole life, a woman had to obey someone else. She had no choices and no rights. It was like belonging to somebody else. And that was true for all women, rich or poor.

My father's brother's wife was very young when her parents died, so she lived with an uncle. But he treated her so badly she moved into her married sister's house, the one who made the marriage arrangement with my uncle, and they lived with his family. But they were both very young at the time, and they hardly knew each other. When they were married, my uncle was still in senior middle school. Then he went to a university in America and when he came back, they soon found they had very different ideas. He became a famous doctor in China, but his wife didn't even know how to write her name, so it was a very bad marriage, and they couldn't get a divorce because his parents had arranged the marriage. That was very typical in those days. When he finally fell in love with a girl at the university, his wife also wanted a divorce, but he could not divorce her. And she tried to do everything to please him. When he returned to China, she cooked and served him his favorite food, she washed his face and his feet, she tried very hard to make him happy.

When they were both fifty years old, he finally realized he had not been very good to his wife and decided to go back to her. But it was too late to have children, so she had nothing, and soon after, she died. On her deathbed, the only words she spoke were "I'm sorry," because she couldn't please him.

My mother's life was different because she was the only daughter out of five children, so her parents loved her very much, and they allowed her to be educated. From the time she was very young, she wanted to go to school and be independent because she had heard all the stories about life for a woman in China. They had a teacher coming to the house to teach the sons, and my mother wanted to study with him too, but the teacher said he would not give lessons to a girl. My mother used to place herself outside the window and listen to the lessons, but one day he discovered her and hit her on the hands with a ruler. In the 1920s there were a few schools opening for women, so she went to one and, after graduating from middle school, she went to the university. And that education was very important in her life because when my father died, she had to support her five daughters. Of all the children in my mother's and father's family, they were the only ones who arranged their own marriage.

In China having sons is very important. Everyone in the family thought my mother was a very high-level woman. But when she had her first daughter, then a second, and then a third, everyone looked down on her. By the time the fifth was born, my father's parents hardly spoke to her anymore, and her position in the family became very low. But when the war ended, we moved to Shanghai and things were better. Big-city ways are different from those in small towns.

When the Communists took power I was only four years old, and by that time my parents were living in an apartment at the university. It was a big apartment, and they didn't take it away from him because his position at the university was quite high. He was director of his department. After he died we could not live there because the housing went with the position. But the university officials were very kind to us. They knew my mother had five children and her mother living with her.

In old China a man could have more than one wife, and my mother's father had two. My mother was the daughter of his first wife, but it was his second who lived with us and she was loved by all the family. We called her grandmother. She had grown up in very poor circumstances and one year, when her people had nothing to eat, they decided to sell her for food. First she worked as a servant in my grandparents' house, and later my grandfather married her. But she always took care of us and helped my mother a lot when she had to go to work in an office. Nobody believed my mother could support the whole family after my father died. My uncle told her she was still young and beautiful and if she wanted to marry again, her children could go and live with my father's brothers. But she said, "No. When I lost my husband, I lost my happiness and I cannot let my children lose theirs."

And I had a happy childhood. It was not a rich life, but it was nice and quiet. I liked my friends, I had enough food and a place to live, and I liked school. I think not being as rich as my parents were taught me how to treat people and face difficulties. When you have to do everything by yourself you try harder.

I never did want to be just a housewife, and after the revolution everybody in China had to work. The salaries were lower, so if they wanted to support a family both parents had to work. I also saw my mother working very hard, and I knew that if I wanted to be independent, I had to have knowledge. I also thought being a housewife would be boring, especially after I entered the university.

When I went to the university, only six of my thirty classmates were women. That's not because women are not as intelligent as men, but only because in middle school the girls had to do house chores, so they had more responsibilities. The boys could put all their energy into study. I have some women friends who are very intelligent, but they did not have high grades in middle school because their parents made them clean house while their brothers were encouraged to study.

Also, when women apply for jobs in offices or in factories, they are often turned down in favor of men because the unit leaders feel that the women will get married and have children to care for, so they will take more time off. But compared to my mother's and grandmother's generations, Chinese society has progressed a lot. It has given me the chance to change my life, so I feel very lucky and grateful.

Everyone took a uniform examination just before graduating from middle school. Then they gave us a form to fill in, telling which university you wanted to attend and which major you wanted. There were some fifty choices, and you had to select in the order of your preference all the way through the list. It was really a hard job. They made their decisions according to your school record. If you had good grades in all your studies, they would give you your first, second, or third choice. Competition was very high because they didn't have enough places for everyone. Each school has a specialty, so because I wanted to do research, I chose the University of Science and Technology, which is where I was sent. It was in Peking at the time, but they moved it to Anhui during the Cultural Revolution.

My husband and I were classmates. We met when we entered the university in 1962, and we were married in 1971, two years after we graduated, so we knew each other for nine years.

During our courtship, my husband said, "You are a nice girl," but we never talked about love. We just helped each other study and tried to do things for each other. After we were married, he said, "I like you, how about you?" I said, "Well, we will try to make a good life together."

Soon after our graduation, we were separated because we didn't work in the same place. We graduated in 1969, during the Cultural Revolution, and I was sent to a farm in northwest China, close to Mongolia. It was hot and dry, and I worked there for a year and three months, doing farm labor. The mud hut I lived in was like a dormitory, because there were 140 other students living there too. All those who graduated from universities at that time had to go and work on farms or in factories.

I hated it because I had not studied science to work on a farm as a laborer, but I had no choice. The life was okay. At that time I was very young, only twenty-two, and I was strong so I could do anything they asked of me. I also believed that if I worked hard I could change my life for the better. I knew if I allowed myself to be depressed I would just go down. All the students I lived with were about the same age and sometimes we argued, but generally we got along. After finishing work every evening, I couldn't stand on my feet. But after a good night's sleep, I could work again.

My fiancé was sent to do hard labor in a factory in Lanzhou, so he was in a city. On the farm it was worse. No one could visit you, you could not get married, and if you already were married, you could not have a child. We just worked and worked. My fiancé was also working hard, but he got twelve days vacation every year, so he could visit his family. Then I was sent to work in a factory in the same city where my fiancé was, and in 1971 we were able to marry.

Everyone had bad experiences during that time. My oldest sister, who is now a teacher at Peking University, was a student. They sent her to a farm, too, so her education was interrupted. The Red Guards controlled everything, and though some were kind, most of them thought all educated people had bad qualities, and they were very rough with us. My other sister, the one who is living with us now, majored in music and she was a very good singer. Before the Cultural Revolution, she was starting to become famous, but they told her that because of her family background, she could not sing anymore. You see, one of my father's relatives was vice president of Taiwan when Chiang Kaishek was president, and all of us were contaminated by that. My sister was sent to Shanghai to labor in a factory, but she continued to study music and after the Cultural Revolution she was able to go to university. Now she's at USC, working on her master's degree.

. After our marriage the factory where I was working gave us a small apartment—one room, no kitchen, and no bathroom. But all during that time we kept trying to get back into the work we had been trained for. My husband has always believed that if you allow people to work at what they enjoy, they will do a better job for the country. We filled out many application forms, telling what kind of education we had and what we wanted to do. Then, after three years, we got lucky. In 1975 Deng Xiaoping came into power for a short time, and we heard he was saying if people wanted to work in their specialties, they could try. So we tried again and finally succeeded. One of the science institutes was being divided into two sections, and every department needed new people, including those who had our type of training. Some of our former classmates who were working at the institute helped, and both of us were transferred to the physical chemistry branch in Lanzhou. The apartment they gave us was the same size as the one we had at the factory, but we didn't care. We hadn't transferred for better living conditions; we just wanted to do our work. We cooked on a hotplate in a corner of our small room. There was no refrigerator, so we had to shop every day after work or during break time. We ate very simply.

Our son was born in 1972, but he didn't live with us. First I was working in the factory, and then, when we got jobs at the institute, I had to work hard during the daytime and study every night. And my husband encouraged me. He said, "You want to go up like a mountain, so you cannot take care of the child." My mother offered to take care of him, so he went to live with her in Shanghai when he was only three months old, and I saw him only three or four times in ten years. Now we are so happy to have him with us. Having our family separated was the most difficult part.

When we were at the institute, we begged them for a chance to go on for higher studies. Then, in 1978, the government opened a graduate school in Peking, and we found out that if we passed some examinations we could enter. We studied hard and passed the test and were sent to Peking, but again we were separated because we had to live in separate dormitories. My husband lived at Peking University, and I lived at the University of Science and Technology. After we were there about a year and a half, my husband's auntie, who lives in Los Angeles, came back to China for a visit. She knew we had very good backgrounds and offered to sponsor us if we wanted to go to America and work on our doctoral degrees at a graduate school. We agreed and she applied to UCLA for us. When we were accepted, we were able to come here on student visas.

When we arrived my cousin met us and said, "Hello, how are you?" But I couldn't speak a word, so I just laughed because I didn't know what to say. It was also very difficult in classes, so I took English lessons at an adult evening school for two months. My husband had studied English for three years when we were at the University of Science and Technology fifteen years ago, but I studied Russian because the Russians were our friends at that time. At graduate school in Peking, I learned a little English, but only enough to look up science references in an English dictionary.

I could not understand the instructors at first, but I could read the textbook and I got good grades. It's hard learning by yourself, and I really feel I'm too old to study now. I still hate the Cultural Revolution because it took the best ten years of my life. My husband helps me a lot with the housework because we both have to study. When we first came to Los Angeles, we lived with his auntie for six months and then, two years ago, the university offered us this apartment.

I know there are some limitations for foreign students here because of the language handicap, and at first I also thought there was some prejudice. When we first arrived three years ago, we applied for some finanical support, and after we entered school, we found that everyone had it except us. We didn't understand it at the time, so we just decided to study hard and show what kind of people we are. Three months later, we got support, too, and they told us the delay was because we were the first students here from China and they didn't know about the educational level there. That was reasonable, but at first we felt we were not being treated equally.

I also feel handicapped sometimes because of the language problem, but our living conditions are much better here and that makes life easier. I'm not only a student, I'm also a mother and a housekeeper; after working all day, I have to come home and cook dinner, prepare lunch boxes for everyone, and do the housekeeping. My husband helps a lot, but I do most of it. It's much easier here. In China we had only one day off a week, Sunday, and we had no washing machine. Sometimes my husband and I had to wash clothes by hand for two or three hours. Then we would wait in line to buy vegetables and meat and come back home to cook and clean the house. We had only a short time to relax. Here you can buy food that is easy to prepare, and you can cook ahead. On Saturday I usually cook a lot and freeze it, so when I come home from school, I spend only half an hour fixing dinner. My husband and sister help, too, so I can study or relax after dinner.

Life in America is much easier. Chinese women, especially in the countryside, work so hard Americans wouldn't even believe it. I saw women work like men in the fields and then come home and cook and clean. And the men never help. In fact, men, children, and guests eat first and the woman stands aside until they are finished. It's still the way it was in my grandmother's time.

Everyone said it would be impossible to bring our son here, but again we tried very hard and we did it. We said the reason he had to come was that his grandmother had cancer and could not take care of him any longer. He has been here a year now and likes it very much. He didn't know any English before he arrived, so he didn't want to go out and play with the other kids because they didn't understand him. I told him to watch TV so he could pick it up, and at first it was boring for him, but now his English is better than mine. And I like the American educational system. It's much more open than China's. His school has some special programs for foreign students, and that helped a lot. He started in fourth grade last year and when he was halfway through fifth grade, they chose him and some other good students to enter a special junior high school program for classes in language, art, and science. Now he goes bowling with his friends and he likes school. In fact, he's hardly ever home.

I don't know if it's possible for us to become American citizens, and though my husband has over thirty relatives in the United States, mine are mostly in China or Taiwan. But his family wants us to stay here, so if we can get good jobs and the situation is right, we probably will. It's so hard to decide because my mother is still there and I miss her. If we went back, maybe I could do some research work, but then again, with our background, we had too much trouble during the past fifteen years.

I also think it would be good for my child to stay here, at least until he graduates from the university. Students need some competition, but when the competition is as great as it is in China, it makes them focus on just one thing, A's. America's method of teaching is better. Competition for grades is not emphasized so much, which allows children to develop more rounded personalities. I don't think getting A's is as important as having good ideas. A's are just marks on a paper, not on your mind.

I don't think I've really entered into American society. I just go to school every day and then come home. I have some friends, but Americans are not like Chinese. They may work together, but they don't socialize together after work. In China we used to go to a friend's house, talk a little, and then go home. But here we haven't entered into the society, and I'm afraid I'll never get used to that. I also miss my mother, though it might be easier to see her if I stayed here. In China I couldn't see her for long periods of time because even when I had a vacation, I had no money to travel. If I worked here, it would be no problem to go and visit her.

I like the closeness of families in China. I suppose Americans have family ties, but not like in China. Of course, on the other hand, sometimes close family ties cause a lot of trouble for people. In China old people are the rulers and you have to listen to what they say because they are very respected. In America they are not; it's the young who are listened to. But having very close relatives makes you feel warm.

I think the hope for the world is in the younger generation, so I want my son to have a good education. I once wanted two children, a son and a daughter, but I always had so little time, I couldn't even consider it. And if I'd had another child, I could not have come to America, because I would not have been able to go to graduate school. I think you have to lose something to gain something. I have some independence now, which is quite hard for a women to get, especially a Chinese woman.

JENNIFER YANG

Computer Scientist

Jennifer Yang was the first woman I interviewed for this book and her story was the most shocking. The others I spoke to, both in

China and the United States, had experienced the horrors of the Cultural Revolution and, having lived through our own Mc-Carthy era of unjust persecutions, I was always amazed to find they expressed no bitterness. They preferred to forget and go on with their lives. All, that is, except Jennifer Yang.

In August 1983 she was living alone in a small apartment in a rundown, predominantly Hispanic and Oriental district of Los Angeles. A tall, slim, pretty woman, she was then forty-four years old, but could have passed for thirty-four. The apartment, with its ten-by-twenty-foot living room and small kitchen and bath, was hot, airless, and drab, furnished sparsely with an old sofa and lounge chair, a few nondescript tables and lamps, and a pull-down Murphy bed. But Jennifer, who had been living with relatives since she emigrated from China three years previously, had moved into her own place just a month before and was very happy to have some privacy. Her only complaint was the cockroaches.

The murder of Jennifer's father, Yang Chengzuo, during the Cultural Revolution received world-wide press attention at the 1980 trial of Jiang Qing, Mao's widow and leader of the Gang of Four. Yang was one of two Furen University professors tortured to death on the order of Jiang, according to evidence presented by the prosecution.

Jennifer recounted the terrible ordeals she and her family experienced in China with very little expression in her voice, denying any feelings of anger, but coming close to tears when she told of the death of her father. Her only resentment, she insisted, was the terrible loss of dignity she suffered. When we met, she was studying computer sciences at the University of Southern California and also working there. A year later I learned she had been successful in her efforts to bring her husband and twelve-year-old son to the United States and the family was reunited.

People Against People

I was born and raised in Peking. My father had studied economics at Columbia University in New York from 1927 to 1932 and then returned to China, married my mother, and become a professor at Qoinghua University. When the Japanese invaded Peking in 1944, that university was moved to another province, so my father began teaching at Furen University, a Roman Catholic school in Peking. Though I was only four or five at the time, I still remember the Japanese breaking into our home and destroying everything. I hated them.

But after World War II when the Japanese were defeated, my family had a very nice life. My sister and two older brothers and I lived with our parents in a nice house with a pretty little garden. We had two maids, and my mother never worked because she was raised under the old system; she had very little education. When she finished junior middle school, my grandfather didn't allow her to go any further because she was a girl. Girls were just supposed to get married.

My family was not political, but they sympathized with the Communists, at least in the beginning, because the Chiang Kai-shek government was so bad. Although I was under ten when the Communists took power, I still remember the winters when I saw people die in the streets of hunger and cold. And everyone complained about the inflation. My father earned a good salary, but my mother was always saying that there was not enough money to buy food and clothing, so we welcomed the liberation in 1949. My parents hoped the new system would be better, and it was for the first five or six years, even though the country was rather poor.

Then the Korean War began, and we paid a lot for that in arms and soldiers. In fact, my brother volunteered to go to Korea at the age of sixteen because he was so patriotic, and because of that he never went to university. My other brother and I went, but not my sister because she was ten years younger and the Cultural Revolution interfered.

After the Communists took over, it became very common for girls to go to university. In our last year of senior middle school, everyone who wanted to go had to take a very difficult test. I studied very hard and passed, so in 1957 I entered Peking University, where I majored in chemistry. The course was six years, but we were supposed to have a master's degree when we graduated.

Unfortunately, the Great Leap Forward began in 1958, and the government insisted that all the students go to the country-side or to factories to help make steel in backyard furnaces [crude iron-smelting furnaces, built at workplaces and farms, in re-sponse to Mao's campaign to speed up production during the Great Leap Forward era, 1958–60]. Most of us didn't want to go because it was obvious even to the peasants that the steel was no good. And because classes stopped for long periods of time, I would say that during my six years at university I had only three years of education.

Before the Great Leap Forward, I believed everything the Communists told me and I supported them. Then, gradually, I became disillusioned with the party, but my life didn't really change until the start of the Cultural Revolution in 1966. I had graduated in 1963 and been assigned to work at the Synthetic Fiber Research Institute in Peking, which was part of the Na-tional Chemical Industry Department.

The Cultural Revolution was a time of great persecution, mainly of intellectuals, and my family suffered a great deal. First the Red Guards came into our home and took away our jew-elry, furs, and books. My grandfather loved books and owned some very valuable ones, including one from the Sung dynasty that was more than 1,000 years old. Then they jailed my par-ents for a few days and later forced them to clean the streets. But the worst part came a year later when they were both ar-rested and charged with being American spies.

When my father was teaching at Furen University, Wang Guangmei, who later became the wife of the head of state, Liu Shaoqi, was a student in the physics department. She lived just five doors away from our house, and she and my parents were friends. After World War II, some American Army officers vis-ited Furen to give some lectures and they wanted to visit the homes of some professors while they were there. Because my parents spoke English, it was suggested that the officers come to our house. We had a party for them and invited some other people, including Miss Wang. Later she went to the Communist area and married Liu Shaoqi, and during the Cultural Revolution, when Chairman Mao and the Gang of Four wanted to get rid of Liu and his wife, they used that party as an excuse to charge her with being an American spy and my father with being her link to the Americans.

So in 1967 my parents and Miss Wang were imprisoned in Qin Cheng, the top-security prison just north of Peking, where Jiang Qing, the leader of the Gang of Four, is now. I never saw my father alive again. My mother was there for eight years and we thought she was dead, too, because we never heard anything about her until the fifth year, when a policeman came to our house and said we could visit her. My sister and brothers and I went to the prison and she told us she hadn't known about my father's death until a guard told her just a week before. She cried and said that all she had wanted all those years was to see her family, but after they told her that Papa was dead, she just didn't care anymore, that all her hopes were dead, too. Our visit lasted about three hours and everyone cried except me. I had no tears left, and I was angry with my sister and brothers for crying. I didn't want them to have the satisfaction of seeing our tears.

Less than a year after my parents were jailed, I, too, was arrested and kept in a jail at my workplace. Because so many people were arrested during the Cultural Revolution, they didn't have enough prisons, so every unit—institutes, universities, factories, stores—had its own jail. There were about 500 workers at our research institute, and sixty of us were charged with being reactionaries and imprisoned. They held no trials. They just set aside an area and kept us prisoners. We couldn't go home or contact our relatives or friends. The lucky ones became laborers and the others, including me, were just locked in a room and beaten with rubber hoses.

No Denunciation

When the Communist Party took over the country, I was less than ten years old, so they really couldn't charge me with doing anything bad before then. And because they had such a tight security system, with everyone watching everyone else, I couldn't have done anything after that without it being known, so they had nothing to charge me with. They just wanted me to denounce my parents, which I would not do. They kept me prisoner for twenty months. When they set me free, my spine was so injured from all the beatings I had received, I had to use crutches in order to walk and I was black and blue all over. One day they made me stand bent over double continuously for eight hours when they were trying to make me denounce my parents. I lived in a small space under a staircase, which they had enclosed with some boards, and it was so cold in winter I sometimes woke up in the morning with frost on my blanket.

Both of my brothers were jailed, too, including the one who had volunteered to fight in Korea. My sister was only sixteen and a student, so they did not persecute her, but the schools were all closed, so she lived all alone in our house. Everyone was so frightened in those days, no one would talk to her because her background was bad, so it was almost like being in jail. And because she was alone so much, she gradually stopped talking at all. She just sat there for days at a time. The government continued paying my salary, which was about fifty-five dollars a month, and they took twenty dollars out to send to my sister, so she could buy food.

But the most horrible time of all was a day in 1970 after I was released and living with my sister. Two policemen came to our door and told me my father was dead. They said he had been transferred to a prison hospital and died there of a heart attack and that I could come to the hospital with them and collect his body. I didn't want to go because I was so ill, but I knew that if my mother was still alive, I would never be able to face her if I didn't.

It was about 1:30 in the morning when I rode to the hospital with them, and even though it was cold and windy, they made me wait outside for almost four hours. Then they said that before I could see my father, I had to sign a paper, giving them permission to cremate his body. I don't know where I got the courage, but I stood there on my crutches and said, "No, I want to see him first." Finally they agreed, but at the door to the morgue a policeman said, "Your father was a reactionary, so you are not allowed to cry when you see him." Then they took me into the room, and I saw him for the first time since he had been arrested. There are no words to describe the expression on his face. It was so sad. But I did not cry. I just said goodbye to him in my heart. Then they put the coffin on a truck and told me to climb up and sit on it. But I just opened the front door and got in next to the driver. I must have looked horrible because he asked me how I could come there all alone in my condition. But I was my father's favorite child and, no matter how horrible the situation was, I still loved him. They drove me to the crematorium, where I chose the cheapest coffin they had, and then I took the ashes to a burial place. But you are only allowed to keep them there for a short time because they have so little space. Two years later I brought them to my room, a very small room with two bunk beds, one above the other. I put the ashes in the upper bunk and slept under him.

About a week after our visit with my mother, I went to my research institute and the leader told me I had to go and work in the countryside within five days. He threatened me for almost three hours, but I said I could not because of my spinal condition and walked out on my crutches. I went back to my room and stayed in bed for the next two years. The hospital gave me a certificate saying I could not do hard labor, so they just accepted the situation and left me alone. I was payed 70 percent of my salary so I ate simple foods, just enough to stay alive, and my sister lived with me half the time and with my brother in Harbin the other half.

A year after I was released from jail, I married a man whose family background was also very bad. His father was jailed because they said he had traded with the Japanese, and he also died in prison. My husband was an engineer. He had been a classmate of my brother's, and they were working together in Harbin. He was a very nice person and he looked me up when he was visiting his family in Peking. When he asked me to marry him, I told him everything about my family and then I said, "Now, if you still want to marry me, that's fine." He did, so we went to the police station and got married. His mother had invited a few guests for a wedding dinner, and he asked if I could put my crutches aside just that one day to make his mother happy. I tried very hard, but I couldn't stand unless I used at least one crutch. My condition was a little better by then because I had taken some traditional Chinese massage treatments, the kind where a man stands on your back. They were very painful, but they really helped.

After the wedding he went back to Harbin and I stayed in Peking. During the ten years of our marriage, we tried very hard to work in the same city so we could live together. But we never could, so he's really a stranger to me, and whenever I needed his help, he could not be with me. We only saw each other on our twelve-day vacations every year, but I do know he's a nice person and very honest.

In 1972 I finally had to go to work in the countryside. My son had been born by then, and I left him with a friend in Peking because my mother-in-law was too old to take care of him. Though many of my friends were allowed to stay in Peking and work at a chemical factory or a research institute, they would not allow me to do that. When I asked the leader at my institute, he just looked at me with contempt and that was worse for me than the physical torture. I'll never forget it. I remember his tone was full of scorn. It was as if I was the most horrible person, and I never did anything bad to anyone.

The Chinese have always had a reputation for being very friendly and polite, yet during the Cultural Revolution, everything was turned upside down. I don't understand it. Before that time I had never had any problems with the people at the institute, yet many of my colleagues beat me and I must admit, the worst were the women. They tortured people just to get some praise from the leaders.

I stayed in the countryside for three years, and then they sent me to Harbin for a year, but my husband and I still had to live apart. He lived in a dormitory with other workers, and I stayed with my brother. Then my husband was transferred to a town near the Russian border.

Finally, in 1978, my uncle, who lived in Los Angeles,

sponsored me to come to America and, to my surprise, I was able to get a passport within three or four months. In fact, it was easier to come here than to be allowed to move to Peking. After my mother was released from prison, she lived in Peking, and then my uncle brought her and my sister to the United States too. About a month before we left, my husband was able to move to Peking and he came to the airport with my son to say good-bye. I tried to kiss my son, but he pushed me away. He hardly knew me because I had seen so little of him during the six years of his life. Now they both have their passports to come here, too. I sponsored them as soon as I got my green card.

The United States

When I arrived in Los Angeles, I was very unhappy because I didn't speak any English; I felt like a deaf mute. But it was so beautiful here with all the trees and flowers. I lived with my uncle for three months and took English classes at a college. But what impressed me most was the freedom. People here can criticize their leaders and they have choices. If they study hard, they can do well.

When I was growing up, I heard bad things about this country because at that time China and the United States were not friendly. But my father was educated here and some of my uncles and aunts were living here, so they told me about America, and I had good feelings about this country. At first, having the freedom to make my own decisions bothered me, because most of my life the government made them for me. Also, we were brought up to always consider what others thought about us. If I put on a colored blouse, I thought people might criticize me so I'd better not. Now I like being my own boss. When I first arrived, I found it difficult to tell the difference between the men and women. They all had long hair and wore blue jeans and T-shirts. But my main problem was not knowing the language. It was very frustrating, and I'm really not a strong person. I've always wanted to depend on somebody else, but I never had anyone. I'm in my forties, and it's not easy to start over again at my age. I changed my major because I never liked chemistry. After I graduated from senior middle school, the government decided I should take it. Now I'm majoring in computer science and also working full-time and taking English courses. My brain is not as good as it was twenty years ago when I was at Peking University, so I have to study harder. It's been very difficult to start a new life—a new major, a new language and, above all, adapt to a new environment. I have learned to be more independent, but still, by nature, I'm a weak person. I thought about committing suicide many times, but I finally made a decision to live, and I think the most important reason was wanting to see the end of the Cultural Revolution and the people who did those terrible things to me.

I have some friends here, both Chinese and Americans, but because of the language and cultural differences, I can't get very close to my American friends, and with going to school and working full-time, I don't have very much time to socialize anyway. I also have very mixed feelings about bringing my husband and son here. My boy is one of the reasons I try so hard. I have only one child, and I want him to have freedom and a good education. My husband is a very clever person, but he's by no means aggressive, so I don't know how he will adapt to this country. I feel my responsibilities will be even heavier when they arrive, and I'll have to work harder. This is a bad neighborhood, and I want my son to go to school in a nice neighborhood and have nice friends. At his age, friends have more influence on him than his parents. And though we suffered a lot, China is still our country. I don't want my son to forget his heritage, so his parents will have to teach him Chinese literature and history. And in spite of everything that happened, I miss China and I'm proud of being Chinese. It's hard to replace that spiritual kinship.

CHAPTER

5

EDUCATION

A HIGH PRIORITY

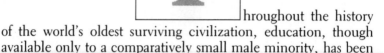hroughout the history of the world's oldest surviving civilization, education, though available only to a comparatively small male minority, has been revered by the entire population.

As David Bonavia writes in *The Chinese*, "On the traditional Chinese scale of priorities, education ranked only one notch below rice. To have a well-educated son was the pride and glory of any family that could afford the tuition fees. . . ."

Under the old Confucian system, education was a long process of rote memorization, primarily of classical literature and philosophy. Very little attention was given to the study of science or to the encouragement of independent thinking. It was the nation's intellectuals, however, under the leadership of men like Sun Yat-sen, a medical doctor who was educated in Hong Kong and Hawaii, who first challenged the old system, starting the movement that led to the overturn of China's last dynasty in 1911.

From the beginning the Communist government tried to wipe out illiteracy through the establishment of a nationwide network of free schools, and also by attempting to establish a unified, national written and spoken language. Youngsters are now being taught a simplified version of the northern dialect, Mandarin and the old, complicated pictograph writing is being abandoned in favor of a romanized Chinese called pinyin. The many different dialects still prevalent throughout the country often make it impossible for Chinese to understand each other if they are from different provinces.

The Communists did, however, perpetuate the old rote system of learning. It became a convenient means for teaching party dogma, which was a major part of the curriculum in schools at every level. And though Mao himself—like most of the founders of the Chinese Communist Party—was a college graduate, he had a lifelong distrust of intellectuals. Fearing that they would establish themselves as yet another elitist and exploitative class, he viewed them as a threat to his conception of China as a classless society. In the end it was that fear that led to the ten terrifying years of the Cultural Revolution, when intellectuals were forced to work in the countryside or factories and "study" under the peasants and workers. During that era, rote learning became even more entrenched, as everyone in the nation concentrated almost exclusively on memorizing and reciting from a "little red book" called *Quotations from Chairman Mao.*

But the most tragic development during those ten years was that, for all practical purposes, the entire educational system in China was abandoned. Youngsters called Red Guards invaded the schools and universities, examinations ceased, and discipline was made the province of students. Teachers and principals were often subjected to insults, beaten, and forced to do janitorial work, and many were imprisoned or sent to work on communes or in factories.

After the death of Mao and the fall of the Gang of Four in 1976, the new government tackled the enormous problem of reinstituting a workable system of education. But China was and still is very poor, and peasants comprise approximately 80 percent of the population. While city schools are state-supported, those in the countryside are maintained primarily by the peasants out of collective funds. And as their priority is usually on children working in the fields, so they can contribute to family income, education suffers. Theoretically all Chinese children are supposed to attend school for a minimum of five years, but in rural areas large numbers actually drop out after only a year or two.

As part of its modernization program, the Deng government is making efforts to combat illiteracy and to raise educational standards. At the June 1983 annual meeting of the National People's Congress, Premier Zhao Ziyang reported that although education in China had made huge strides in recovering from the damage of the Cultural Revolution, the per-student outlay of funds was still too low—only 10 percent of the total national budget—and that one-fourth of China's population was still illiterate or semiliterate. Emphasizing education as an important national priority, Zhao projected a 75 percent increase in college and university enrollment by 1987, and a 280 percent increase in evening and correspondence colleges. He also pledged to improve vocational education for workers and peasants, and to restructure primary and middle school education, predicting that vocational schools would account for more than 40 percent of senior middle school enrollment within five years.

Ironically, in spite of Mao's emphasis on training in practical skills, vocational and technical schools were closed for a full seven years during the Cultural Revolution, while the universities closed for only four.

The practice of conferring master's and doctorate degrees was suspended in 1966, but finally reactivated in 1981 after major universities had been operating normally for about five years.

Though the education of women has increased enormously since the Communists took power, an October 1983 issue of the *Guangming Daily* reported that "for historical reasons, the scientific and cultural level of women is still lower than men and it is urgent for women to further improve themselves." The article urged that "female employees in urban areas . . . be encouraged to take an active part in all kinds of study programs in politics, culture and professions. In the meantime, they should improve their ability by self-education. . . . Women's household chores must be lightened to ensure that they have time for studying culture and science. Social services, such as nurseries, kindergartens, tailor shops and fast-food shops should be developed to socialize housework. Husbands should share housework and education of children to encourage wives to study."

If, as most scholars agree, a nation's progress is largely determined by the quality of its educational system, the ten years of the Cultural Revolution were China's most devastating setback since the People's Republic was established.

The following educators and university students are primarily concerned with the education of women.

DR. XIE XIDE

President, Fudan University

Fudan University had its roots in Aurora University, a Catholic school for women established in Shanghai in 1905. A few years later, a number of students and faculty members broke away from Aurora and founded Fudan as a private, Chinese-owned and -administered coeducational university. Today it is one of the most respected universities in China, and its president, sixty-three, is the only woman head of any college or university in the nation.

Located in the heart of the city, Fudan has seventeen departments of study, including eight research institutes. The older buildings are Western in architecture, but the newer ones, with their tiled roofs flaring up at the edges, are definitely Oriental.

On our visit to the campus one cold, cloudy day in November, we were immediately aware that Fudan was thriving. Large numbers of students, dressed in bright-colored sweaters, skirts, slacks, or jogging outfits, were hurrying to and from classes. We were met by a young woman at the entrance to the building that housed the office of President Xie Xide and ushered up a flight of stairs to a reception room, which by then looked very familiar to us.

Within a few minutes, a short, plump, round-faced woman dressed in a black silk pantsuit limped into the room and greeted us with a warm smile and handshake. I discovered later that, as a teenager, Dr. Xie had suffered from tuberculosis of the hip. Because she had been educated in the United States—first at Smith College, where she received her master's in physics, and then at MIT, where she earned her doctorate—she was able to converse quite fluently in English. Seemingly at ease and very much her own woman, she spoke frankly about the deficiencies of education in China, as well as its accomplishments.

Women Have More to Overcome

I was born the same year the Chinese Communist Party was established, and I feel very honored that we have the same birth-

Dr. Xie Xide, president of Fudan University, Shanghai

date. I was also very lucky to have been born into an intellectual family. My mother died when I was four, but my father and stepmother were both university graduates. I had three stepbrothers and, because our parents believed in education for girls as well as boys, we all graduated from various universities.

When I was six my family moved to Beijing [Peking] because my father, a physics professor, was teaching at a university there. After I graduated from secondary school, I was bedridden with tuberculosis for four years and then, in 1942, I entered university, where I received my bachelor's degree in physics. I worked as a teaching assistant at Shanghai University for a year and then went to America to do my graduate work at Smith College and the Massachusetts Institute of Technology. I received my doctorate in 1952, after the liberation.

When I returned to China, I joined the faculty at Fudan University and have been here ever since, first as a lecturer, then as an associate professor, and later as a full professor. I was appointed vice president in 1978 and then president at the beginning of 1983.

Fudan University was founded as a private school and then, during World War II when it was moved to Chongqing [Chungking], it became a national university. When the war ended, it was moved back to this campus in Shanghai, but it was still very small. The specialties were journalism, humanities, economics, and civil engineering. There were no natural science departments. Then, in 1952, the university was completely reorganized and expanded. Now we have over 6,200 undergraduate and 600 graduate students, and we cover every area of studies except premedical. But since the beginning of this year [1983], we have had a cooperative program with a medical college in Shanghai, so now we can give some premedical training there. Altogether we have seventeen departments, so Fudan is now one of the major universities in China. We have over 2,000 faculty members, and 438 are women. Forty-two of them are associate professors, but only six are full professors. They are still small in number, but that will improve. Most of the women professors are over sixty because promotions were suspended for ten years during the Cultural Revolution, and though they were suspended for men too, as I said before, women didn't have as much opportunity to go to university, so we find it difficult to find qualified women to promote.

About 28 percent of the student body are women, though in some departments like foreign languages and literature, there are more women than men. The percentage of women in chemistry and biology is also quite large, but not in physics. Of the 372 students in the physics department, only fifty-nine are women. Women still feel inadequate in the hard sciences, and I think that begins when they are in senior middle school. They think they are not as good as boys and develop feelings of inferiority. Also, before liberation, there were very few women in universities because most Chinese families wanted only their sons to have an education. After liberation those attitudes changed quite a lot, and the percentage of women students became quite high. Before the start of the Cultural Revolution in 1966, about a third were women.

The numbers dropped after the Cultural Revolution, especially in the sciences, and I think it was the result of those ten years of turmoil. Of the first batch of students who enrolled in our nuclear science department, only 5 or 10 percent were women.

Many of the first batch of students who enrolled in universities after those ten years were quite old, over thirty. They were the ones who had graduated from senior middle school on the eve of 1966 and couldn't go on with their education. But a large number were strongly motivated, so even during the years they were in the countryside or in factories they continued studying in their spare time. But that was easier for boys. By the time they were thirty, most of the girls were married and had homes and children to care for.

Another reason was that during those years it was claimed that any kind of knowledge was almost useless—that you could get along without knowing how to read and write, or learning mathematics, physics, and chemistry. And while families were quite happy seeing girls occupy their spare time with things like sewing, cooking, and cleaning, they still pushed the boys to study because they had to make a living. So, basically, people reverted to the old ideas and women lost a lot of ground during that period. Now things are gradually changing. The enrollment of women students is increasing every year, and eventually it will balance out.

Like many other faculty members, I stayed at the university during the Cultural Revolution, but we were forced to participate in the movement. We had to criticize the so-called revisionist line and also be criticized by the students. I was not subjected to physical torture because in 1966 I had breast cancer and was very weak physically, but I was placed under house arrest for a year. It was very hard for the faculty to see China come to a stop intellectually for so many years, but we had faith in the future so we tried to do our best until we could start teaching again. I began doing some work in 1972, when we started to enroll the peasant workers. The university really didn't close during that period as so many Westerners thought. Enrollments were just suspended, and then students began to come again as early as 1971, but not through nationwide examinations as before; they came through recommendations.

My major goal is to upgrade the teaching and research quality of the university, and also to improve the efficiency of the administration. That will happen through the cooperative efforts of all my staff; I couldn't do it myself. Fudan is quite different from an American university. I have to worry about money, but not as much as American university presidents do. I'm told they must spend a lot of their time raising money. I have to write proposals justifying our requests for increased construction budgets and other expenditures, but I do not have to go around raising funds. And the present government policy of supporting education is very helpful.

There are some women vice presidents, and now that most of the universities are in the process of reorganizing their administrative staffs, I think in the future there will be more women presidents. Since the liberation, legally women have had equal rights in all areas, but it's been difficult to get rid of some of the ideas left over from the feudal society, especially in the rural districts, where boys are still preferred over girls.

Women also have more difficulties to overcome than men.

They play more important roles in raising and educating children and, though husbands share some household chores, women still do more. So it's not that women are inferior in their capabilities, they just have more work to do. For example, we now have nationwide examinations to select students for graduate studies abroad in physics. The program was sponsored by Tsung-Dao Lee, an American of Chinese origin who is now a professor at Columbia University and a 1957 Nobel Prize laureate. The program is now in its fourth year, and this year—out of 600 participants in the examination—one of our women students scored highest. That means women can achieve if their motivation is strong enough.

In primary school, girls usually do very well, much better than boys. In junior middle school, most girls still do all right, but after they get into senior middle school the inferiority complex begins, and it's fostered by families and teachers. We are trying to eliminate that situation by giving girls more encouragement. In Shanghai a senior middle school for girls was recently re-established. We used to have many all-girl schools, but during the Cultural Revolution they became coed. My personal feeling is that separate schools for girls are very important; they give girls more self-confidence because they have no boys to compare themselves with.

I was married quite late. After I finished my Ph.D. work in America, I went to England to join my fiancé and we were married there in 1952. At that time the People's Republic of China was at war with the United States in Korea, and science and engineering students were not allowed to go directly back to China from the United States. I made a detour to England, where my fiancé was studying biochemistry-chemistry at Cambridge and, after our marriage, we returned to China.

But marriage did not interfere with my career because my husband was very understanding. He shared a lot of house chores and we had household help, too, which most families cannot afford. We also had only one child, a son, who went to a day nursery school, and in the evenings we always tried to put him to bed early so we could study.

When I was at school in the United States, very few women were working except those who were single. It was different at Smith College. Because it was a women's college, most of the faculty members were women. But in general, very few women worked after marriage. Now the situation in your country has changed a great deal. Lots of women, married or single, are working—and not just as secretaries. Some are in high-level jobs, but still not enough. For instance, how many women are in high-level positions at the University of Chicago? So, in that sense, the situation for American women is very similar to Chinese women.

But one thing surprised me when I attended commencement exercises at Smith College in 1981. The guest speaker was one of the leaders of your women's movement, and she mentioned that a priority was to fight for the right to abortion. I was surprised because, from the very beginning, we were supported in that by our government.

I also think your child-care programs are inadequate and even though the number of facilities are increasing, they are quite expensive. But the one thing we should learn from the United States is adult education. I spoke to a number of women research workers at various institutions in America who said that they were kept from working for a number of years while their children were small, but then they could go back to school and study for a career. There is no age limit in most of your colleges and universities, but in China, because of the limited number of places, we can't do that. We hope to increase our adult education facilities so that women who were left behind when their children were little can have a chance to to renew their knowledge of books.

Our young people must study the history of contemporary China, especially the period before liberation, or they will take everything for granted. It's easier for the older generation to understand the progress we have made because they experienced what it was like before. And, although we would like to progress faster, our achievements have been tremendous. But these days our young people like to compare their lives with those of people in Hong Kong and other countries of the world. So one of our major efforts is to teach our youngsters about the past and convince them to work harder to achieve our goals.

Crime is also one of the bad results of the Cultural Revolution, and we need time to overcome it. During those ten years knowledge was useless to youngsters, so boys, especially, developed bad attitudes, and some went into criminal activities. But I think the situation is improving because more attention is being paid to the problem. Crime is also a result of our high unemployment rate, which stems from our overpopulation problem. During the Cultural Revolution many city youngsters were sent to rural districts and, when it ended, they had a tendency to come back to the cities. Now the unemployment situation is very severe in heavily populated cities like Shanghai and Beijing. But there are areas where the population is low, and it's easy for people to earn a living. So I think we must encourage youngsters to go to remote districts. We can't keep everyone in Shanghai.

Because of the new responsibility system [the communes are being disbanded and each family is now responsible for its own plot of land] and the encouragement of sideline businesses in the rural areas, living standards are getting better, and that's an incentive for young people to live there. Farmers now sell a percentage of their crops to the state, and they can sell the rest on the free market so they have more incentive to work hard. And, because 80 percent of our population are peasants, if they become wealthy, it will solve most of our problems. All those changes are good if the people do not engage in illegal practices. Earning income through one's own efforts and without exploitation of others is the major difference between communism and capitalism. We are not allowed to hire employees; it must always be a cooperative effort. And everything cannot be state-owned, especially small factories and service businesses, because people must have freedom to meet the needs of the customers.

People must realize that every kind of work is an important part of our socialist reconstruction, and that will come through education. We still have problems in that respect. Some service people in the stores are not very polite. The work units are giving bonuses for better work, but that has to be carried out very carefully. One cannot solve everything with bonuses because the trend is always to ask for more; people are never satisfied.

But I really feel that every problem we have in China would be solved if we could level our population increase. With the use of chemical fertilizers and the mechanization of agriculture, food production can increase somewhat, but no matter how large the production is, you have to divide it by a very, very large denominator and the result is almost zero.

WANG LAN

Primary School Teacher

The Yangtze River Road Primary School occupies a small complex hidden behind a wall in the center of Nanking. Unlike United States city schools with their large, open play areas, distinctive buildings, and prominent identifying signs, one could easily walk past a Chinese primary school and never realize it.

But the moment we passed beyond the wall, we knew this was a school. There was the play area—a hard-packed square of earth with a basketball net, a few swings, and a group of about twenty well behaved ten-year-olds performing exercises supervised by teachers. The buildings were very old, wooden two-story affairs with outside stairways, and though it was a cold fall day, there was no heat in the classrooms. As we toured a number of them, we saw the children sitting quietly at long wooden tables. And unless they had an arm raised in response to a question, both hands remained clasped behind their backs. An American teacher might have been envious of such order.

Wang Lan, a fifty-eight-year-old first- and second-grade teacher [Chinese primary schools include first through sixth grades], was waiting for us in the ground-floor teachers' lounge, a rather plain room with worn but comfortably upholstered armchairs lined up against the walls, interspersed with a few wooden tables. A small, slim woman with a pleasant, expressive face and short, stylishly arranged black hair, Wang seemed very pleased to see us and eager to demonstrate the new teaching method she had been developing since 1978.

Basically, the technique consists of a series of 18-inch-square films, painted with Chinese characters or scenes, which are projected onto a screen made of white cloth stretched on a wooden frame. When one film is overlayed with another, the character or scene changes. Obviously an innovation in China, the same procedure has been used for many years in the United States. But Wang, a dedicated teacher and very proud of her invention, was unaware of that.

Always Wanted to Teach

My father was also a primary school teacher and my mother was a housewife, but they both died when I was a very little girl, so my sister and I were brought up by an uncle. In the old society, very few women had the opportunity to be educated, but my uncle, who was an artist, believed in education for girls, so we attended primary school. After I graduated at the age of thirteen, I went to a normal school, which in those days was like secondary school. I only attended for a year and a half because the Sino-Japanese war brought a great deal of poverty to China, so I had to leave school to stay home and help my uncle. But I continued to study on my own because I really wanted to become a teacher.

Eventually I married a man who had graduated from a teacher's school called Yenjing University, but he could not find a job for a long time. Finally, through one of his professors, he got a job teaching in a middle school in Peking, and I took care of the house and children. It was very hard for women to find jobs at that time. In the old society women were dependent on others economically, and they had no political rights. Women were not as happy as they are now.

After the liberation, the Communist Party set up the women's federation, and in 1951 they helped me find a job as a teacher. By then we had moved to Nanjing because my husband had been transferred to a school here. In the old society jobs were not stable, and he was always being sent from one middle school to another. My first job was at the Chu Chang Road Primary School and then, twenty years ago, I came here.

I was very happy with my job because for the first time I felt independent economically, and I had wanted to teach for many years but couldn't realize my ambition. So I worked very hard and over the years earned the respect of the government and the other teachers. They gave me the title of Special Class Model Teacher and I was selected to be a delegate to the Nanjing People's Congress. Now I'm also on the Congress Executive Committee. [The local people's congresses elect delegates to the National People's Congress, which is the national government's legislative body, according to China's constitution. In reality, however, power rests with the Central Committee of the Communist Party.]

I always tried to combine teaching theories with child psychology, and eventually I created this new method to stimulate the interest of the students. I use what is called an overhead projector. I put a sheet of film that has a Chinese character painted on it onto the projector, which enlarges it and projects it onto a screen. Then I overlay a second film with another character on it, and that changes the first character into another word. For example, the first one was *kung*, a one-word character, and the second was also one word, but when you put them together, they make still a third word. So instead of having to draw each character on a blackboard, I can just move the pieces of film around and make the words change right on the screen. The children find it interesting to see the changes, and they are also in color and much bigger than when they are written on the blackboard. Another important result is that the children learn how to write more easily because they don't have to learn to write each character stroke by stroke. Instead, by just putting two familiar words together, they can see how to form a more complicated word. This method helps remove mental blocks, and they remember what they learn.

Most of the films are hand-painted by me and a few other teachers. At first only I used the method, but now all the teachers think it's good and it's being used in all the grades. It's a little difficult for primary schools to buy such expensive equipment, but since it has proved so effective, I have had the support of the school president. Now we have eight of these machines and also a few smaller ones that can do the same thing; they just project smaller pictures. But the films must be made by the teachers because you cannot buy them.

I also made some films that help students to understand the meaning of objects. For instance, I have one that shows a picture of a child paddling a canoe, and I can make the paddle move. This new teaching method is also beginning to be used by teachers nationally, because we teachers learn from one another. They come from other cities to observe me in the classroom, and last October I attended a national conference for primary school teachers, where I demonstrated how to design and use my method. Model teachers exchange views at these conferences and develop more research projects for the future.

Because I love children so much, I prefer to stay at the primary school and just attend conferences and give lectures to teachers. My method has been filmed so it can be shown to other teachers, and that serves the same purpose. Also, I must stay here because I am still developing my work, and I need the children in order to continue. There is no other way to test my theories. I have already made some comparisons that show that the use of this method really helps children learn faster and remember more. Some six-year-olds who were taught with it knew as much as seven-year-olds who were not.

We are now raising the standards for teachers by increasing the length and quality of their education. Most primary school teachers are women because, generally, women are more patient than men, so it's easier for women to be with children. For instance, if you hire a man to teach kindergarten, when a child is very naughty, the man will lose his temper. Another reason is that in the old society, women were less educated than men, so after liberation the only thing they could do was primary school teaching, while men could teach at higher levels. That's what happened to me.

My children are grown up now and working, but when they

were small, I took care of them while my husband made a living. After liberation, when I was finally able to get a job, with my education the only thing I was qualified to do was primary school teaching. Some kindergartens and nurseries had already been established, so I sent my children to a boarding kindergarten, and I never had any problems about child care. My husband and I also shared the house chores when I began working.

LI LIN TSING

*Director, College Preschool
Education Department*

In comparison with the United States, China's concept of government-supported, low-cost, or free child-care facilities is more advanced. Unfortunately, the reality has not measured up to the theory, due primarily to the still burgeoning population, the lack of funds, and the years of political upheaval that seriously affected the training of competent nursery and kindergarten teachers.

Like most visitors to China, we were shown through a number of model factory, farm, and city child-care facilities, and found them impressive as well as enchanting. The teachers were paragons of patience and loving concern, the equipment was simple but plentiful, and the children were irresistible from the moment they greeted us in unison with a cheery, "Hello Auntie," to the songs and dances they performed perfectly—even to the most minute movements of their tiny fingers—and, finally, to their smiling, "Goodbye Auntie," chorused again in unison.

Unfortunately, as I was told again and again by the Chinese women I spoke to in the United States, these facilities were not the norm. They really were, as described, models. There is still a shortage of child-care facilities in China, and many that do exist are below the standards acceptable to most Chinese parents. The few really good child-care centers, such as those we visited, have long waiting lists.

The shortage was discussed openly in the September 1983 is-sue of China Reconstructs, *an official monthly magazine pub-lished mainly for overseas distribution. Zhou Cuifen, vice direc-tor of the Child Care Office of Canton, admitted that there are just not enough kindergartens and nurseries for parents who need them; that the area has over 546,000 children of kindergarten age but facilities for less than 211,000. To alleviate the situation, she said, her office has been encouraging more work units to build nurseries and kindergartens, and urging that already established ones open their doors to the general public if they have space. Also, neighborhood committees have been asked to organize child-care centers, using retired workers and teachers to staff them. She admitted, however, that because of "the ten chaotic years of the Cultural Revolution," most preschool teachers now have only a junior or senior middle school education or a short-term training course in child care. In other words, there is a shortage of quali-fied teachers.*

Because I was feeling under the weather from a bad cold, Li Lin Tsing, chairperson of the preschool department of Chong-qing's Southwest Normal University, was kind enough to come to my hotel room to be interviewed. The Mansion is one of the strangest hotels I have ever encountered. A monster of an edifice with over a thousand rooms, it was built in the 1950s during the height of Sino–USSR friendship and managed somehow to com-bine the worst of both Russian and Chinese architecture. Though warm and comfortable enough, those surroundings, viewed through my rheumy eyes, imparted an almost surrealistic atmosphere to our conversation.

Short and heavyset, with her hair pulled back from her face, the sixty-four-year-old Li seemed a very sweet woman and most eager to please. She was dressed in a Mao-era dark blue pant-suit, with a shirt and tie.

Men Are Not Qualified

Because he was very advanced for his time, my father believed in education for girls as well as boys. He was also very involved in Sun Yat-sen's revolution and supported liberation for women. He would not allow his daughters to have their feet bound.

I attended Christian missionary schools in Peking and Chongqing and, as a young girl, I had many ideas about what I wanted to do in life. Because my father was a professor of law and political science, I wanted to follow the law but I also wanted to become a writer or a teacher. I was full of ideas in those days, and the teachers, who were mostly foreign women, encouraged us to be whatever we wanted. But in those days women had no real status. They were oppressed by society, so I felt I must do something for women.

When I was fourteen my father passed away, and my family wanted me to support myself. I was attending a Christian middle school at that time. Oberlin College in the United States had set up a branch in Shanghai and I was selected to attend. I studied biology and public health for three years and then, in 1946, I came here to study teaching. In those days it was called Chongqing Normal School and it was only for women students. After the liberation, the name was changed to Southwest Normal University, and it became coeducational. In my department, we train only preschool teachers, grades from birth until age seven, but we also have departments that train teachers for the higher grades.

Women are more suited for preschool teaching. But there are men among the students and faculty in the upper-level departments. A preschool teacher must have very good moral standards, a high intelligence, and she must study hard and be physically and intellectually well. If she is not physically strong, she cannot do well at teaching preschool children.

There are some male preschool teachers in China. If a man loves children very much, he can try to pass the examination to become one. In fact, some boys who graduate from senior middle school apply, but I found that those who applied to my department were not qualified. Perhaps in other normal schools the requirements are not as strict.

I have four children who are now grown. My husband was a middle school teacher, but he is retired. Sometimes he teaches an evening class at a factory, and many workers ask him to give them private lessons so they can pass their examinations. So actually, he is semi-retired. He volunteers to do some tutoring for the good of the society.

When my children were small, they were taken care of by my mother, and sometimes my husband shared the housework. In China, by law, men and women are equal, but that doesn't mean that women have no problems. China is a large country with a long history, and the feudal ideas are still very strong in various areas of the country. Women in our society are still discriminated against by men and their families. The most important thing is that women should love and respect themselves and make a great effort to be economically independent. That's the only way women can liberate themselves.

Although I am sixty-four, I feel young enough and strong enough to do more in preschool education. I like it very much and, as I'm in good health, I would like to continue working. I would not like to stay at home and be idle. The retirement age is coming, so I will not be able to stay in my present position, but I can become an advisor. I feel a great responsibility because I am now one of the representatives to the Political Consultative Conference [one of the many local- and national-level consulting groups that make recommendations on various issues to the government; they have no real power], a delegate from the Women's Federation of Chongqing, and also a member of the Education Association Committee. So I have much work to do for the society, and I feel I must do it well and contribute more.

I thank you for interviewing me. It is a great honor, and I hope that through you understanding and friendship between China and the United States will be further promoted.

YEH LING AND LIU FANG

Students at Wuhan University

Wuhan University, set in the hills above the busy Yangtze River port city of Wuhan, boasts a large, pleasant campus overlooking beautiful East Lake, one of the area's outstanding scenic attractions. The campus, with its many trees, shrubs, and grassy spaces, is a peaceful retreat from the bustle of this large industrial city of over four million inhabitants.

Established in 1913 as a teacher's college, over the years the school has grown into one of China's most prominent general universities, offering a wide variety of liberal arts and science courses.

When we arrived on a sunny October day, we found students and faculty members in the throes of decorating the green tile-roofed buildings in preparation for the school's seventieth anniversary celebration the following month.

Yeh Ling and Liu Fang, twenty-one-year-old students with smooth, fresh complexions, enhanced by faint traces of rouge and lipstick, were the first women we saw in China wearing makeup except for stage actresses. In appearance, they could have been students at any university in the United States. Liu, with her long, black hair in pigtails, was wearing dark blue slacks topped by a red jacket. The dimpled Yeh wore her hair in a shoulder-length page boy with bangs, and was dressed in blue jeans, a white, round-necked sweater embroidered with flowers, and a beige corduroy jacket.

In comparison to most United States college seniors, however, both were lacking in composure and sophistication. More like many American high school girls, they seemed ill at ease and undeveloped in their ideas about society. I attributed their comparative immaturity to strict prohibitions against students dating or engaging in other social activities while they are in school. Because of the huge competition for college positions, most young aspirants for higher education in China study all the time they are not sleeping or eating.

Some interesting information was also elicited from two Foreign Office representatives, Mr. Zhou (I missed his given name) and a young woman named Huang Ling, both university graduates.

Although Liu and Yeh were English majors, their grasp of the language was still rudimentary, and the interview was conducted through my interpreter.

Boys Are Naturally Smarter

YEH: We were classmates at Wuhan Foreign Language School, which is like a middle school. At the age of thirteen, we were chosen to attend the foreign language school because we did well in our general studies at primary school. But I could have gone to another school if I didn't want to study foreign language; we had a choice. They taught several languages at the school, but we studied only English because that's what we were asked to do.

HUANG: That was in 1975 and the foreign language school had just reopened. It was closed during the Cultural Revolution and they were among the first group of students accepted into the school at that time.

LIU: We were asked to study English because they needed a certain number of students in that class, and we were chosen by the school authorities. We also studied the other subjects that were given to regular middle school students. The difference was that they didn't stress mathematics or science as much. It was mainly language, literature, and history—what we call liberal arts. We like English and we do not find it as difficult as French, which we are studying now.

ZHOU: Comparatively speaking, from the middle school level on, there are more male students than female. But all the schools are open to both sexes, and the entrance requirements are the same. There are 5,200 students at this university and the ratio is about three-fifths male to two-fifths female, though it varies according to the different departments. For instance, in the foreign language department, there are more female students than male. So maybe females are more suitable for language learning.

LIU: At the foreign language school we attended, there were more men than women because it was a special school. Not everybody could go there, and the standards were higher than at the general middle schools.

HUANG: Men do better than women and I think the fundamental reason is the chromosomes. There is a biological difference in the intelligence of men and women.

Yeh Ling and Liu Fang (right),
seniors at Wuhan University

YEH: We did better than the men.

LIU: If I wanted to study, my parents would do the household work themselves. They did not interfere with my studies.

YEH: It was the same in my family, but I think boys become smarter when they grow up, especially in the science courses.

HUANG: The university examinations are very difficult, especially in science, so perhaps that's why more men than women are enrolled. I think women have more talent in languages, and men have more talent in science and technology.

ZHOU: We have more than 300 professors at this university and about one-fourth are women. In the early days, immediately after liberation, there were fewer women students than men because of the old feudal ideas, but we are making our best efforts to change the situation. As I said before, the university has the same enrollment standards for men and women, and if anyone can reach the standards, they will be accepted. There is no discrimination against women here. All the women sitting in this room have higher-learning education because they all took the entrance examination and were accepted without discrimination.

But I think another problem is that some women look down on themselves because of the old ideas in the society. And it's even more serious now that the state is implementing a family-planning policy. Some couples, not many, prefer boys because they still have the idea that boys will take care of the parents in their old age.

HUANG: Many prefer boys and I will give you an example. My roommate, who married the son of a university professor, gave birth to a daughter and the whole family, including the old professor, was unhappy about it. So the prejudice against girls does not necessarily go with a low education, and I still think that although women are not stupid, men are smarter.

ZHOU: I can give you examples to prove that in our country men and women enjoy equality both in work and in the family. There is a Chinese film called *The Model Husband* that encourages the husband to share house tasks with the wife. Every day after school, I go home and change into a model husband.

My wife is a statistician, and she works later than I do, so I cook dinner every evening while I'm waiting for her to come home. But after we eat, my wife does the cleaning and I do nothing. And sometimes I think she's smarter. I often have to ask her to solve some problems, and, of course, she also asks me. Some people have the idea that men are smarter than women, especially after middle school, because fewer women are accepted into universities, not because of government discrimination, but because they cannot pass the exams. But I really haven't studied the subject. I can only compare myself with my wife and I feel I am not smarter than she is.

HUANG: I think he has difficulty in answering your question because if he agrees with me, women will think he's a male chauvinist.

ZHOU: I'm the only man here, and if I say men are smarter than women, I will be attacked by all the women.

YEH: I think women in China are treated equally. We are not very much looked-down-upon, so there is not much talk about that kind of thing. I want to get married, but I plan to continue working even after I have a child.

LIU: In China, it's natural for women to work after they are married. And I would rather work. Staying home is meaningless.

MINNIE GAN

Visiting Scholar

When we met one hot September afternoon just a month before my journey to China, Minnie Gan, fifty-eight, an English professor from Shandong Normal University, had already been in the United States a year. Looking more like a benevolent grandmother than a student, she was enrolled as a visiting scholar in UCLA's Teaching English as a Second Language program and also working for China America Film & T.V., Inc., a company that exhibits films from China to promote friendship and understanding.

Minnie Gan, visiting scholar at UCLA

Our meeting took place in the company's office in an old downtown Los Angeles building. Throughout our two-hour conversation, which focused more on her life than on education, she never stopped smiling, even as she described the hardships she and her family had suffered. As with all of the women I interviewed both in and out of China, Gan loved her country very much and was proud of her heritage.

Mao Should Have Listened

In my time, women like me described their lives as "the three gates." We went from the home gate to the school gate to the government gate. I went to elementary school, middle school, and college, and then, after my graduation in 1950, I went to work for the Communist government as a middle-school teacher. In the 1950s the Russian language was very popular, so although I majored in literature at university, I also learned Russian, and at first I taught it. Then, when we had a falling-out with the Soviet Union and all the Russian experts were thrown out, I began teaching English.

It was very usual for women to go to university by the 1940s, but only for people with money, not for poor people. I went to a Christian school in Chengdu called West China Union University. It was run by missionaries and about 50 percent of the students were women. But during my childhood women were very repressed. They dared not even go to public places, and I can count the number of conversations I had with my father, only three or four. He seldom talked to his daughters. We had meals together every day and my father sat in the highest place at the table. The next-most-respected place was set for my brother, and my mother had the lowest seat. The table was round, and with ten children it was very crowded, but the women were forbidden to talk or leave anything in their bowls. We had to just eat without making a sound, and we could not even reach across the table for food, so we learned to be silent and obedient.

When I started primary school in the 1930s, the government had already established schools that were open to girls. And since my father worked for the Kuomintang government, we had a decent life. He could support his family quite well. But the majority of the people were very poor. I saw a great deal of poverty and inequality, and my schooling helped me develop a very strong conscience. For instance, I felt very sorry for our servants who were young orphan girls that my parents had bought. They were treated like slaves and I pitied them.

When the Communists took power in 1949, my father lost his job and became very depressed. He was nearly seventy by then, and he died a short time later. We had nothing to live on, so my mother gradually sold all the family belongings, and all the children tried to find ways to earn money. My two elder sisters' husbands were supporting them, and after my graduation, I was planning to marry a man I had met at university. At first my mother objected because he was only a poor student. But I would not listen to her and, because it was 1950 and the new Marriage Law had passed, she had to agree. After our marriage my husband said, "Since your father's death, your family has collapsed. You should send your sisters and brothers away to make their own lives." So two sisters and one brother joined the army, and only one younger sister and two younger brothers were left at home. My husband and I got teaching jobs at a middle school in another province, and I sent my mother half of my salary every month.

We were able to rent a very luxurious room in the home of a former capitalist. You see, those who were wealthy before 1949 became poor, but they could still own their houses and they rented part of them out. The rent was cheap, because the government subsidized it. In the early days after liberation, people could still rent privately, because no one knew what to do. The socialist system was not in place yet, and we had what we called a socialized capitalist system. We had a beautiful room with a lovely view of the sea, and we lived there for thirteen years.

We moved when I was selected to teach English at a university in another city, and my husband and son, who was ten by then, went with me. The three of us lived in one room in a university dormitory that seemed like a prison, and it was very crowded. Each floor had long corridors with rooms on both sides, and we shared a public kitchen and bathroom with the fifteen other families who lived on the same floor. After living there ten years, I was finally offered an apartment, but I never got it because by then I was alone. My husband had died, and my son was working in another city. There's a waiting list for new apartments and as they become available, they're given out according to the number of people in a family—the more the better.

When I became an associate professor, the authorities decided I should have more space, so they gave me another room in the same building. I continued living in the one I already had and used the other for tutoring individual students.

If I had stayed in the same province, I might have been persecuted because of my father's background, but I moved away, and I also married a poor man. His background was considered very good because his father was a bankrupt merchant. But the rest of my family was labeled reactionary or capitalist, so it was hard for them to find jobs or go to the better schools. That's why my younger brothers did not receive a good education. They had to go to work right after they finished middle school. I was also fortunate because I had just about finished university by the time liberation came. But I was never as trusted as the other members of the university faculty.

During the Cultural Revolution they called me a reactionary capitalist academician, and I was put in what they called the cowshed, a place at the university they set aside as a prison. There was no government control. Everything was run by people who labeled themselves workers, peasants, rebels, and Reds. That was encouraged by Mao and the Gang of Four, and no one dared do anything about it. Because I had a very bad origin, I was not part of that group, but even if they had asked me to be a Red Guard, I would have refused because I knew it was all wrong. I had lived through so many political movements I felt it was dangerous to become involved, because you are never quite sure which side is correct.

So in 1969 I spent a year in the cowshed, and actually it

was very comfortable. They just selected all the people who did not have the right background and kept us all together. The school was closed and we could not go anywhere so we just studied or worked in the vegetable gardens and orchards. After I was released, I was allowed to go back to my department, but all we did was sit and talk politics. However, I began receiving my salary again, and they gave me all the back wages for the year I spent in prison. My husband was in the cowshed only two months, because his background was better than mine. We were kept in the same dormitory but not in the same room.

I had sent my son to live in another city with my husband's sister and brother-in-law, who had studied Western medicine. He was a very famous surgeon, a big shot. My son was only fifteen when the Cultural Revolution began, and it was such a turbulent life, I didn't want him with me. Soon after I was released from the cowshed, the whole university was moved to the countryside and I was there for three years, but I was happy because I was well treated and allowed to teach. The peasants said that everything that was going on was the fault of ignorant students, and they wanted me to teach their children. My husband was with me, and though we lived in a mud hut with a dirt floor, we were happy. I knew that many people had been tortured to death, and I felt we were fortunate to have survived.

Let me tell you about my eldest sister's life and you will see how women's lives were changed after the Marriage Law was passed in 1950. She was very pretty, and when she was in middle school the son of a general saw her and pursued her. The tragedy was that my sister fell in love with him, too, and they wanted to marry. But his family objected because they had already arranged his betrothal to the daughter of another general. So my sister and this man eloped to another province, and later they wrote saying they had a son, but if the father's parents did not bless their marriage, they would never return.

The parents wanted their grandson, so they had to tell the other general they could not accept his daughter. They gave back the dowry and told my sister and her husband to come home. But though their son and grandson were treated well, my sister was treated like a maid because they said she had disgraced the family. And they took her son away. Later she gave birth to two more sons and a daughter, but her first son always belonged to the grandparents. She could do nothing about it, because she was economically dependent on them.

After the liberation the whole family fled to Hong Kong, but my sister's husband and his parents were always quarreling. Because he was so spoiled, he did nothing to support his own family. He just took money from his parents and always wanted more. Then my sister received a letter from a cousin in Shanghai telling her that women had been liberated, and she could come back to China and live a decent life. She and her husband decided to go, but they could take only their two younger sons and daughter with them. The grandparents took the oldest child to Taiwan. In China her husband still tried to live the life of a playboy, but because of the new Marriage Law, my sister was able to divorce him. She got a job as a nursery-school teacher and was able to support her children. So she lived a very nice life and retired at the age of fifty-five.

Now she is here in America. She wanted to see her eldest son, who was sponsored to come here by our cousin after his grandparents died in Taiwan. The same cousin sponsored my sister and her other children, so now we are all together here and we are very happy.

My son became a successful doctor. He never came back to live with me after I sent him to his uncle, but I visited him every year on my vacations.

My sister, who is living here, asked me to come to the United States because I was alone after my husband died. It was impossible for me to get a transfer to the city where my son was living, and I was very unhappy. I came here a year ago, but then I had nothing to do, so I applied to become a visiting scholar at UCLA. I have a lot of friends who are visiting scholars here, and because I worked at a university, I knew a lot of university people. They arranged a meeting for me with the chairman of the English department, and I was accepted. I have another year to go in the program and then I will go back to China and teach American literature.

Right now my country says it needs me, but my sister says

she needs me, too, and she is trying to persuade me to stay. If I do stay, I would still want to work for my country. China Films is part of the cultural exchange program between my country and the United States. It's an effort to promote good relations. What I would really like is to have a green card, so I could come and go.

In China I was never discriminated against because of my sex. I became a university professor because of my ability, and I never saw any discrimination against women. In fact, when we needed to appoint a new department chairman, the authorities often chose a woman over a man who was more qualified just to keep things equal.

Because of the different political systems in China and the United States, the life-styles are different. In China, we don't have to worry about our lives at all. Everything is planned, we are taken care of, and we know exactly what is going to happen. That's good for the old people, not for the young; but American society seems to be only for the young, and I have heard a lot of complaints from old people. They say they are not treated well, that they are pushed aside. In China old people are respected.

On the other hand, in America you have the freedom to choose your jobs and to leave them when you want. We never leave a job, because once you are placed in a position, you will never get another if you quit. You will be unemployed your whole life. I feel they should do something to rectify that policy, and that politicians should be a little more considerate. They should not separate families, and they should listen to the complaints of the cadres. And if they are valid, they should do something about them.

But I hear things are changing now. There is still no choice of work, but families are being reunited. I know the government must place people where they are needed, but the leaders must be wise and considerate, even though it's hard to plan for a billion people. Also, if you give some people full freedom like you have, they will ask for too much and will never be satisfied. So I really am sympathetic to the government, but the leaders must be wise. When Chairman Mao was alive, he wouldn't listen to any opposing ideas and that was bad. It's the reason he made mistakes. He should have listened to ideas from people like Chou En-lai, and even from the Kuomintang and other minority parties. Now I think they are starting to do that.

CHAPTER

6

WRITING

A HAZARDOUS PROFESSION

Chinese, especially city dwellers, love to read and have traditionally held writers in the highest regard. Since the end of the Cultural Revolution, when the new government began easing restrictions that for ten years had confined literary expression almost exclusively to dreary socialist propaganda, writers have again been plying their craft in ever-increasing numbers. And though still under heavy censorship, they are allowed to explore a considerably wider range of topics.

One day Buff and I walked to the large Xinhua Bookstore, located on a busy thoroughfare about two blocks from our hotel in Peking. It was one of the few times we went anywhere in China without a guide, primarily because our busy schedule allowed us little free time, and also because the language barrier made our attempts to "experience" China and its people so frustrating. Cities in China are not like those in most other countries, where one can usually hail a taxi and be driven back to familiar territory. Except for those available at a few major hotels, there are virtually no taxis in China.

The country's overpopulation was especially evident to us that day as we threaded our way through throngs of people crowding the sidewalks, and streets jammed with fast-moving automobiles and bicycles, all vying for the right of way and often avoiding collisions by a hair's breadth. But even more disconcerting were the stares. "Big noses," a pejorative term used for Caucasians since the days of Western imperialism, are still a curiosity, even in big cities. Being openly peered at was a rather uncomfortable phenomenon we encountered again and again throughout China.

The two-story bookstore was filled with men and women avidly perusing the glass-enclosed cases where the latest books and periodicals were on display. Later I learned that the demand is so great that anything new is quickly sold out. That is especially true for translations of foreign literature that had been banned for so many years. After we made our selections from a limited number of Chinese novels translated into English, a clerk gave us a ticket and we joined a long queue at the cashier's window, where we had to pay before picking up our purchases.

For the next few nights, my bedtime reading was the well-known novel *The Family*, revolutionary author Pa Chin's first book, written in the 1930s. Based on conflicts in his own family of wealthy landowners during an era when the younger generation was beginning to rebel against old traditions, the story was interesting for its portrayal of social change. I found a more recent book, *A Small Town Called Hibiscus*, by novelist Gu Ha, a well-written, ironically humorous account of how the Cultural Revolution affected individuals in a small village. Writing about those ten years of turmoil and injustice is now permitted, and the period has become the subject of a large number of current books and articles.

But many China-watchers, like Jay and Linda Mathews, in their book, *One Billion: A China Chronicle*, contend there has been little great literature produced in China during the twentieth century. "Why has the last century been such a cultural desert? Where are the Faulkners, the Solzhenitsyns?" they ask. Some attribute the dearth to the political turbulence that has occupied most intellectuals for some 100 years and, of course, to censorship under the Communist regime. Yet, throughout history Chinese writers have lived under the yoke of censorship. In the old days, they were an elite group living under the patronage of emperors and warlords and allowed to write only what was approved by their benefactors. Later they were censored by authoritarian governments like the Kuomintang and the Communists. Thus the quality of Chinese literature has always been determined largely by governmental taste. During the Tang dynasty (seventh and eighth centuries), for example, art and literature flowered; in other centuries, books were often destroyed and their authors imprisoned or put to death. Under the Communists, who devised one of the world's most well-organized and pervasive government spy networks, even the old street storytellers, whose tales sometimes evolved into classics like the great eighteenth-century novel, *Dream of the Red Chamber,* are gone. And the underground newspapers and magazines that flourished during the early revolutionary days (from the mid-nineteenth century until 1949) are now virtually impossible to produce and distribute, especially if the writers hope to earn a living.

The current Deng regime has eased—though certainly not lifted—restrictions on content, and the Chinese now have a significantly wider range of reading material in books, newspapers, and magazines than at any time since the Communist takeover. Previously, the optimism of news and feature articles in China's newspapers could well have been compared to the philosophy of Dr. Pangloss in Voltaire's *Candide,* "In this best of possible worlds . . . all is for the best." Now the people are also being informed of such realities as crime, unemployment, economic hardship, and social injustice. In the *China Daily,* a national newspaper printed in English, we read criticisms (albeit mild) on all sorts of issues in feature stories and the Letters to the Editor column, as well as a fairly accurate roundup of national and international political, economic, scientific, and sports news. Nevertheless, writers and publishers, always fearful of changes in government policy, tread slowly and cautiously. They know from bitter experience that what is permitted today may be banned tomorrow, and even many years later, transgressions could be used against them ex post facto during a new political upheaval.

Chinese women writers began to emerge with the social and political changes in the middle of the nineteenth century. Though still comparatively few in number, women now occupy a significant place in Chinese literature and suffered equally with their male colleagues during the bitter years of the Cultural Revolution. One famous example is the novelist Ding Ling, who was "rehabilitated" in 1979 at age seventy-five after spending thirteen years at hard labor on a farm and in prison. An early revolutionary, she was also a victim of the Hundred Flowers Campaign of 1957, but she still expresses her faith in China's future under Communism.

The following dialogues with women writers in China and in the United States reveal a similar faith and optimism.

LIU ZHONG YING

Magazine Editor

I met with Liu, the editor of Women's Life *magazine, in Chengdu, the capital of Sichuan province, China's most important farming area. I was amazed to learn that Chengdu has a population of close to four million. Its broad, uncrowded, tree-lined streets, profusion of flowering shrubs, and mild, almost tropical climate create an atmosphere more like that of a peaceful small town.*

We met in a private dining room at my hotel. A short, slightly stout, pleasant-looking woman in her mid-fifties, Liu wore the usual blue man-tailored jacket, gray pants, and white shirt, buttoned up to the neck. Her straight, black hair was cut short and brushed back behind her ears, but her somewhat severe appearance was lightened by eyes bright with intelligence and humor. She was eager to answer my questions and also, as a journalist, to question me about American publications.

"Dear Abby"—With Clout

Before liberation I was a literature student at a university in the northern part of the province. A year before I graduated, I joined the revolutionary forces in Yenan. I was assigned to edit a small university newspaper, and I also began doing some interviews and writing articles. I never had any ambition to be a writer. I was assigned to do it and learned from experience over many years. Then last year, when the government began publishing *Women's Life,* I was appointed editor and I'm also doing some of the writing.

We started with a circulation of only 20,000, but in one year it climbed to 200,000. I think I was chosen to be editor because while I was working at the university newspaper, I also worked for the local women's federation. The government thought my combination of newspaper and women's rights experience qualified me to edit a women's magazine.

Women's Life is mailed to women who pay twenty-five cents a year for a subscription, and though it's really a provincial magazine, it can be ordered from all over China. The articles mainly reflect the lives of women in Sichuan province, but we also publish stories on the achievements of women from other areas. We discuss the problems women have in marriage and love affairs, taking care of family chores, health, and education of children. And we answer many questions. People write letters, and we print them with answers in the next issue. The most popular articles are on love, marriage, and women's morality. We try to use the magazine to educate women on good behavior. For example, in this issue there is an article about a woman who does not have a good moral attitude in her marriage; she has love affairs with many gentlemen and our magazine criticizes that kind of behavior.

Through the magazine we want to educate women on the difference between right and wrong. So every article we publish has our own point of view. There are also many stories about women's rights, which we feel should be protected, not only by law, but by people's attitudes and behavior. Before liberation, women had no political or social status, and the new government focused great attention on women's rights. But although the law protects us, we women still have problems. From time to time, we find cases of abuse of women and children, and there may be even more that we do not know of. Discrimination against women still exists because of feudal ideas. In an individual family, for example, a husband may still beat his wife. But now, when that sort of thing happens, the women's federation or the magazine encourages the woman to tell the truth, and to fight against her husband, not just to accept it. Some women still think they should suffer, but we encourage them to fight back.

The women's federation plays a great role in women's rights. They are almost like mothers protecting the women of our country. The majority of women in China know that legally they enjoy equality, but they still feel in reality it's hard to win that kind of status. To do it, women must have self-respect and fight for it. Without their own efforts, they will have nothing.

I am responsible for answering letters to the editor, but of course I don't have the time, so I take responsibility only for the ones dealing with marriage and child education. For example, I recently answered one from a happily married young girl who suddenly found out her husband had been in love with another girl before their marriage, and he did not tell his present wife about it. She became very angry when she found out, and even though her husband treated her quite well, she kept thinking about it and was very jealous and unhappy. So she wrote asking our advice, and I answered that the gentleman had a right to see other girls before he was married, but he married her, so he must have felt she was the best. I told her, "Your husband treats you well, you have not suffered any abuse from him, so it's not necessary for you to be angry and seek a divorce."

Many readers regard the magazine as their trusted friend. When they have difficulties, they don't tell their parents, they write to us for advice and we give it to them. And if a case is a little complicated, a staff member or someone from the women's federation will visit the home or workplace and make an investigation. We do everything possible to help resolve the problem.

There was one case where a leader from the federation went to a machine factory to deal with a problem between a husband and wife who had two children. They had been living separately for ten years because the wife was suspicious that her husband had fallen in love with another woman. She did not seek a divorce because she still loved him, and also because she wanted to keep an eye on him. After the woman from the federation investigated the facts, she mediated between them and persuaded this couple to reunite. Two years ago China launched a campaign calling on all married people to be model families [comply with the one-child requirement, work hard, and respect each other, their neighbors, and their co-workers]. We want to preserve the stability of the family in this country.

We also publish marriage advertisements from men and women who are looking for suitable partners. The majority of our stories are about real people, but we also publish fiction stories, novels in serial form, poetry, and we have one very popular column called Women's Life Knowledge. It tells women how to do everyday things like making clothes, caring for babies, and cooking.

The provincial government subsidizes the magazine now because we began only a year ago, but if we are not self-supporting after two years, they will close it. We take paid advertising from businesses that sell washing machines, sewing machines, clothing—all those that want to reach women. And if we can build that up, we will survive. In fact, after just one year, we are already earning a little money. In this country if a magazine can reach 100,000 circulation, it usually makes money, and we are well above that. And our staff is small, only twelve writers and editors and one photographer, so our expenses are low, but we are all very busy.

My husband also studied literature but he's been in administrative work for a long time. Right now he's working at a very famous film studio in Sichuan province. We have three children, two boys and a girl, and they all went to university. My eldest son, who is twenty-five, majored in architecture; the second son is in television production; and the youngest is now at a university, majoring in Chinese literature. Most Chinese parents would like their children to go to university, but right now that opportunity is not open to all middle-school graduates. We have places for only a small portion, and the others are assigned to do various kinds of work. If middle-school graduates can get any sort of job these days, they are satisfied; at least they are not unemployed.

And women today have the same chance to go to university as men. It depends on their capabilities, on whether they can pass the examination. Actually, only 30 percent of the university students are women, though in some specialties like teaching and nursing there are more women than men.

This stems from traditional ideas in the society and also from the natural differences between men and women. Women have more patience for child care and nursing, and because of their physical limitations, women could hardly take jobs mining or working in iron and steel factories. So that's why there are fewer women in heavy labor.

There are some women who can do engineering and scientific research. In fact, we have a famous woman who does mineral research and is always climbing mountains. But generally people in China think women are not suitable for certain jobs. Just after liberation, we tried to train women to do all the same kinds of work that men do. In 1950 we trained them to be railway engineers, airplane pilots, parachute jumpers—in fact, to work in almost every area—and they really did a wonderful job. But eventually we found they could not do those kinds of work for as long a period of time as men because of their physical limitations. They do fine when they are young and before they have children, but gradually, their physical condition becomes weaker, and they cannot keep it up as long as men. So now we women must admit we have this natural problem, that there are physical differences.

HUANG QING-YUN

Writer

There is a beautiful park in the center of Canton (Guangzhou) that is like an oasis in the largest, most heavily populated city of southern China. As we strolled along its winding paths amid lush, tropical flowering trees and shrubs, intricately landscaped small gardens, and ponds filled with blooming water lilies, we came upon the small house that was the meeting place for my interview with writer Huang Qing-Yun.

At sixty-three, Huang is a bright, energetic, sophisticated woman, active in literary circles. She began her career as the editor of a children's magazine and children's-story writer, later widening her scope to books and stories for adults. Over the years, in addition to short stories, she has produced fifteen novels and is also a visiting lecturer at universities throughout China. A member of the Canton Writers Association, she was recently elected vice president. The position is prestigious and enhanced by a salary that, combined with the money she earns from writing, enables her to maintain a living standard well above that of the average Chinese worker.

As the mainland city closest to Hong Kong, Canton residents are greatly influenced by the West, especially in their appearance. For the first time, we saw large numbers of people in Western-style dress. At our meeting Huang wore a dark blue silk dress, subdued but well-tailored to enhance her small, trim figure. Her softly-curled black hair, carefully arranged around her face, created the impression of a woman who takes pride in her appearance.

The small garden house, which Huang said she often rents for meetings with colleagues, was furnished with a comfortable sofa and lounge chairs. As we sipped our tea, she spoke freely of her life as a writer in China, and because she had been partly educated in the United States, she was able to converse quite well in English.

A Better Writing Atmosphere

The Sino-Japanese War broke out while I was a student at Sun Yat-sen University, which was one of the few state-supported colleges in those days, and my family moved to Hong Kong. There I completed my undergraduate work and went on for a master's degree.

Very few girls were in the universities in those days, but then there were very few students at all, because it was hard to qualify. Of all the students who took the entrance examinations, only 5 percent were admitted. In my Chinese literature classes, only one-tenth of the students were girls, and there were even fewer in the science courses. I graduated in 1939, and in 1941, after finishing my postgraduate work, I began editing a children's magazine in Hong Kong.

World War II began in December of that year, so I moved to Kweilin, which is in the interior of China, and continued to publish the magazine there. I was the editor in chief, and one of my professors subsidized it. When the war ended in 1945, we moved the magazine back to Hong Kong; and then, in 1947, I received a scholarship from an American organization called the China Aid Council to study for a year at Columbia Teachers College in New York.

In the old days most children in China were very poor and uneducated. When my family moved to Hong Kong, I saw many refugee children, and I joined an organization that was trying to help them. I often went there to tell them stories, but in those days there were very few children's books. So when I ran out of new stories to read I began making them up, and that's when I became interested in children's literature.

But even before that I knew I wanted to be a writer, and that's why I studied literature in college. I was twenty-three when I returned to China from America, but I went to Hong Kong first because Canton was such a mess. The Kuomintang was still in power, and it was terrible. I remember seeing three bodies of children in the street after one cold night. They had died of starvation and the cold. I made up my mind then to dedicate myself to the welfare of children, and since I was a writer, I wrote for them. My stories were first published in a semimonthly magazine called *Modern Children*, and they were very well received. I was the publisher, editor, and a writer for the magazine, and it became self-supporting through the sale of subscriptions. After the liberation in 1949, I moved back to Canton and continued publishing the same magazine, and then, ten years later, I stopped publishing and devoted myself only to writing.

I joined the Writers Association of Canton and also began writing for adults, but I found that although I was a Chinese writing for Chinese people, I didn't know them well enough because I had always lived in a very small area of China—Canton, Shanghai, and Hong Kong. I was like a foreigner; in fact, some foreigners had traveled more in China than I and knew more about it. I began traveling to other places so I could become more familiar with the people, especially the peasants. If a person doesn't know the countryside, she doesn't know much about China, because the majority of the people are peasants. First I moved to a rural area just a short distance from Canton, and eventually I traveled to other places like Hainan Island in the south, where I lived with national minority people and wrote about them. But I've always written mainly fiction. My children's stories are directed toward ages nine to fifteen, though in recent years I've been writing for a younger group. I find most children are interested in fairy tales and myths, but recently they have also come to like science fiction. I write some science fiction, but not as well as I write fairy tales.

There are many publishing houses in China. Sometimes they ask you to write something, or you can try to get a contract for one of your own ideas. The publisher pays us a fee, but they don't pay royalties. If they publish a second edition, they give you more money, but less than for the first edition.

I work with the Writers Association of Canton, which was organized by writers but is subsidized by the government. Because I'm vice president, I receive a salary whether I write or not. The other members only receive money from their published work, and amateur writers, the ones who are just starting, usually must work at some other job to support themselves until they can sell their work to a publisher. But if the writer is a member of our association, we sometimes help by requesting a leave of absence from his workplace, so he can still receive his wages. In that way he is subsidized while he is writing. But we do that only if we feel his work has merit. For instance, there was a farmer who wrote some short stories, and then he planned to write a novel about his life. His work was not as polished or artistic as most professionals', but still we decided he had talent. So the association not only requested that he receive a leave of absence from his job, we asked some of our members to go to his farm and teach him how to write. Now he is a very, very famous writer in China, and one chapter of his book is being made into a film. His name is Wang Sing-yuan.

Most publishing houses are owned by the government, but there are a few owned by literary associations and other organizations. Those are collectives as opposed to government-owned, and they pay their publishing costs with profits earned from the sale of books.

There is no censorship. Any ideas can be published in China today. It's up to the publisher. During the Cultural Revolution, a great many writers were persecuted, but I must say I was a lucky one. I was sent to a May 7 Cadre School in the country-side to be re-educated and I had to do farm labor, but I did not suffer very much. [On May 7, 1915, the Japanese, one of the World War I Allies, submitted demands, later ratified by the 1919 Versailles treaty, that they be allowed to occupy large areas of China and have a voice in the government. In China, May 7 is observed as National Humiliation Day, and the farm labor camps where intellectuals were sent during the Cultural Revolution were called May 7 Cadre Schools.] All of the association officers went there, too, so we were together as before, but we were not allowed to write, only work on the farm. I was there almost three years.

We all thought of the Cultural Revolution as a great destruction. Nothing was written but revolutionary drama, so literature became very stereotyped, dull, and mediocre. I began writing again in 1973 before the Cultural Revolution ended. I was ordered to come back and edit a magazine for adults, and eventually I wrote some adult stories too. I didn't want to write children's stories because everything was upside down; teachers were being taught by children.

When I lived with the minority nationalities, I collected some interesting material, so I wrote about those experiences. The stories were published because they were not political or controversial; they were about people. You know, we have some minorities living in the high mountain areas who have changed a great deal since liberation. Before, they lived like savages; they had no clothes and were illiterate. They didn't even know how old they were. But that has changed a great deal because the government has been educating them and improving their living conditions. So I wrote about those things, and they couldn't accuse me of being a rightist because I had a clean background.

The climate for writers is good now in China because you can express your own ideas. For instance, the magazine I edited for children before liberation took all my energy, but the circulation throughout China was only 8,000 copies. For the past two years I have been editing a small children's newspaper with a circulation of over 200,000, and that's not considered very large these days. That's because more people can read, and they are eager for newspapers, magazines, and books.

We have more women writers since the Cultural Revolution, but in comparison to men the proportion is still rather small. For instance, there are 555 members of our association and only one-tenth of them are women. You see, in China we have a feudal history that is thousands of years old. Few women were educated in those days, and even those who studied literature and wanted to write had families to care for, so they just didn't have the time.

I'm a widow. My husband died two years ago, and I have four grown children. But when they were babies I still managed to write. When I traveled, my husband stayed in Canton and took care of the family, and of course we also had a nurse to care for the children. My husband was a writer too, and now one of my daughters is writing children's literature.

I used to be prejudiced against women. When my children were young, my daughters always appeared cleverer than my sons, but when they grew older, the boys seemed cleverer and more concerned with world affairs. Now my concepts have changed. I see that in senior middle school, girls do just as well as boys.

We have the All China Women's Federation, which campaigns for women's equality, so we don't need any other organizations. True equality for women is just a matter of time, a question of getting rid of the old ideas that still persist with some people. Some factory leaders still don't like to hire women workers because of their physical limitations, and they also think women will take more time off for household chores or having children.

As secretary of the Canton Pen Center, another writers' association, I recently attended a congress in Toronto, and last year the Mexican government invited me to visit as part of a cultural exchange. This year I went back to the United States for the first time since I studied there many years ago and found big changes. Some things were worse and some were better. But I went there to learn, not to criticize, so I won't discuss it.

WEI JUNYI

Publisher

Wei Junyi, a writer and head of the People's Literature Publishing House, lives in one of Peking's large, walled-in compounds occupied long ago by the wealthy. Now shabby and run down, it is divided into housing for three families but still retains traces of its old grandeur—huge red double gates now in need of paint, red-tiled roofs, small stone statues, and intricately carved details on the walls.

Wei occupies one of the largest units—six rooms—and the small brick-paved garden area fronting her entrance appeared carefully tended, displaying a number of flowering shrubs and a little shade tree where she often sits and reads. The rest of the courtyard was dry and neglected, with various bits of wood and other refuse strewn about.

Cool and dark, the interior of Wei's home was a welcome respite from the heat of the unusually warm October day. Apparently happy to see us, she graciously showed us through the old rooms with wooden floors and walls hung with fine brush paintings, family photographs, and calligraphy. One piece of calligraphy, of which she was particularly proud, was done by a famous poet who had been forced to commit suicide during the Cultural Revolution.

Wei shares her home with her daughter, son-in-law, and six-year-old grandchild, who was in a boarding kindergarten and home only on Sundays. The outstanding feature of her own room, where she works and sleeps, was a huge old wooden desk, cluttered with books, magazines, and newspapers. There was also a telephone, a symbol of high position in a country where private phones are virtually nonexistent.

Married thirty-nine years to the vice president of the Institute of Social Science, Wei had been widowed the year before at age sixty-five. She is a short plump woman with a rather plain face, made more attractive by a pleasant expression. Her short, gray-streaked black hair, combed straight back behind her ears; her spectacles; and the dark blue mandarin-collared jacket she wore gave her a conservative appearance that contrasted with her liberal outlook.

A Family of Achievers

My father was an intellectual who studied railroad engineering in Japan, and when he returned to China, he became a railway manager. Although women did not go to school at that time, my mother learned how to read and all the children in my family were educated. My elder sister is a retired university president, my younger sister is an associate professor at the National Minority University, I have a younger brother who is vice minister of the ministry of water resources and electric power, and the youngest brother is a mechanical engineer with the architecture department.

In those days, only girls from the wealthier families went to school, and because my father was an intellectual, he encouraged us to go. He also took part in Doctor Sun Yat-sen's revolutionary activities and believed in equality for women. While I was at university, the war against the Japanese broke out, and the school was moved to Kunming in southwest China's Yunnan province. I continued studying there for another six months and then had to leave again because of the war. But I recall that there were only 108 girls in the whole school, out of more than a thousand students.

Both my parents died about five years after the liberation, but by then my youngest sister had already graduated from college, so we were all supporting ourselves. I was editing and publishing a magazine called *People's Literature*. It's now the biggest one in China.

In 1941, when I was at the Communist base in Yenan, I wrote an article and it was published in one of their newspapers. It was about the young people at the revolutionary base and how the Communist movement had changed their minds and their lives. I was only twenty-four at the time, but I had already been with the revolutionary army for three years. The reason was simple: The Japanese were raiding China, and I felt the Kuo-

Wei Junyi, publisher and writer, at home in Peking

mintang reactionaries would never fight them. Our only hope was the Communist Party. Many of my friends went to Yenan with me, but before that we all took part in the anti-Japanese uprising in Peking, which is now called the March 9 movement. After we were defeated, we joined the Mao forces in Yenan.

Over the years I've been mainly an editor and publisher, although I wrote some articles and short stories in my spare time. But looking after the magazine with a staff of 150 people never gave me much time to spare. In recent years I've been semiretired because, as I grew older, I did not have the energy to look after the whole magazine and 150 workers. So I've been spending more time at home, and over the past three years I've written two books. One is a collection of short stories and the other, of medium-length stories. Right now I'm working on a novel about veterans and their lives.

During the Cultural Revolution, I was sent to a May 7 Cadre School in the rural area of Hebei province. They were called schools and I was sent there to be re-educated. Actually, there was no education, only hard labor. I was there three-and-a-half years and was not able to do my own work during that time. That happened to all intellectuals.

In 1950 the new Marriage Law gave women legal equality, but actually women are not equal in any corner because the old feudal ideas still exist among the Chinese people, especially in the villages. The peasants always want to have sons rather than daughters because, according to the old tradition, if you have only a daughter, after she is married she will move to her husband's home, and you will have no labor force in your home. That's the main reason, and those ideas will change only when girls have the same income as boys. Then they can help support the family, and parents won't care if they have a boy or a girl.

In the city things are a little different because more and more women are working, so we have two-paycheck families, especially in the younger generation. And even older women are doing collective work at the small factories set up by the neighborhood committees. They organize the old women into sewing groups or other collective businesses. And city women earn the same salary for the same kind of work as men do. It's illegal to pay them less.

But sometimes a man is hired before a woman who has the same capabilities because the work leader thinks the woman will take more time off for household chores. And women do have more responsibilities at home than men. When I hire people, I don't think about their sex, only who will do the best job, and now in China we are encouraging men and women to share home responsibilities. We are also trying to build more nurseries and kindergartens. That's another method of socializing family work. But the main problem is changing people's attitudes and that takes a long time.

Most women think they are basically equal with men because they do not feel very much discrimination nowadays. But as a writer, I see things from many angles. For instance, I see quite a number of girls who like to find husbands who are more capable than they are. Recently my daughter's girlfriend got her master's degree, and now she thinks she must have a husband who has a doctoral degree. She still feels the man should be the intellectual leader in the household.

And many people still think that men are more intelligent than women because, while it is noted that in primary and even in junior middle school, girls get better scores, when they get into senior middle school, the boys do better. Some people say it's because girls think about too many other things while boys concentrate on their studies. And sometimes girls have difficulty studying at home because their mothers make them do more house chores, while they allow the sons just to study. They still feel it's more important for a boy to go on to university.

TIEN FAN

Playwright

After I returned from China, I met Tien Fan, then in her mid-forties, for lunch one afternoon at the old, but elegant, Hun-

Tien Fan, playwright, on a visit to California

tington Sheraton Hotel in Pasadena, California. A resident of Peking, she was visiting Los Angeles relatives and had not yet made up her mind about applying for a permanent visa. The interview had been arranged by a young Chinese-American newspaperwoman, who also acted as interpreter.

Tien was enthusiastic and open, clasping both my hands in hers in warm greeting as we were introduced in the hotel lobby. She could not speak a word of English, but communicated quite well with vivid facial expressions and body language, especially when she saw the lavish variety of foods displayed on the buffet table in the hotel dining room. Her pleasure was unmistakable as she helped herself to portions of watermelon and strawberries, which, she said, were very rare in China.

Democracy Would Bring Chaos

Both my parents studied in Japan, and before liberation my father was a capitalist. He worked for a United States–British tobacco company in China, and my mother was a pediatrician.

In those days China was being invaded by imperialist countries, mainly Japan, and my family supported the Communist effort to unify the country and resist the Japanese invasion. First they supported Doctor Sun Yat-sen, but later, when the Nationalists were fighting the Communists instead of the Japanese, they lost the support of most Chinese people, including my parents. I was very young at that time, but my parents told us about the Japanese killing people and burning their houses. They were very brutal.

I am the eldest of four children, two girls and two boys, and I majored in drama at university because I wanted to become an actress. My college specialized in training actors and actresses, and they set a ratio of two-thirds men to one-third women, but only because the demand for male actors was bigger. Those ratios do not apply to all colleges, only a few specialties.

We had complete choice, though we were counseled by the teachers on our abilities. But they only made suggestions; they had no right to make assignments. Of course, if a person who couldn't act took the exam for acting school, it's very likely that person would not be accepted. But you had the right to take all the exams you wanted to. When I was younger I really liked acting, and I was prettier than I am now.

At my university they had male-female social activities. For example, we went to the beach and other places together. And if a young man and young lady insisted on dating, they could, but there was social pressure against it. They were criticized because traditionally the Chinese think students are too young to date.

When I was in college, the population problem was not as serious as it is now, so the government did not really discourage people from getting married early. At that time girls could marry at the age of eighteen. But then the population exploded, and the government tried to discourage marriage with slogans like Don't Date, Get Married Late. The accepted dating age was later, and in 1981 the legal marriage age for women was pushed to twenty. Nowadays they don't think about dating until they're in their third or fourth year of college.

Though school officials try to discourage dating, if they really insist on it, girls can date; they just can't live with men. Living together is prohibited. During the Cultural Revolution, if an unmarried man and woman had sex and were found out, the criticism was very serious. But it wasn't the sex that created the problem. The couple only incurred harsh punishment when, because of their sexual relationship, they were not working as diligently as they should, and it interfered with their productivity. Before the Cultural Revolution, they would only be criticized in private by their party or production leader. For instance, the work unit leader or the party secretary might have a talk with them. Since the end of the Cultural Revolution, there is a more liberal outlook, and those things are not considered very serious. The party and work unit leaders are also more understanding. If two young people are really in love and want to marry, but they don't have the financial means or cannot find housing, the leaders will be more tolerant if they have a sexual relationship. People sympathize with them.

But China used to be a very feudal society and women had to be pure. It was okay for a man to take concubines, though not so good for the concubines, and socially there is still a double standard for men and women in China.

Chinese women are very shy and passive. They never initiate anything, and those who do are considered shameless. I think men who disapprove of women initiating sex are very hypocritical. They enjoy having a passionate lover yet they despise women who are passionate and active in lovemaking. It's a very conflicting attitude. There's a well-known Chinese proverb that says a woman should behave as if she is half pushing her partner away and also as if she is half submitting.

My courtship was very typical of two people in China at that time. We went to the same university, and because he paid extra attention to me, I knew he cared for me. For example, if he had tickets to the movies, he would invite me. If we wanted to be alone, we would go to the park and sit behind some bushes or meet on a quiet street corner. Youngsters today do the same thing, but they are much more open than they were in my time. Parks are so crowded now that two couples have to share a bench. They just face in opposite directions and pay no attention to the other couple.

I was divorced after the Cultural Revolution. It was very difficult before that, so after the downfall of the Gang of Four, the divorce rate skyrocketed. The government is now concerned about that, and they are trying to talk people into working things out together.

In my time, when both the husband and wife wanted a divorce, they just had to get the approval of their work unit leaders and their neighborhood committee. The committee would first investigate as to whether there was a property agreement and the children were going to be well taken care of. If they found there was nothing to worry about, they would give their approval, and the couple could just take the signatures to a registry and get the divorce. The period of the Cultural Revolution was so abnormal, there's no use in talking about it. The years after, however, can be divided into two segments. Around 1979 and

1980, if one party wanted a divorce, he or she stood a very good chance of getting it because the government put a lot of emphasis on individual feelings. But within the past few years, because the government saw that the huge divorce rate was creating a lot of social problems and many women were complaining, they began tightening things up again.

If one partner wants a divorce and the other doesn't, the one who wants it goes to court and files a lawsuit stating why. The court investigates and then makes a final judgment on whether or not it will be granted. That sometimes happens when one partner suspects the other is being unfaithful.

It's not common, but it's only natural that sometimes an extramarital affair will occur. When two people are in love, before they get married they usually pay a lot of attention to each other. But often, after the marriage, they stop making any kind of effort and it's natural for them to grow apart. Love is like a plant. It needs to be watered every day so it can grow.

In my time, youngsters were more idealistic. They sacrificed a lot for love. But nowadays youngsters are becoming more and more practical. Girls look at the boy's work rank, and I think that is very feudal. We don't have social classes in China now, yet if a boy's rank is very low, girls prefer not to marry him. For instance, coal miners are well paid in China, but they get very dirty every day, so they don't have a high status and girls don't want them. Another kind of work that's looked down on is service jobs; women don't want to marry servants.

And, of course, income is a big factor. When youngsters start working, their salaries are all about the same, so the young ladies look at the financial standing of a boy's parents. They are also concerned about whether he has a place to live because, although rent is very reasonable, it is difficult to get a housing unit. You need a connection or help from the family.

I was a professional actress from 1962 to 1966, the year the Cultural Revolution began. Then, because my family background was considered complicated, the government decided not to continue cultivating my career. I have tried to be very objective about that. I was the only college graduate in my work unit, the Provincial Drama Company, and I was very spoiled, quite proud, and not very considerate of other people. So when the Cultural Revolution began, they all started criticizing me. In the beginning I thought the criticism meetings were very positive because they taught me how to get along better with people, but later things got out of control and people suffered unjustly. When the intellectuals were sent to the countryside for reeducation, I was sent there, too, for three years. But I received the same pay as before and ate food provided by the government. The peasants ate their own food, but even though we were doing peasant work, the government provided food especially for us.

Then some officials from another province heard that we were pretty good actors and they requested our services. We were fortunate, because soon after we went to the other province they had a decentralizing movement, and the individual provinces lost their right to control people to the county governments. It was ridiculous because county officials are often very ignorant. They're illiterate and receive less pay than the people they control. But during that transition period, I was taken to another province and began acting again and also teaching youngsters how to act. We were required to write plays, and one I wrote for my students was chosen to be performed in Peking. The Gang of Four was in power, so it was a play about the life style of the intellectual youth who went to the countryside and learned to overcome their weaknesses and become better workers. In those days, a play had to be written that way, but after the Cultural Revolution when everything opened up, the subjects of my dramas changed.

Around 1957, before the Cultural Revolution, there was a movement called Fighting Against the Rightists. I was very young at that time and didn't understand what was happening, but according to the older generation, it was the best time. They say they felt free. But in my opinion, people want to go back to that period because the whole situation was much less complicated. The country was unified under one conviction, and the economic and political climate was steadier, so life was stable. But that doesn't mean people had more freedom. There were problems, but the larger environment was better. Everybody had a single purpose; they were very simple and naive and excited about making an ideal society. Actually, that atmosphere provided the warm bath that led to the Cultural Revolution. The Gang of Four could lead them wherever they wanted. I think the present is the best time because the Cultural Revolution encouraged people to rebel. Now they have a certain amount of individuality, and the only problem is convincing them to continue to do what's best for the country. For instance, a shoemaker should try to do his job perfectly. If he decides he wants to study to become a nuclear expert, that's too far out. He should be proud of what he does and do it well. That's why I talk to young people a lot and try to encourage them to try and do their best at the work they are in. Now every youngster would like to study a foreign language and be a translator, but that's not beneficial to the country.

I can't speak for others, but I think I can write whatever I feel like writing. I happen to agree with Deng Xiaoping and the other current leaders, so whatever I write is likely to be accepted. After the Cultural Revolution, I was sent to the Institute of Movies and I studied screenplay writing. Then I was borrowed by a work unit in Peking because my second play was also well received, and they wanted me. I wrote a lot of plays that won awards from the central government, so they felt I belonged in Peking, and I was able to stay. Now I work for a national organization called the Drama Institute of Chinese Youth, and I receive a salary from the government.

I'm considered fortunate by my fellow workers. My plays have always been accepted, though sometimes they do make corrections because of party policy changes. But usually the changes are only from an artistic point of view. I love to write about women and ordinary people in the society—their life styles and how they feel. A lot of writers suffer because they cannot write what they really want. I think they are being too extreme, and I don't feel that criticizing the government is effective. If they say they don't like the society, it will not help the country. Things will not be any different if they are allowed to express their views.

The basic function of an artist is to portray the beautiful side of life. If we portray the dark side, it will not be a good influence on the people.

What China needs now is stability. We don't need any more revolutions. I agree that the Communist Party has made a lot of mistakes, but it learned from them. If a new group takes over the country, they will only make more mistakes, and China will be in great turbulence again. I don't believe any new party can do as good a job as the Communists are doing right now. China is like a very sick person; don't treat it vigorously or it will die. It's like a shabby ship; you have to let it move slowly or it will sink. The problems we're facing now are cumulative, starting with the feudal society, the Nationalists, and then the Communist government, and they can't be solved in one day. Because of the extremely serious economic situation, it's hard for the government to please everybody—the intellectuals, the farmers, the workers. One group cannot get better treatment than the others because resources are limited, and they have to keep a balance.

A lot of people think the government separates husbands and wives intentionally, but I don't. It's a very troublesome arrangement, but I feel neither the government nor the work unit leaders like to see husbands and wives separated. It doesn't happen often to newlyweds, because they just don't choose to marry a faraway person. They usually meet in their school or work unit and start courting. At one time, a man from Peking, who was visiting Shanghai on a work assignment or vacation, might meet a girl and marry her, thinking that eventually one would be transferred to the city where the other lived.

Actually, it's very simple to solve that problem. People prefer living in certain areas like Peking, so if a man from Peking wants to work in an isolated area where his girlfriend is, he can get a transfer. But his girl cannot come to Peking because everyone wants to live there. In other cases, both the husband and wife are very skilled in their work and needed by their own work unit, so the unit leaders just won't let them go.

If you want to move to another place, the only way to do it is to go to your superior and ask for a transfer, and perhaps it can be arranged. You can't just quit and go. I think that's both good and bad. It's human nature to want to live in a nice, comfortable place and hold a more important job even if the person does not have the ability. So if the government controls mobility, it's good because they do not let people without ability move around. We need people to do all kinds of work. But I agree that some bad things go along with government control. It limits a person's ambition and personal development, which is not right. The Communists really believe everyone should be able to do their best, yet the government curtails a person's ability to do it. But that's more of an ideal than a practicality. Even in your country, everyone doesn't do their best.

I don't think the Chinese have the ability to enjoy democracy because they don't understand it. If you gave them democracy, there would be chaos because they would not know what to do with it. And that's not the fault of the present government. It's because of our 5,000-year history. In the family, when the father is dead, you must obey the grandfather, and that's a longtime tradition and habit. Throughout history the Chinese have always needed someone to tell them what to do, so if they suddenly had democracy, there would be chaos.

I'm a person who usually says what's on my mind, but a lot of people are more careful of what they say and to whom. It depends on the individual. The average person is afraid of being reported, but I'm not concerned about that.

You interviewed many women in China, and I don't think they would lie to you, but I'm sure they had reservations about what they said. For instance, if you asked them the year they were born, they would give you the right answer, but some questions they might not answer at all or just omit certain information. People are afraid of more changes in government policy and are cautious about talking. Recently, there was an anticontamination campaign in China that ended very quickly, but people became frightened again.

I feel women in China are equal to men politically and economically, but not in other things. For instance, if a man has extramarital relationships, he may be criticized a little, but a women who does that will suffer much more criticism. If a man is very famous, people will admire him, but if a woman is famous, they find reasons to criticize her a lot. If a woman wants to get to the top, be independent, and travel around the country, her behavior will be very closely watched. People look at her disapprovingly and wonder what's the matter with her.

Rationally, they can accept the idea that if this woman wants to be successful, she has to be a little more aggressive. But emotionally, they just cannot accept that a woman should behave that way.

I'm visiting relatives here, and I haven't decided whether or not I'll stay. I would like to stay and work in my profession if that's possible. I would be miserable doing nothing. But even if I stay for a while, I will eventually go back to China. I want to remain Chinese forever. Also, my favorite subject is Chinese literature and if I stay away too long, I will lose contact. How can I continue being a Chinese writer without living there? Right now I'm learning about the American people, and I'm especially interested in overseas Chinese because that will complete my understanding of the Chinese world.

Everything is very convenient in this country. You have all kinds of help like washing machines and dryers, and that's very good. But if you moved all those things to China, I don't think it would work because the people can't afford them. Here, when you go to a supermarket, things are well packaged and they need very little preparation. In China people can't pay for prepared food; the economy forbids it.

Here I go to a laundromat to do my laundry. It takes twenty minutes and costs me seventy-five cents, and it's very convenient. But in China it costs me only a dime to wash by hand even though it takes hours. In America you can use the time you saved to make more money. But in China you cannot, so if I have the time anyway, why not save the money?

CHAPTER

7

VISUAL ARTS

AN ESCAPE FROM MONOTONY

Beyond food, shelter, and education, nothing is more important to the Chinese than spectator entertainment. Movies, television, plays, art exhibits, and sports events offer the only relief from work that is often routine, boring, and tedious.

China has produced some of the world's greatest literature and art. Traditionally, the arts were mainly regarded as a means of educating the people about ethical behavior. Mao Tse-tung also believed in the philosophy of art for education, but only in the political sense. As early as 1942, in a series of lectures at the Yenan Forum on Literature and Art, he decreed that all cultural expression would be directed toward educating the masses on the glories of socialism. "In the world of today," he said, "all literature and art belong to some one definite class, some one definite party. . . . Our literature and art are first and foremost for the workers, peasants and soldiers."

After the Communists took power in 1949, cultural expression was, for the most part, restricted to dull, uninspiring party propaganda. Portraits of Mao Tse-tung and, to a lesser extent, other revolutionary heroes, hung on the walls of virtually every public building and home throughout the nation; sculpture and painting were mainly depictions of victories of peasants and workers against the evil forces of capitalist imperialism; and music was largely limited to strident marches and songs extolling the virtues of Mao, "the Great Helmsman." Morning, noon, and night the people heard the pedestrian strains of "East Is Red" blaring from loudspeakers in the streets and workplaces. Even the traditional ink and watercolor washes, for centuries the hallmark of Chinese art, were considered relics of feudalism along with the ancient songs, dances, and the famous Peking opera.

During the Cultural Revolution, Jiang Qing, Mao's wife and leader of the Gang of Four, imposed an even more repressive censorship. Convinced that her short and undistinguished career as a Shanghai actress in the 1930s had given her expertise in all forms of art, she established herself as the supreme commissar of esthetics, restricting movies, plays, ballet, opera, music, and painting almost entirely to promotions of Marxist-Leninist-Maoist thought.

She also banned the traditional Saturday night dances at factories, offices, universities, and community centers and closed Peking's Beihai Park—where families had long enjoyed strolling among the beautiful gardens, lakes, and pavilions—as well as the Peking National Fine Arts Gallery and other museums that exhibited traditional art. Ancient festival celebrations and religious observances were prohibited, and the Red Guards were unleashed on the Buddhist temples and other places of religious worship. Most were ransacked, and many statues and relics, some irreplaceable works of art, were destroyed. Depending upon Jiang Qing's whims, the bans on each form of cultural and religious expression lasted anywhere from two to ten years. Thus, during the Cultural Revolution, entertainment in China became a wasteland and cultural expression, a mediocrity. China's leading painters, performers, and composers were beaten, jailed, or banished to the countryside along with the nation's other intellectuals. Some were even forced to commit suicide.

Currently, though the Deng Xiaoping regime still imposes censorship, it is far less restrictive and the arts are again flourishing. Performers, composers, and artists who survived the Cultural Revolution have been "rehabilitated." Traditional ink and watercolor wash paintings are again on exhibit in museums and galleries throughout the nation, along with more contemporary oil paintings. There is also a widespread movement to revive ancient Chinese music. During the 1984 Olympic Arts Festival, twenty-three musicians from the 250-member Central Ensemble of National Music came to Los Angeles and performed compositions like the seventh-century *Prince Qin Storms the Enemy Lines*, which had been reconstructed from ancient museum scores. Many of their instruments had been unearthed by Chinese archeologists from tombs dating as far back at 6,000 years.

In Peking we were taken to see a performance of the Hubei province singing and dancing troupe, famous for its interpretations of the works of Quyuan, a Hubei poet born 2,400 years ago. The production, with its exquisite scenery, costumes, and talented performers, was a delight. Most amazing, however, was the music, provided by sixty-five huge chime bells and other instruments unearthed from a fifth-century B.C. tomb.

Though we saw many portraits and statues of early revolutionary heroes like Sun Yat-sen and Chou En-lai in homes and public places, rarely did we find any of the formerly venerated Chairman Mao. When asked why, one of our guides just shook her head and said, "He made many mistakes."

As I scanned the *China Daily* radio and television listings in Peking, I was surprised by the large variety of programming. On a typical day one could listen to radio broadcasts of music by Chinese composers as well as that of Westerners like Tchaikovsky, Mendelssohn, and Beethoven. The two television channels included programs on health, hygiene, English, pinyin, and gardening; American and Chinese movies and cartoons; a travel documentary; and Peking opera. The entertainment page listed five stage productions and an even larger number of films.

During our two-month stay in China, we saw three or four beautifully choreographed and costumed song-and-dance reviews; a performance of Peking opera; a vaudeville show with talented acrobats, jugglers, and a slapstick comedy team; a well produced and directed film on martial arts; another on the life of the Ching dynasty's cruel Empress Dowager; the Shanghai Circus; and a traveling troupe of dancers and vocalists who performed at one of our hotels, delighting the predominately Western audience with a rather unusual rendition of "Oh, Susanna" as the finale.

Increasingly large numbers of Western art exhibits, films, concerts, and plays have also been touring the nation as part of the government's cultural exchange agreements with other countries. An exhibition in Peking from the Brooklyn Museum drew 10,000 viewers a day, according to an article in the July 1984 issue of *China Reconstructs*. The only criticism, according to the writer, was that Chinese artists "regretted the show did not contain more paintings by famous American artists like Sargent, Whistler, Winslow Homer, Thomas Eakins and Thomas Hart Benton, whose names are well known in Chinese art circles."

That same month, the CBS television network reported signing a deal with the Chinese network to show a variety of American sporting events as well as programs like "60 Minutes," Walter Cronkite's "Universe," the twelve-part series, "World War II," and four Dr. Seuss specials. The Chinese announced that they were also negotiating for programs from other United States networks.

When playwright Arthur Miller went to Peking in 1982 to direct a Chinese production of his classic, *Death of a Salesman*, he was amazed to find how well the Chinese related to the American story. Every performance was a sellout. In fact, tickets for most movies and stage shows, especially those that are departures from the old propaganda fare, are usually sold out because of the insatiable Chinese desire for entertainment.

Like women writers, women artists and performers are enjoying a new prominence on the Chinese scene.

ZHAO YOU PING

Painter

There are two categories of artists in China: those who are officially recognized and belong to professional organizations that pay them regular salaries, and a sort of underground group, who have freed themselves from government control by working at other jobs to support their art. The latter, many of whom are members of an unofficial organization called the Xing-Xing (Stars), have even managed to exhibit their works occasionally on sidewalks and in

Peking's Beihai Park without interference. The new government, it seems, has still not made up its mind about art and culture.

Zhao You Ping, fifty-two, an officially recognized artist and one of China's leading impressionist painters, lives with her artist husband at Peking's Central Art Institute.

When we arrived at the entrance to the old, graystone institute building in the heart of Peking, Zhao was waiting to greet us. She led us up three flights of stairs and down a long, dingy corridor to the large studio that serves as the couple's working and living quarters. The ambiance, created by huge, wired-glass windows and bare, wooden floors, reminded me of the industrial lofts in New York and Los Angeles, converted by artists into studio/living areas that have become fashionable places in which to live—indeed so fashionable that most young artists can no longer afford them.

Zhao's was divided into two areas: a work space crowded with tables, easels, and art tools; and a living and sleeping space furnished with a small hotplate, a sink, a bed, a dining table and chairs, a sofa, two comfortable lounge chairs, an upright piano, and book-filled shelves. The couple's oil paintings were stacked on shelves and displayed on the walls. Zhao's were reminiscent of the French impressionists—soft, colorful, and full of light. Her husband's were dark and somber and more in the style of the early Dutch and Italians.

The Art Life

I wanted to become an artist since I was a little girl, but received no encouragement from my parents. At that time women were not supposed to have careers in art, and my parents wanted me to become a doctor. I had many interests, but I loved art most of all. Finally, when my parents realized I was not going to listen to them, they allowed me to do as I wished.

Just before the liberation, when I was sixteen, I passed examinations in sketching and creativity and was admitted to the Central Art Institute. At that time about 30 percent of the stu-

*Zhao You Ping, artist, in her studio-home
at Peking's Central Art Institute*

dents were women, and all the teachers were men, but we were all treated equally, and I learned a great deal. I was encouraged by my teacher to study sculpture because I showed talent in that medium, but my early interest was in watercolors. Later, after I was exposed to Western art, I began to love painting in oils, and now that's my specialty.

At first I was influenced by artists like Michelangelo and da Vinci and later by the French impressionists Delacroix, Daumier, and Degas as well as some Russian painters. But during the early years of new China, it was very difficult for people to understand my kind of art. They were used to traditional brush-and-ink paintings. My work is mainly representational.

I like to meet the people who buy my paintings. If I feel someone really loves a piece, I usually make a copy for him, but I will not sell the original. I don't mean to say I keep all of my original paintings. The government has some of them, and some I keep here at home. I did sell one painting from an exhibition at the institute. The subject was a flower, and the manager of an airplane company in England loved the piece so much he begged me to sell it to him. I just couldn't say no, so I sold him the original, and later nine reproductions of it were sold to American artists.

I keep part of the money from those sales and part goes to the institute. They pay me a salary, and my husband and I are also allowed to live here. Not all the artists can live at the institute. We had priority because of my reputation. Actually, this was a classroom, not a living space, but because housing is a big problem in China, we consider ourselves fortunate to have such a large area in which to live and work. We also teach here. In fact, when I came here as a student, my husband was my teacher.

Women artists now enjoy the same opportunities as men, but before the liberation, women had a very low status, and they suffered much discrimination and oppression. The new government made a special effort to give women greater opportunities, so I would say we are not only equal but more than equal.

The younger generation loves oil painting very much, but middle-aged and older people still prefer traditional Chinese art, watercolor and brush-and-ink painting. I've also found that city people appreciate oil painting, while rural people like traditional art.

My work has been shown in France and the United States, and nine pieces were sold from those exhibits. The shows included the work of many artists, and a few were selected by the government to travel with the exhibitions. I was not one of them, but that doesn't mean I will never go. I feel it's important for an artist to see original works of other artists throughout the world, and soon I will have that opportunity. A few of us have been chosen to study in Belgium for a year, and it's a rare opportunity. We will be copying famous paintings in the museums, so we can learn their methods of color and design. I also want to go to France and Italy someday to study the work of their artists.

We suffered a great deal during the chaos of the Cultural Revolution. Many of our paintings were destroyed by the Red Guards when they searched our home, and we felt very badly about losing our work. It was also impossible for us to paint because they were always watching us. We spent three years in the countryside, and when we came back to the institute, they said we had to rehabilitate ourselves at self-criticism meetings, so our work was interrupted until the smash of the Gang of Four. We lost ten years.

XIA JUHUA

Acrobat

In Shanghai I thrilled to the most astonishing circus performance I have ever seen. Housed in a large, new auditorium, the circus ring was luxuriously covered with a thick, bright blue carpet, and all the performers—including the trained baby panda—were superb. Unlike the European and American acrobatic, high-wire, and trapeze acts I had seen, the Chinese did not rely on danger to enhance the entertainment. Each performer was visibly protected by a wire or cord attached to a belt around the waist, and thus excitement was provided only by their amazing skill.

Acrobatics is an ancient and highly developed Chinese art form, though historically, acrobats and other circus performers occupied a low rung on the social ladder, along with actors. After the Communists took power, special schools were established for talented people in all the arts, and in recent years, Chinese acrobatic teams have performed throughout the world. When the Chengdu Acrobatic Troupe (part of the China Performing Arts Company) played in Los Angeles during the 1984 Summer Olympic Arts Festival, one reviewer commented, "The company delivered exactly what it intended: people's art—accessible, edifying and almost awesomely masterful. . . . Seven women doing handstands from a leaning tower of eight chairs. Three men tossing enormous ceramic jars and catching them on the backs of their necks. A woman riding a bicycle across an elevated wire while balancing a vase on her head—and, of course, pausing to kick a bunch of flowers up into the vase."

In her mid-forties, former international champion acrobat Xia Juhua was still graceful and attractive when I interviewed her in her office. Now director of the Wuhan Municipal Cultural Bureau, she described vividly the contrast in the lives of circus performers before and after the Communist revolution.

A Circus Performer in Old China

My childhood was very miserable. I was twelve years old when the new China was founded in 1949, and though thirty-four years have passed, I still have very fresh memories of my childhood in the old society.

My parents lived in the countryside, and we were very poor. My grandfather worked in the fields for a landlord, and he died when he was only thirty-eight, so I knew about him only through my father. After my grandfather died, my father worked for the same landlord. There were two children in my family, my younger sister and me, and when I was five the Kuomintang government began drafting peasants into the army. My father was in his twenties then and very strong. He was afraid of being

*Xia Juhua, acrobat, performing
the Pagoda of Bowls in 1965*

called to be a soldier, so he ran away from our town. Only my grandmother, my mother, my sister, and I remained at home. My grandmother was in poor health. She was suffering from what we call "big neck" [goiter], and we had no money for medical treatment. There was no one to work the land, so my mother took my sister and me out begging.

After my father left, he joined a circus troupe and, soon after, the troupe came to our village to perform. My father was with them, and when they left again, he decided to take me along. My grandmother didn't want me to go because in those days circus performers were looked down upon, and life was very hard for them. But if I went there would be one less mouth to feed, and maybe they could keep from starving to death.

My father was not a performer with the circus, just a handyman, so the money he received was not enough to feed me, too. The circus boss and his wife had no children, and they adopted me. Their two children had died, and there was an old superstition that if you adopt a child, your own future children will be healthy.

The boss gave me a few lessons, and I became an acrobat at the age of six. In the old society, acrobats were exploited and their lives were very hard. We had no real home. We just traveled from province to province and performed in open fields. Because we were looked down upon, we were not allowed to perform in theaters, so our lives were very hard and miserable. I still have very clear memories of living in broken-down temples and abandoned huts.

And the children were even more miserable. Acrobats were given no real training, as they are now. Today performers go to school and are under the protection of the government. In my time, we just learned a few tricks, and then we had to perform. My first act was having my pigtails tied to the top of a high pole and I had to swing around by them for about ten minutes. It felt as if I had needles in my head, but even though it was very painful, I dared not cry. If I did, I was beaten by the boss. I was very bold—bolder than the other children—so I performed on the highest pole, and they had no safety wires or nets. Once I saw an acrobat fall and break his neck, and others were seriously injured. I was lucky. I didn't fall from the pole, though once I fell from the top position of a pyramid of acrobats. We were performing at night, and because there was no electricity, they used oil lamps, which attracted a lot of insects. The man at the bottom got a fly in his eye, and when he tried to brush it away, he lost his balance, and we were all toppled to the ground. I was unconscious, and they found I'd broken my collarbone. There was no money for a doctor, so they just pressed it back into place and put some herb medicine on it. If you didn't perform, you got no pay, so even though I was not fully recovered, I began performing again in a week. I was only six years old, and it was very painful.

The life was very hard: not enough to eat, no warm clothes, and no place to live. On fine days, when we could perform, maybe we could buy a little rice. But when it rained we could not perform, and we had nothing to eat.

I was very popular with the audiences because I learned many different acrobatic stunts, but my salary was all taken by my adopted father. After each act was finished, he would ask the audience to give money, and because I enjoyed a high reputation I earned a lot, but it all went to the boss. And after each performance I had to do housework for the boss and his wife—laundry, cooking, cleaning—and she did nothing. So that was my childhood, very miserable and hard, and I was only one of thousands of poor people who had similar sufferings.

In 1949 acrobats were liberated along with the rest of the Chinese people, and the hard life was gone forever. We were taken care of, given a decent wage, and could perform in theaters. I came to Wuhan with the circus in 1950. The government organized all the acrobats from various areas into groups, and we were given training and better living conditions. And we were respected because the government looked upon acrobatics as an art like the other arts. So we were liberated socially, politically, and economically.

After the liberation, my adopted father also changed. He learned the new ideology and did not continue in his old habits.

He was educated and reformed, and we studied together at a school organized by the government.

After the circus arrived in Wuhan we disbanded, and because I had been adopted by the Xia family, my father could not take me with him when he left for a new job. But two or three years after we left our village my father went back there again, and when he returned to the circus, he told me my grandmother had starved to death, my younger sister had been sold to another family as a child-bride, and my mother had married another man. So the whole family was split apart.

After the liberation I became very serious about acrobatics as an art. In the old society, I had been forced to be an acrobat and do very dangerous things because the boss wanted to thrill the audience and make money. After liberation, the danger was eliminated, and the real art of acrobatics was developed. And, because I was only twelve and my body was naturally very flexible, more so than most people's, I learned to perform very intricate acts like the Pagoda of Bowls. It involved balancing twelve bowls stacked on top of my head while I bent from the waist all the way to the floor. I began practicing that act in 1952 and perfected it after many years of hard work.

In 1956 our troupe toured France, Great Britain, Italy, and Belgium, and my act was the main attraction of our performances. In 1957 I won a gold medal for acrobatics at the Sixth World Youth Festival in Moscow. But I was not satisfied and wanted to make even further progress, to create new acrobatic feats. In 1962 I won another gold medal for an action I developed myself. Since ancient times, the bowls were always placed on the head, but I created a new act by balancing them on my feet while standing on my hands. So using the old art as a basis, I've gone even further. It's a very difficult thing to do because you cannot see the bowls; you can only feel them with your feet. During countless hours of practice, I broke countless bowls and I was so tired I could not walk. By then I was in my early twenties, but I was determined because I felt that since the government had done so much for me, I should dedicate my youth to the state.

Because I had performed so much, many people knew me and that caused some problems. For instance, I received many letters expressing admiration, love, and encouragement. Some boys even wanted me to be their girlfriend, but I had to ignore them and concentrate on practicing. Of course it was impolite not to answer those warm messages, but if you want to create something new, you must give it all your time and energy. You cannot allow yourself to be distracted by other things.

The people of Wuhan know very well about my experiences during the Cutural Revolution. I was criticized and attacked, not only spiritually and ideologically, but also physically. I was seriously beaten and, as a result, my performing career was shortened. My back was injured, and I had to leave the stage earlier. All famous people were attacked in those years, but it's past history, and we should now look to the future.

I did not marry until I was thirty-four. My husband is a teacher at a radio technical school, and we have two daughters, aged nine and six. I stopped performing in 1972 when I was thirty-five, but I have continued to enjoy great honor and high prestige from the party and the state. I am a delegate to the National People's Congress and also a member of the Communist Party, but the happiest occasion of my life was when I had a private audience with Chairman Mao.

After liberation most of the problems for women were solved. Now women in general enjoy equality with men because that is the government policy. For instance, the central government makes sure that women take part in all the important state activities, and the old revolutionaries—like the widows of Premier Chou En-lai and Marshal Chu Teh—are senior cadres. But some of the old feudal ideas still persist in the society. As you know, our country was under a feudal system for thousands of years, and though we have made great progress, it's impossible to change all the old ideas in only thirty-four years.

But the government is very concerned about that and is making efforts to educate people. Some people still look down upon girls and prefer boys. We have a serious population problem, yet when the first child is a girl, some couples want a second child. If the second is again a girl, they want a third, and they keep having more children until they have a boy.

I have been to many countries and found that foreign people prefer to have fewer children, not like in China where in the countryside, especially, they prefer big families. The state leaders are also urging women to have more self-respect. We have outstanding women in many fields—education, science, and in every industry—but women could advance even more if they had greater respect for themselves. As Chairman Mao once said, "Women can do whatever men do." All Chinese people are working hard to realize the Four Modernizations and women should not lag behind.

ZHANG RUI FANG

Actress

One of China's most famous film actresses, Zhang Rui Fang was sixty-five years old and still very beautiful when I interviewed her at the Shanghai apartment she shares with her husband, writer-artist Yen Li. I was told later by the reporter from Shanghai's Wen Hui Bao, who arranged the interview, that Zhang's hair had turned snow white from the beatings she received during the two years she was forced to do hard labor on a farm during the Cultural Revolution, and that since that time she had dyed her hair. That day, dressed in a well-tailored, black wool pantsuit with a burgundy turtle-necked sweater, she looked very fashionable.

The daughter of a wealthy warlord, Zhang became a revolutionary at age nineteen, beginning her acting career with the Communist forces in Yenan. She has appeared in more than forty stage plays and twenty-five films and is still working hard. When I asked her how she managed to look so young, she laughed and said, "I think it's because I always try to feel happy and not worry about pressures. I'm an optimist and I also enjoy being with young people. I feel they keep me young, too."

Her prominence has brought her special privileges such as a higher salary, a private telephone, and a car always at her disposal. Hers was one of the loveliest apartments we saw in China. Located in one of Shanghai's older, European-style buildings, the unit had six spacious rooms, beautifully polished wood floors, and was furnished with a number of exquisite Chinese antiques as well as attractive and comfortable Western furniture. The many books, green plants, and paintings, combined with the warm afternoon sunshine streaming through the large bay windows of the living room, provided a pleasant and relaxed atmosphere. As we sipped our tea and chatted, a caged canary sang cheerfully in the background.

We were told that Zhang had become very ill the night before and had been taken to the hospital for treatment, but she did not wish to cancel our meeting. Yen, very solicitous of his wife, interrupted the interview periodically to inquire about her condition, but Zhang insisted on continuing. It was important, she said, to promote good relations between the women of China and the United States.

The Warlord's Daughter

My father was a warlord, so my family were landowners and very rich, but we moved around a lot because in those days the warlords were always fighting among themselves. My father passed away when I was eleven, but because there was money in the family, we were still well taken care of.

My grandfather did not approve of girls going to school, so soon after my father died my mother brought me to Peking and sent me to school there. Around 1935, when the Japanese were invading China, there was a big student uprising in Peking against the Kuomintang because they were fighting the Communists rather than the Japanese, and the younger members of my family joined in. Then, gradually, one after another, we joined the Communist Party. So my generation of the family became revolutionaries, even though we were wealthy.

Zhang Rui Fang, film star, with her husband,
writer Yen Li, in their Shanghai apartment

When I was seventeen, I entered the National Painting Institute because at that time I wanted to become an artist. Then, in 1937, after I had completed two years, Chiang Kai-shek officially declared war on Japan and I left school to join the Student Federation [a political activist organization], and that was when I began my acting career. Students everywhere in China were taking part in the campaign against the Japanese, and I became active in drama, singing, and dancing. We went to the front lines to put on plays for the soldiers, and then I went to Chongqing, where the Kuomintang government had moved their capital, and I began acting in films. I worked for a production company owned by the Chiang Kai-shek government. During that period the Communists and the Kuomintang had united against the Japanese, so Chou En-lai was in Chongqing representing the Communist Party, and he was also in charge of the film company. That's when we became friends and also when I met my husband. Yen Li was head of the film company's art department. During the war he joined the army as a playwright, but he was also an artist.

After the liberation, the biggest change was that our lives became more stable, and conditions were much, much better for making films. The Kuomintang government had treated artists very badly. They considered us low-class people, so conditions were not good for us. We were also forbidden to perform progressive plays, so we were very limited.

Yen Li and I were married soon after the Communists took power. We moved to Shanghai and have lived here ever since. We have one son who is now twenty-eight and attending a law university in east China.

I've often had to travel abroad for my film work, but my husband works at home writing plays, so he could take care of our son and do some household chores. We also hired a maid, and our child was in a boarding kindergarten until he was three. Then he became a day student. Family life is a little easier for a film actress, because when you finish a film you can take a holiday and spend time with your family.

I love my son very much and, of course, I would have liked

to be with him more. But I'm also very dedicated to the Communist cause, so I couldn't spend as much time with him as I wanted. At a very early age I taught him to be very independent, to study hard, and to have self-respect. He learned to rely on himself because his mother and father were very busy with their work. And he was very proud of us because he thought it was unusual to have such successful parents.

I feel that the separations from our son made our relationship stronger. When we do get together, the three of us sometimes talk all night. In fact, our neighborhood committee wanted to select us as a Model Family, but we refused because we felt there were others who were even more deserving.

There are no conflicts in our family because I always support my husband's work, and he supports mine, and our son supports both of us. He can cook even better than we can, because during the Cultural Revolution I was sent away, and he often had to cook for himself.

Nothing happened to my husband and son during the Cultural Revolution, but I went to prison for two years because I was very close to Chou En-lai. Everyone who was close to him was singled out for persecution. Premier Chou did many great things for China, and the people loved him very much. That's why so many people demonstrated in Tiananmen Square when he died.

There is still a great deal of inequality in the rural areas between men and women, and also some in the cities, but not as much. In the rural areas, there are many feudal ideas left over from the past, so many people still think women are not equal to men. For example, they are still disappointed when they give birth to a girl, and abuse of women still exists. We must fight strongly against that. So, right now, men and women in China are actually not equal, but it's not because women are less intelligent than men; it's because of the old ideas.

In China, if you are in good health, you can act all your life. I'm also teaching. I work at the Shanghai Film Studio, and recently I organized a drama company there to teach young people in our profession. I'm chairman of the company, and that keeps me busier than my own acting. Sometimes an amateur acting group will call on me for help, too, so that, combined with my responsibilities as a delegate to the Political Consultative Conference, the National People's Congress, and the women's federation, keeps me very busy.

I also travel to other countries. I've been to Japan and Korea three times, to India seven times, and to Egypt and Russia. Many actresses in other countries complain that they don't enjoy a happy life at home. In Japan especially, some film stars become involved with very young men, and they leave their husbands. The actresses are flattered that younger men worship them so much and want them. That type of thing rarely happens in China. Divorces are very rare here because we have very strong family relationships, stronger than in other countries. And if a family does have problems, the neighborhood committees and the work leaders always try to find ways to help solve them, so usually the situation can be worked out.

I think Western ideas are affecting our younger generation a little, but while the old generation is still alive, they will continue to teach them traditional values. You know, our films are not made only for entertainment. We try to reinforce the old ideas, and films have a great influence on the people. That's also true of writing and the other arts.

I feel I'm too old now to have new ambitions. My hope lies with the younger generation, and that's why I'm helping to develop young film stars. But I do have one other goal. Because I joined the Communist Party when I was very young, and I knew Chou En-lai and many of the other great leaders, my colleagues have asked me to write a book about my early life. Now I just have to find the time.

Some people worry about what they will do when they retire, but my husband and I will have no trouble keeping busy. There are still so many things we want to do. Yen Li writes and paints, and I can write my autobiography. My only problem is finding a quiet place to work. There always seems to be a crowd around me, not only admirers and curiosity-seekers, but also those who want me to teach and lecture.

HONG XIEN NIU

Actress

A leading actress with the Canton Drama Company, Hong Xien Niu, which means Red Thread Girl, was fifty-six years old when we met at the company's rehearsal center, an old and rather shabby complex of wooden buildings in the center of the city.

Having been told of her status as one of China's most popular stage performers, I was surprised to be welcomed by a rather unpreposessing woman, not the colorful personage I had expected. When I asked why she was named Red Thread Girl, she said, "It was a name given to me by my old drama master. There is an ancient Chinese legend about a very talented woman warrior who could also act. My master thought I had those characteristics, so he gave me that name and I kept it."

As soon as we were seated at a long wooden table in what seemed to be the company's meeting room, Hong explained that she had a very busy schedule that morning and could give me only an hour for the interview. However, she was very warm and open, answering my questions in a forthright manner. When we finished, she invited me to watch her direct a new musical play the company was rehearsing.

The old rehearsal hall was a bedlam, with singers, actors and musicians all practicing individually, but Hong soon restored order. She had a commanding presence and seemed highly respected by the performers.

The Red Thread Girl

My father owned a drugstore in Canton, and though we were not rich, he was able to feed his family. When I was almost ten, the Japanese took Canton, and my family moved to Hong Kong, where I had an uncle who was an actor. My father could not find work, so I could not go to school. Instead, I got an acting job with a company that performed Canton drama, a type of drama that had originated in Canton and was also popular in Hong Kong and Macao.

After the Pearl Harbor incident in 1941, I returned to China with the drama company, but this time to Guangxi province. I was only fifteen, but already I was playing leading roles. Life at that time was very bitter because of the war against the Japanese. Our company could perform only on the streets, and it was even worse after the Japanese surrender, because the Kuomintang government was in power and they looked down upon drama companies. I was very unhappy and I returned to Hong Kong.

I knew very little about politics and the Communist Party. I just wanted to find a good place to develop my talents. During the next few years I continued to act, and I also studied art and literature in school. Actresses were also looked down upon by Hong Kong society, but I had a few roles in films and concentrated on my stage work. In 1949, after China was liberated, lots of Chinese in Hong Kong returned to the mainland, and I began hearing about the new China. Everyone said it was different than it was under the Kuomintang, that things were much better. I didn't really believe them, but finally I decided to go back and see for myself. I returned in 1955, and after seeing the changes, I decided to remain.

By then I had already been married and divorced. I was married at age fifteen, too early to know anything about real life. After I had my daughter and two sons, I found out that my husband was unfaithful, so I left him, but it was very painful. I had been married ten years and was only twenty-five when I was divorced. I remarried a few years later, and my daughter also became an actress. I was her teacher.

My mother looked after the children, and I also hired a maid to help. There are other young actresses in our drama company who manage to have good family lives. One way is having the children looked after by their grandparents. Another is sending them to boarding kindergartens. As far as the husbands are concerned, Chinese women enjoy equal status with men. The husband shares in the household chores, and he supports his wife in her work. Of course, that is not always the case, but I would say it's true in the majority of marriages.

When the wife travels, the husband makes sure the children are taken care of. He usually sends them to his mother-in-law or to a boarding kindergarten and brings them home on the weekends. So there is harmony in the family, and I think that's a very important part of new China.

I suffered a lot during the Cultural Revolution. I was under arrest for a long time and was not permitted to perform. But some of my friends helped me. They secretly sent me messages and good food, which made it much easier. Many of the messages said they were crying for me because I had done nothing wrong and it wasn't fair to treat me that way. I told them not to feel sorry for me, that sooner or later it would all be cleared up. I was in prison for five years and could not perform for thirteen years. After I was released from prison, I was assigned to other jobs like teaching. Jaing Qing controlled all performances in China, and she only allowed a certain kind of drama. Only what she approved could be staged. But that's all over now, so let's forget it.

In new China the government treats actors with respect. We are looked upon as architects of people's feelings, because they learn from our dramas. Also, the conditions are much better for actors to develop their talents. For example, in Hong Kong, my boss would tell me in the morning what role I had to perform that evening, so there was no time for rehearsal. In new China it is quite different. I'm given a play and asked to read it. Then I'm told that if it's too difficult, they will make changes, and they also give us at least a month to rehearse before the performance. So there is enough time for me to be creative, and that's a very big change.

Also, though I received enough money to make a living in Hong Kong, my life was very narrow. All I did was work, work, work, and my mind felt empty. But in new China, I do many things besides performing. I teach young people, I direct, and I also travel to other countries, which makes my life very rich. Even when I first returned from Hong Kong, my talent was recognized—and now even more so. I'm the leader of my company; I've performed in Korea, Vietnam, Singapore, America, and Russia; I've been a representative to the National People's Congress for many years; and I'm also the vice chairman of the Drama Association of Guangdong province. So I've had the chance to broaden my entire life.

Since the founding of new China thirty-four years ago, I feel there has been a great change in the status of women, but there is still room for improvement. Some men still look down upon women; they regard them as inferior creatures. That's true only among a minority of people, but if we want to rid ourselves of discrimination completely, I think women should make a bigger effort to fight against it.

CHAPTER

8

THE HEALTH REVOLUTION

Potions concocted from snakes, lizards, turtles, fossils, scorpions, and herbs; skewering the patient's body with long needles; a bath of smoke from burning root of artemisia—these are just a few of the exotic practices Chinese doctors have used for centuries to cure the sick, sometimes with a surprising degree of effectiveness. In China today, these methods are called traditional medicine, as opposed to Western medicine.

Most Americans first became aware of Chinese traditional medicine in 1972, when columnist James Reston, a member of the press corps accompanying President Nixon on his visit to China, reported that acupuncture treatments had relieved his pain following an appendectomy in Peking. Since 1979, when United States–Chinese relations were formally re-established, hundreds of American doctors and scientists have flocked to China to study their traditional remedies, and have reported good results with a number of techniques. Some herbal remedies, they say, may be even better than modern manufactured drugs. Acupuncture has been proven extremely effective as an anesthesia, and with fewer side effects than Western methods, although neither Chinese nor Western researchers can explain why.

Yet, from the middle of the nineteenth century, when Westerners began to enter China in large numbers, until the Communist Party took power in 1949, Chinese intellectuals had rejected their ancient medical practices as useless relics from the past. In their rush to emulate American and European political and social ideology and to modernize their country, they also embraced Western medical science. Children of the elite were sent to study at universities and medical schools in America and Europe, or to those established in China by Christian missionaries. These children included some of the early revolutionaries:

Sun Yat-sen received his medical degree in Hawaii; Chou En-lai was educated in France.

In China's city hospitals, Western medicine was practiced exclusively, while the use of acupuncture and herbal medicines was relegated to a few old men and women who operated out of dusty old neighborhood offices and shops.

However, like education, Western medical treatment was a luxury that could be afforded only by the wealthier class. For the vast majority of the population, poor factory workers and peasants, the old folk remedies continued to be the main method of treatment, along with superstitious rituals that were believed to be effective in appeasing the various gods who might have brought illness to a family or an individual.

Today, despite many flaws, China has established one of the least expensive and most pervasive health systems in the world. By 1982, just thirty-three years after the Communists took power, infant mortality had decreased from 200 per thousand to 34.68 per thousand, and the average life expectancy had increased from 35 to 67.88 years. These figures, taken from the July 1984 issue of *China Reconstructs*, are actually modest compared to those reported by Western journalists. By any standards, however, progress in health care has been nothing short of phenomenal.

In the late 1940s, when it became evident that the Communists would succeed in their fight to depose the Chiang Kai-shek government, many Western-trained Chinese doctors fled to Taiwan, the United States, or Europe, and the new government faced an acute shortage of physicians. Mao decreed that those who remained should study the ancient traditional methods, combining the best with Western medicine. The old practitioners were re-instated in the medical schools, teaching from the more than 8,000 ancient treatises that were found in museums. Currently, medical schools and hospitals have both Western and traditional medicine departments, but most Chinese still prefer being treated with herbal remedies and acupuncture before resorting to Western methods.

The greatest improvement in the health of the Chinese people came, however, with the introduction of modern sanitation and hygiene, combined with the use of pesticides (which destroyed disease-carrying insects) and drugs to control infectious and endemic diseases. Typhoid fever, schistosomiasis (snail fever), malaria, and other epidemic diseases, which for centuries had caused the illness and death of millions, have been largely wiped out. According to surveys, in 1957 the leading causes of death in China were diseases of the respiratory system, acute infectious diseases, and tuberculosis. By 1982 those had fallen behind cerebrovascular disorders, heart ailments, and cancer—the same as in Western countries.

The shortage of trained physicians was further exacerbated by the ten-year interruption of all education during the Cultural Revolution. Medical educators, like others, were forced to obey students, and classes consisted largely of recitations of Mao's thoughts. Consequently, medical students during those years received inferior training. Today patients commonly check the certificate on the wall in the doctor's office to make sure he or she received it before 1965. The shortage of doctors is most acute in the rural areas, since many are reluctant to leave the superior hospital and laboratory facilities in the cities to live and practice under crude conditions in the countryside.

Shortly before the start of the Cultural Revolution, the Communists introduced the concept of "barefoot doctors." Each village selects one or two men and women to attend a training course given by physicians at local hospitals or clinics. Then they return to their villages to teach sanitation and hygiene, and to provide primary medical care such as delivering babies, setting broken limbs, giving innoculations, and dispensing drugs for minor illnesses. Serious cases are referred to hospitals for treatment, with the patients often transported on wagons or carts. After a few months of practical experience, the barefoot doctors go back for another period of training, and then for periodic refresher courses.

In the cities there is a shortage of hospital beds. In 1980 there was reportedly one per 10,000 people and, although many more hospitals and clinics have been constructed since then, that figure has probably remained roughly the same because of the population increase.

To Westerners, the lack of cleanliness is disturbing. We visited four major hospitals in China—one in Peking, one in Shanghai, and two in Canton, and found the atmosphere depressing. The walls, usually painted a bilious green, were peeling and dirty; doctors' and nurses' uniforms were stained and gray-looking; and the patients were wearing their own clothing—shirts, pants, and sweaters.

But the affordable cost makes medical care available to all Chinese. Students and workers in government offices and educational institutions receive free services. Factory workers are covered by labor insurance, which also pays half the fees for their families. However, townships (formerly communes) are responsible for their own health systems, as they are for education. According to a 1984 report in *China Reconstructs*, all of China's 2,100 counties now have hospitals, child and maternity clinics, and sanitation and anti-epidemic stations, while 87 percent of the villages (formerly brigades) have clinics. With the change from collective farming to the individual family responsibility system, where each family farms its own plot of land, the system of medical payment has also changed. There are now private clinics set up by doctors, as well as those owned by the villages, and some peasants prefer paying medical charges themselves instead of a monthly fee for cooperative medicine. Those who cannot afford medical costs are helped by the village public-welfare fund.

As the ensuing dialogues reveal, women play a significant role in China's health services.

DR. YOUNG AI-LAIN

Surgeon

The First People's Hospital, built in 1953, is a huge, graystone affair, but hardly noticeable among the tightly crowded buildings along one of Canton's busiest thoroughfares.

A young male intern from Dr. Young's department met us at the entrance to the 800-bed hospital, and led us through a

*labyrinth of dark, dingy halls crowded with people, to an eleva-
tor that took us to the third-floor office where the director of thoracic and cardiac surgery was waiting. Looking far younger than
her fifty-seven years, Dr. Young was stylishly dressed in a blue-
and-red checked jacket, white cotton blouse, and navy blue slacks.
She was only about four feet eight inches tall, with tiny hands.
Yet they were hands that opened the chests of three or four patients a day, a surgical procedure that takes a great deal of
strength.*

*Though warm and receptive, Dr. Young seemed nervous dur-
ing the interview, giving terse answers to my questions but providing some surprising information about the status of women
doctors. When we finished, she insisted that I visit some of her
patients, becoming more animated and relaxed each time she
displayed the results of her work. The first patient was a young
woman in a ward with seven others. When we requested permission to photograph the patient with Dr. Young, she gladly gave
her consent. Later we were shocked to learn that the woman had
undergone open-heart surgery only one day earlier. In American
hospitals, such patients are usually kept isolated from public
contact for at least a few days.*

*Next she took us to a similar ward, where we saw another
young woman who had had heart surgery weeks earlier. Dressed
in faded pajamas, she was sitting on a chair, and without any
request for permission, the doctor unbuttoned the woman's pa-
jama top in order to display the neatness of the incision. In another ward, Dr. Young displayed the healed incision of a young
man in whose heart she had replaced two valves a couple of months
earlier. He was almost ready to go home.*

Prognosis: Equality

I had a very average childhood. My family was neither rich nor
poor. My father had an administrative position with the Kuomintang government and he made enough money to take care
of his family.

My parents believed in education for girls as well as boys,

so I was sent to primary and middle school, and then I entered the Sun Yat-sen Medical Institute here in Canton. I received a subsidy from the government because it was too difficult for my father to pay all of the tuition.

Before liberation there were only a few women doctors, but when the Communists came into power and women began to enjoy equal status with men, the government emphasized that women should be trained as doctors because there was a shortage. And I loved surgery very much. I was twenty-four years old when I graduated from the medical institute in 1950, just one year after liberation, and I was assigned to a hospital to do general surgery. Four years later I began to specialize in thoracic surgery.

One-third of our surgeons are women. Most of them work in the hospital wards, and a few in the outpatient clinic. The most common type of surgery we do on women in this hospital is tumor removal, but we also do a lot of plastic surgery on fire victims.

When I began my career I was doing only chest surgery, but gradually it became difficult to separate chest and heart surgery, so I learned how to operate on the heart. Now I do mostly heart surgery.

I'm very proud of my work, and I feel respected by the male patients and doctors. I'm director of my department, and the seven doctors who work under me are all men, but they seem to believe in me. The head of the inspection office team is also a woman, and that office is very important because the staff must carefully monitor the patients for forty-two hours after an operation to see that they are reacting normally. Women enjoy great status and respect in this hospital.

Quite often we have doctors from other countries visiting this hospital. I believe we are far behind other countries in medical equipment, but in surgical skills I feel we are doing very well. There is no shortage of doctors in China now, except for the rural areas. Most doctors don't want to live in the countryside because the medical facilities are not as good as in the cities, living conditions are not as comfortable, and there are very few cultural activities.

Occasionally I am invited to give lectures to medical students at the institute. And I'm beginning to see as many women as men students in the classes these days. It's almost half-and-half, though there are still a few more men than women.

My husband is a radiologist and also practices at this hospital. We have two children who are grown now, but when they were young, my household duties did not interfere with my work because I had a maid.

Medical conditions are much better than they were before liberation, but we need more and better equipment. And because of our population problem, there is still a shortage of hospitals. I also feel that women are still not totally liberated, but that situation is also better than it was before.

NURSE WANG MIN LI
AND DR. NING SHOU-PAO

Shanghai First Medical College
Children's Hospital

When we drove into the courtyard of the Shanghai First Medical College Children's Hospital, we found a large and beautifully decorated Chinese pictograph poster (these are called big-character posters) standing on an easel at the entrance. It read, we were told, "Welcome journalists from Los Angeles."

Standing beside it was a smiling committee of eight or ten hospital personnel dressed in snow-white coats, including Wang Min Li, deputy director of nursing, and Dr. Ning Shou-pao, a male specialist in pediatric cardiology and deputy director of the hospital.

Wang and Dr. Ning led us into a new-looking, white brick building, to the ground-floor staff lounge. A large, sunny room, it was pleasantly furnished with a long conference table, comfortable, upholstered sofas and chairs and, of course, a giant thermos of tea. A pleasant-looking woman in her late forties, Wang was shy and unwilling to express opinions or to provide very much information. I was told that Dr. Ning, a tall, slim, and attractive man of about forty-five who had studied in Canada, was there to help translate for Wang, but, as it turned out, he was also a good source of information.

After the interview, Dr. Ning toured us through the children's wards, and we found that—unlike the newer entrance and lounge wing of the building—the eight-story hospital was as gloomy as the others we had visited. The halls and rooms badly needed fresh paint, and the iron beds were old and rusted.

Both Wang and Dr. Ning had assured me that nurses were treated as equals by the doctors. Later, however, one of our guides told me that his daughter, a nurse at the same hospital, complains that nurses are not respected and are treated more like maids than professionals. He confided that the doctor and nurse had to say what they did because equal treatment is government policy.

Nurses, Doctors, and Health

WANG: My father was a bank clerk, and our lives were very comfortable because he earned money to support the family. In the old society, girls were usually not as highly educated as boys, but my parents believed in education for girls, so I was sent to primary and middle school. But because we were not wealthy, we all had to stop attending school for short periods of time. Then, when the family could afford it, we would go back again.

In 1949 there was much more economic stability. After the liberation, my elder brother got a job, so he could help support the family, and I was able to go to nursing school. One of my middle-school teachers had encouraged me to become a nurse because before liberation only two professions were open to women—nursing and teaching. I attended one of the nursing schools affiliated with this medical college. It has a number of nursing schools, and after graduation nurses are sent to the six teaching hospitals affiliated with the college. When I graduated in 1954, I came to this hospital and I've been here ever since. I was appointed deputy director of nursing in 1982.

Nurses are still mainly women, but there are a few male nurses in some hospitals and departments, such as the hospital for psychiatric diseases and the surgery departments.

Before liberation nurses were looked down upon by doctors,

but that has changed. After liberation our leaders, Chairman Mao and Premier Chou En-lai, put more value on nurses, especially those working in the children's hospitals. I think it's very important to encourage children's nurses, because they take care of the younger generation. So, in the new society, nurses are respected. They are of great help to the doctors, and I feel we have equal status. In fact, one day I saw a film on television that showed a nurse serving a cup of coffee to a doctor after an operation and I felt badly. I did not like to see a nurse behaving like a maid.

NING: It's true that Chairman Mao emphasized the importance of nursing, and many people agreed with him. Just before the liberation, doctors and nurses in the People's Liberation Army were not really separate in their work; doctors did some nursing and nurses did some medical work. Everyone did what they had to because it was an emergency situation. So army doctors had already increased their respect for nurses, and because most of our leaders were in the army, they saw that doctors and nurses could work together as equals—that one should not have to be subservient to the other.

We have also discussed the issue for a long time in this hospital. I joined the staff in 1956. Two years later China entered a period called the Great Leap Forward, which was something like an early Cultural Revolution. At the time we talked about the problem a lot, and some of our nurses entered a special training course to become doctors. In fact, some of them are now working as doctors in this hospital, but most of them went back to nursing after the end of the Cultural Revolution in 1976 because they did not have enough training. Only those who went on to medical school are still doctors.

During the Cultural Revolution, I learned some nursing techniques myself because the majority of the workers in this hospital thought that doctors should learn from nurses, and nurses should learn from doctors, so we could take better care of the children. I worked as a nurse in the wards for a couple of weeks, and I feel it was good for me. Now I understand nursing much better, and I cooperate more with nurses because I learn more about the patients from them. But I still think the medical profession should be divided. We can't mix doctors and nurses, because there is still a big difference in training.

WANG: During that time, the Red Guards didn't think the head nurse was important. She was criticized with big-character posters and had to stop working for a while. Just a few nurses were allowed to take responsibility for the patients and go on doing their work.

NING: Fortunately I was not deputy director of the hospital at that time, because if you were the head of a department or a director, you received more criticism. Criticism is not a bad thing, but not in the way it was practiced then, like writing about people on big-character posters. There were so many criticisms and so many problems, but at least this hospital continued to function. We didn't stop for a single day even though everything was disturbed.

I was really very upset because I couldn't do some very specialized techniques for the patients. For several years the atmosphere did not permit it, because the Red Guards thought the only thing that was important was politics, not technical work.

WANG: If a nurse really hasn't done her job well, she should be criticized. But if she worked well and the doctor still did not treat her with respect, he would be reported to the administrators who will deal with the problem. In this hospital, out of a staff of about 600, only 210 are nurses, so the doctors and administrators value them very much.

NING: There is one process here that is quite different from the hospitals I trained at in North America. All the Shanghai hospitals have a staff study meeting once a week. We study the works of Chairman Mao or Deng Xiaoping, and sometimes important editorials in the *People's Daily* [the official Communist Party newspaper]. We also usually have criticism and self-criticism sessions, and the doctors and nurses join in. In Canada doctors always met with doctors, and nurses with nurses. There's a big difference, because here we have more communication. During a meeting a nurse may complain that a doctor has not been very kind to her, and then others give their opinions. That usually solves the problem, because the doctor would be afraid to continue his bad behavior or he would be criticized again at the next meeting—not only by the nurse but also by the doctors. As I recall, those meetings started after liberation, because the new government told us we should have them.

WANG: On the average a nurse makes sixty to seventy yuan a month and a doctor earns about ten to twenty yuan more. In Shanghai, as in all of China, there is always a housing shortage because we have too large a population. But in this hospital, the administrators are attentive to housing for doctors and nurses. In recent years they built several big apartment buildings so we could have adequate living conditions. My husband is a schoolteacher and we have a child, so we have one of the new apartments. But my parents are not in good health, and they cannot take care of my child, so I sent her to boarding nursery school and kindergarten, and I was able to do my job.

NING: Housing is still a problem, but we have two kinds— the new apartments at the hospital for doctors and nurses, and some that are unattached to the hospital. I am now living with my family in an apartment that belongs to my neighborhood district, not to the hospital. It's a small building with only four floors, so it's quite different, and because I have only one child, it's big enough. The hospital provides housing only for those who have no place to live or those whose homes are too small. One of my colleagues recently got a new apartment that has 40 square meters [about 430 square feet], and if you're a professor, you receive an even bigger one. They go according to your rank.

But, to get back to medicine, the health situation in China has changed a great deal over the past thirty years. In the 1950s we had more infectious diseases, but now those are down, and we see more chronic diseases like heart problems, kidney diseases, and cancer. The most frequent kind of cancer in children is leukemia. They also have nearly all the malignancies found in adults, but the incidence is certainly not as high. First the children are seen at a neighborhood clinic. Then, if they need hospitalization or special treatment and care, they come to the hospital. There are three hospital levels in the city: the district, the municipal, and the teaching hospitals like this one, where they receive the most specialized care.

It's rare that we have children who are emotionally disturbed, certainly not the high numbers I saw in Canada. We do have some handicapped children, and there is a special facility for them called the Children's Welfare Institute. They care for deaf, blind, and crippled children. But we have much fewer mental disorders or learning difficulties than in North America. In our hospital, when we encounter such problems, we just give some advice to the parents. None of the children's hospitals have psychology departments; only the adult hospitals have them.

I don't know why there's such a low incidence of mental illness in Chinese children, and I discussed that subject many times with Doctor Simmons, the psychiatrist at the Toronto Children's Hospital. There is a Chinatown near that hospital, and although he is interested in the mental problems of all the inhabitants of Toronto, and he has a lot of patients, only a few are from the Chinese community. He asked me why many times, and I thought of a few possibilities. The first was that Canadian families try to make their children independent as early as possible. At sixteen, a boy may even leave his family and have his own apartment. That does not happen in a Chinese family. The children usually stay with the parents, so that they have more influence on them.

Doctor Simmons once told me, "You know, I hoped that one of my three children would become a doctor, but none of them liked medicine." A friend of mine who is a Canadian Chinese hoped his son would be a dentist, and though the child said he didn't want to, my friend put pressure on him, and now he's a good dentist. My Chinese friend didn't let his child decide for himself at such an early age. I think parents in the United States and Canada allow children too much independence, while here we feel that we must educate and influence our children. Certainly, however, there are two sides to it; some things are good about our system and some are not.

I also found that there are many single parents in North America. We, too, have such problems, but they are rare. There is more stability in Chinese families. There may also be a genetic factor to explain the high incidence of American and Canadian children who can't read or write properly. A visiting American doctor suggested that to me a few days ago.

Another difference is that we have more women than men in our medical schools, while in the West it's just the opposite. After liberation the number of women students increased steadily, and now I think they make up about 55 percent of the classes. But there is a difference in the specialties. For example, more surgeons are males and more pediatricians are females.

We also have a good system of medical care in the countryside. In 1974 I joined a mobile medical team. We had twelve people—four were doctors and the rest were nurses and technicians. We went to a commune in Guangxi province and worked in their hospital. We were there for a year, and although my main duty was to consult with the hospital officials, I also gave lectures to barefoot doctors. They were men and women selected directly by the peasants, who had shown that they were serious and devoted workers. They were sent to the commune hospital for a special three-month training course. The courses were given in the winter, when they had less farm work to do. The reason they were called barefoot doctors is because they also worked in the fields. Actually they wore shoes, but it was a colorful way to describe them and distinguish them from regular doctors. Most were males, but there were a few females, too, because many rural women like to have a woman doctor when they give birth to a child. So they had at least one female doctor in each brigade to work as a gynecologist. Most of them were not married because married women have more responsibilities.

The training we gave them included some basic anatomy—skeletal, muscles, heart and lungs—some basic physiology, and we also taught them about the common local diseases. They needed a pediatrician very much because the parents are always much more worried about their children, so I had a lot of work to do. The most common diseases were respiratory infections and diarrhea. We taught the barefoot doctors how to use the basic drugs for those illnesses.

The local doctors also explained traditional medicine to us. They have a lot of experience in the use of herbs and acupuncture, and sometimes those methods are really effective. So I learned from them, and they learned from me. For example, you can stop abdominal pain when you acupuncture a certain point in the hand. It's not effective for appendictitis, but it is for an intestinal spasm, even during diarrhea. We did some experiments at the medical college on rabbits and dogs, and found that when you hit certain points, the intestines start to move and the spasm is reduced. It's not clear why, but clinically it works, and it's very simple and has no side effects. The only problem is learning which points you can't touch. On the chest, for instance, you have to be careful of the lungs and heart, and you also must avoid the great blood vessels.

I gave two courses to barefoot doctors at that time, and I'm sure that someday I will give additional ones. It's really an effective method for getting medical care into the rural areas, but I must say that they have less knowledge than the nurses in our hospital. Certainly they're better than nothing, and they're trusted by the peasants because they're so close to them. We already have more than a million barefoot doctors in China.

One of my friends, who was a barefoot doctor, is now studying at medical college. He got the chance because he is very, very intelligent and he passed the entrance examinations. China has such a big population. If peasants had to wait for doctors from the city, it would be impossible.

WANG: I think my future looks promising. Medicine is progressing in China very fast, and I feel it will go even further, so I'm always learning new techniques. I love my job very much and would like to do even better, so I can make a greater contribution to the motherland.

NING: We are entering many new fields in medicine, like the implantation of internal organs. We're planning to do a kidney implant soon, and for us, that's a new procedure. But we've been doing open-heart surgery for about five years, so the nurses are learning many new things, and they have a lot more to learn. During the Cultural Revolution, Miss Wang was very upset. She told me she would never be a head nurse, but just a year ago she was promoted to deputy director, so now her spirits are high.

DRS. WU KAM GING
AND LOU XIO HONG

Herbalists

Located on a narrow side street in the heart of Canton, the Medical Hospital of Canton Province can be distinguished immediately from other buildings crowding the area by the red-and-white ambulances that are parked in a spacious front courtyard enclosed by large wrought-iron gates. Obviously built in the Russian-influenced period of the 1950s, the hospital itself is a huge, twelve-story, graystone structure, dark and gloomy both inside and out.

Drs. Wu and Lou, herbal medicine practitioners, received us in a fourth-floor reception room furnished with the usual cotton-covered, pleat-skirted lounge chairs and a few nondescript wooden tables. Former classmates at medical college, both were around fifty, of medium height, slim, attractive, and dressed in white hospital coats, their hair covered by surgical caps.

Although they tried hard to explain the ancient science of herbal medicine, they found it difficult. According to my interpreter Zhao Yaqing, most of the terminology had never been translated into English.

After finishing the interview, they accompanied us to the pharmacy department on the main floor, which was crowded with outpatients waiting for prescriptions. We were quite surprised to see that only one small room was reserved for Western medicines, while a number of large ones were devoted to the preparation and storage of herbal medicine. The corridors were also lined with large baskets filled with herbs that had been recently gathered and brought to the hospital.

In one room we saw workers steaming various types of herbs in large, stainless-steel cauldrons; in another, the herbs were being sorted and dried; a third contained more than 100 drawers and bins built into the walls; and in the last room, workers were busily wrapping the finished products in small, brown-paper packets and labeling them for dispensing.

Natural vs. Manufactured

WU: I was born in Hong Kong, but because of the Japanese aggression, my parents moved to Canton. When I was five they both passed away, and I went back to Hong Kong to live with my grandmother. I had many relatives in Hong Kong and Peru, and they all contributed to my support.

After I graduated from middle school, I went back to Canton and joined the Red Cross Institute, and then, in 1956, I entered the Canton Chinese Medical Institute and graduated in 1962. About 70 percent of my time was spent on learning Chinese traditional medicine and the other 30 percent on Western methods.

LOU: My father is a doctor of traditional Chinese medicine who is still quite famous in Canton. He's now seventy-one and still takes care of patients at his home. Because of his profession, he was able to support our family quite well, but we were never rich, because I had so many brothers and sisters.

Doctor Wu and I were classmates at the medical institute, so we have been friends for many years. In those days there were 120 students in our class and only 36 were women; we were a minority. The teachers were also mostly men, but they treated the women students with equal respect.

WU: Our traditional medicine is very different from Western because Chinese medications are made from natural herbs collected in the mountains, while Western medicine relies on manufactured drugs. The philosophies are also different. We feel the patient's health is influenced by environmental factors like the weather. Doctors that practice in the Western style put more emphasis on tests—X rays, blood samples, and others.

It's very difficult to describe how we practice Chinese medicine, because until recently the terms were never translated into English. At medical school we learned only the Chinese words.

LOU: I'll try to give you an example. If a patient comes in complaining of a stomach pain, I would ask if he had a bowel movement recently. If not, I would give him an enema. If his eyes are very red and he feels weak, I would put some herbal drops in his eyes to clear them, and I would also ask if he has some emotional problems that might be affecting his health. So we consider many aspects.

Wu: We usually try Chinese methods first and if they don't work, we try Western. But it depends on the disease. We know that certain diseases cannot be cured with Chinese methods, and as I said, we have also been trained in Western medicine. Of course, I believe that Chinese treatment is better than Western, but when I have to do any testing, I use Western equipment. For treatment, however, I believe more in Chinese methods like herbs and acupuncture. This hospital also has an acupuncture department, but acupuncture involves a series of treatments, so the patient must be admitted to the hospital. It cannot be done for outpatients. Dr. Lou and I specialize only in herbal medicine.

Lou: Even though they learned Western methods, most Chinese doctors accept the value of traditional medicine, especially if they are on the staff of this hospital. Almost all of them want to learn more about it, and now hospitals in most of our cities have a Chinese department even if they practice Western medicine primarily. When patients come to a hospital, they are usually allowed to decide for themselves whether they want Chinese or Western treatment.

Wu: Since we established diplomatic relations with the United States, many Western doctors have been coming to our medical schools to learn about Chinese methods. They are very curious about our traditional medicine.

Though most of the books and scrolls on the practice of traditional Chinese medicine are very old, some of our recent experiments on the use of herbs and acupuncture have been published in medical journals, and many of those have been translated into English at the Foreign Language Institute. We also give lectures at the medical college, but mainly we just teach postgraduate students here at the hospital. In America I believe they are called interns.

One of our problems is the people who still practice traditional medicine at home and base their treatments on superstition rather than on proven scientific evidence. Many patients, especially in the countryside, go to them instead of a doctor, and that can be dangerous.

LOU: Many eye diseases respond better to herbal medication, and we also believe that it's better for curing broken bones. For example, if a person breaks a leg, first we X-ray it. Then we use a splint or board to brace it and wrap it tightly. Doctors who practice Western medicine would put the leg in a cast, but we find that using only splints shortens the healing time.

For heart problems, we use Western and Chinese combined. First we give the patient an electrocardiogram and then some Chinese and Western medicine. If the problem is serious, Western- and Chinese-trained doctors consult with each other and decide on the treatment. There is no competition between us. We try to keep up with the new discoveries in Western methods, and each year we hold classes on them, so our decision is made on the basis of what is best for the patient.

Chinese medications are all made from natural plants, and some of them are very difficult to get. Our pharmacy department usually organizes groups of people to climb the mountains and look for them, but some can be planted in a garden. Generally the quality of wild plants is much better than those that are cultivated. For instance, there's a certain herb we use for headaches that is very hard to find because it grows only in the high mountain areas.

NI HUI-LAN AND LIANG HUI-LI

Barefoot Doctors

Since the abandonment of the communal farming system in China over the past few years, the term commune has been changed to township, and the brigades, which were the smaller units within the commune, are called villages. However, because the change has been relatively recent, those names are still being used interchangeably by the peasants themselves.

The San Yuan Li township, located in a suburb of Canton, is the largest and most prosperous of the three farming communities we visited in China. It has a population of 50,000 people serviced by a comprehensive health-care system composed of three hospitals, seventeen village clinics, and 108 barefoot doctors.

Ni and Liang, two of the township's barefoot doctors, both forty-three years of age, were waiting to greet us when we drove up to the large, two-story, cement-block community meeting hall on a warm morning. With them was the local women's federation representative and, after about five minutes of introductions and warm welcomes, we were ushered upstairs to a pleasant veranda furnished with umbrella-shaded iron tables and chairs, where we were served Coca-Cola and orange drinks.

Liang, the taller of the two, had been born in the township. Ni, who had moved to the township from another village in 1961 when she married, had received more training in medicine. But it was obvious that Liang was more respected, most likely because she had made more than $5,000 that year from raising milk cows as a sideline business.

After the interview, we were taken on a tour of the community and then served an unforgettable thirteen-course feast in the meeting hall's dining room. It included such delicacies as roast goose and duck, soup with quail eggs, and many vegetable, pork, and beef dishes.

Country-Style Medicine

LIANG: I became a barefoot doctor five years ago, and Ni eight years ago. We are both married and have children. Originally, I was in charge of a production brigade, and because I was a good worker and we were short of barefoot doctors, some of the commune leaders asked me to go for the medical training. I told them I knew nothing about the clinic or medicine, but they said I could learn.

NI: I was an accountant in the commune silk-weaving factory when the representative from the women's federation asked me to become a midwife so I could help the women deliver their babies. I did that for two years, and because my patients liked me so much and I loved that kind of work, in 1977 my brigade sent me to the Provincial Chinese Medical Institute for two years of study. My specialty at the institute was pediatrics and gynecology.

LIANG: I studied at the commune clinic for about a year and a half. I also specialized in women's and children's diseases, and I learned how to be a midwife, but I am not as highly educated as Ni.

Our priority is medicine, but we also work in the fields when we have free time. There are also male barefoot doctors at this commune. The women mainly take care of the women and children, and the men take care of the men. This commune has 108 barefoot doctors for a population of 50,000 people. There are 20,000 families in the seventeen brigades or villages of the commune, and over 14,000 women and 12,000 men in the labor force.

NI: The township has three hospitals with a staff of 165 formal doctors, and each of the seventeen production brigades has its own clinic, so we have a fine system of medical care on this commune. In the villages all the midwives are barefoot doctors, so normally the pregnant women do not ask for a formal doctor because they are a little too far away. For all the minor things, like a normal child delivery, we go directly to the patient's home.

We treat colds, pneumonia, stomachaches, and other problems like that. Sometimes we use acupuncture and sometimes medicine. I learned a great deal about herbal medicine at the institute. We can also set broken arms or fingers, but we can not perform major operations. For that, the patient is sent to a commune hospital.

LIANG: First we give the patient a general examination. Then we ask the opinion of the clinic doctors, and we may give the patient some medicine for perhaps three days. If the patient feels she is getting better, we continue the same treatment. But if she is getting worse, we draw some blood and send it to the hospital laboratory for testing. Then, if we do not feel we can cure the disease, we will suggest that the patient go to the hospital.

NI: We give immunization shots every year, and we also educate people on how to stay healthy. We tell them what they should or should not eat, that they should not smoke, all the things we know about how to keep people healthy. We also write articles sometimes and give talks on the commune radio station.

The most difficult problem is delivering a baby that is turned wrong. We have to correct the direction, and that is a difficult thing to do. But that doesn't happen very often because we check the mother quite often during the pregnancy, and if we can see this problem before the delivery, we send her to a hospital. But sometimes it happens suddenly; the baby turns in the wrong direction while the woman is in labor and there is no time to take her to the hospital, so we must do the delivery.

The second problem is that even though we try to educate people about public health, some parents don't pay attention. They don't send their children for the injections that will protect them against some diseases. That's very difficult to deal with, and often we just go to the homes and persuade the parents to allow us to give their children the shots.

LIANG: We are very careful not to practice any medicine we are not capable of. If we feel we can't cure a patient, we will definitely send that patient to the hospital. We always keep in mind that we are the lowest base of grass-roots doctors, that our training is not as good as a formal doctor's, so we would never attempt to do anything that could be dangerous to the patient. A few years ago we found that a few barefoot doctors were not practicing correctly. They were giving patients wrong advice and treatment. So first we checked the person's attitude to see if he would like to correct himself by taking advice from his colleagues and if he did, he could go on working as a barefoot doctor. If not, of course, we would report him to the women's federation or to the commune administrators. There are also times when barefoot doctors feel their skill is not good enough and they retire voluntarily. But if they do not, the others will report them, and they are made to retire.

We must also keep our knowledge up to date. There is a rule that we must attend classes at the commune hospital one day each month.

NI: The old common diseases like smallpox and cholera have been gotten rid of. Now the most common disease is infantile paralysis among children. It's a disease where one-half of the body or an arm or a leg feels unconscious. So now, about two months after a baby is delivered, we give pills [Salk vaccine]. Then, when the baby is one year old, it will get those pills three more times, and gradually, as the child gets older, it will get more to protect it against this disease. Many of those cases have been eliminated during the past few years.

We have had some cases on this commune where a man abuses his wife or children, and when that happens, we will have a meeting with the cadres [leaders] to discuss how to deal with that kind of man. Usually they call a meeting of the whole brigade and openly criticize the husband. Our laws protect the rights of women and children, so if the man doesn't stop, he can be prosecuted and sent to prison. But those cases have really declined because the new generation has fewer feudal ideas, and the older men are retiring or dying.

The government also asks all families in the cities and the rural areas to be model families. That means good relations between husbands, wives, and children, and also neighbors. So there are less and less of these kinds of cases; in fact, this year there was only one case of wife-beating in this commune. The usual family problems are just quarrels between the husband and wife about the education of the children, or bad relations between a daughter-in-law and mother-in-law.

LIANG: We work in the fields in our spare time, and because there is usually water in the fields, especially in the southern part of the country, we take our shoes off, so the peasants call us barefoot doctors. When we wear our doctor clothes, we are doctors; when we take them off, we are peasants.

CHAPTER

PEASANTS

CHINA'S
NEW
CAPITALISTS

Z hao Yaqing, my interpreter during the entire journey, is a graduate of Peking University, one of China's most prestigious institutions of higher learning. Having served as an attaché with the Chinese embassies in London and Washington, she considers herself a cadre, a member of new China's elite—enjoying, with her husband and two sons, such urban luxuries as one of Peking's new apartments. Like most Chinese, however, she had done little traveling within her own country prior to her extensive journey with us. The life-style she discovered in the rural areas came as a major shock.

"Their living conditions are better than mine!" she exclaimed, wide-eyed with wonder.

Peasants, who account for 80 percent of China's population, have always been its poorest and most exploited class. Prior to the Communist takeover, all agricultural land was owned by only 8 percent of the people, a predominantly wealthy landlord class operating under the centuries-old feudal system of tenant farming. In return for being allowed to farm small plots of land, peasants were required to give a share of their harvest to the landlord as payment. And because landlords could increase their share at will, the system at best allowed peasants to eke out only a meager living. At worst, they starved, especially in times of flood, drought, and pestilence.

In 1949, when the Communists took control, the government instituted a gradual system of land reform. All of China's agricultural land was eventually expropriated from the landlord class and distributed among the peasants. And because of the new government policy of equality, each woman—married or single—received her own deed along with the men. To increase efficiency and productivity, cooperative farming was also introduced. Though the land was still individually owned, eight to ten peasant families pooled their labor and meager farm-animal and machinery resources.

The agricultural system was changed again in 1958 when Mao, in an effort to move the nation's economy forward at a faster pace, launched the Great Leap Forward. The plan proved disastrous. Township and village governments were replaced by communes and brigades, headed by party-appointed leaders, and individually owned land became the property of the commune. The peasants were organized into work gangs and paid under a system of points determined by the number of hours they put in and the type of work they did. Far from increasing the harvest, the new scheme dramatically *cut* farm productivity, because it eliminated the peasant's incentive to produce.

In 1978 the Deng regime, in a more pragmatic attempt to increase food production, initiated what they call the family responsibility system in the rural areas. Realizing that socialist political indoctrination alone does not stimulate hard work, that people need the added incentive of material gain, the government started to abolish the communes and to restore townships. Under this new system, the land is still collectively owned by the township, but a portion is leased to each peasant family on a long-term contract, and the family is responsible for its own production. And, while a percentage of the harvest must be sold to the central government at state-set prices, the rest may be sold on the open market, usually at a much higher price. Peasants are also allowed to operate cooperative industries and private businesses, keeping the profits for themselves. The results? Bumper crops for the nation and a major increase in income for the peasants.

The 1982 constitution of China officially restored the township system of government, and by the middle of 1984, one-fourth of China's some 50,000 communes had been reorganized. People of these townships elect deputies to the local People's Congress, which in turn elects the township leaders for three-year terms. Their duties are to implement directives from higher-level government units and to administer the township's finances, family planning, education, health services, and public

Members of a neighborhood committee in Peking

security. Each village has its own committee with a chairman and vice chairman elected by the village People's Congress, and with responsibilities similar to those of the township leaders, but on the village level.

The *Los Angeles Times* reported in December 1983 that the new agricultural reforms "are already redefining Chinese communism as well as changing the lives of the country's 800 million peasants." So far, according to the article, 30 to 40 percent of the peasants in China have abandoned farming because they can make more money by raising pigs, poultry, and cows to sell on the open market or by engaging in industrial pursuits like the production of machinery, shoes, clothing, and radios. Their land is then divided among other village families.

While this raises the possibility of a return to the days when most of China's farmland was controlled by a few, it doesn't seem to bother the government. For the first time in many years the markets are filled with produce, and party leaders insist that the socialist system will be maintained through the collective ownership of the land, state control of overall policy, and the rule that everyone must earn money through his own work and not through the work of others.

However, reports of peasants earning as much as $10,000 a year, an astronomical amount compared to city workers who average around $700, continue to appear in the Chinese and foreign press. There are also stories of fathers buying shares in rural factories for their sons, which raises the specter of capitalism in the countryside.

During my travels in China, I toured three townships operating under the new responsibility system. Though I'm sure they were carefully selected by my Chinese hosts, they appeared to be quite prosperous. While most of the city women I interviewed maintained that the old feudal ideas about women still persist in the rural areas, the information I received from farm women disputed that theory, along with the one that everyone in the countryside wants to move to the cities. In fact, if the press reports about peasant prosperity continue, the trend may well be reversed.

CHANG YU XHENG

Wu Guei Village
Tian Yuan Township

Wu Guei village was the first farming community we visited in China. Starting out from our hotel in the city of Chengdu one Sunday morning, we drove along country roads lined with lush green fields, and it soon became apparent why Sichuan province is described as one of China's most productive agricultural areas. Located in the southcentral part of the country, it is also one of the nation's most heavily populated areas, with more than 98 million people, some 90 million of whom are peasants.

Chang Yu Xheng, administrative leader of Wu Guei village, was waiting to greet us at the entrance to the new community center, a one-story structure made of brick and topped by one of the charming pitched, thatched roofs seen frequently in that area.

Sturdy and good-natured, the thirty-nine-year-old Chang epitomized the stereotype of a peasant woman. Dressed in black cotton slacks and a blue jacket, her face was round and apple-cheeked, and her jet-black hair was parted in the center and braided. After a kind welcome, she led us into the building's large, cool meeting room, where we were introduced to a representative from the local women's federation who stayed with us throughout our visit.

After the interview we were conducted on an extensive tour of the village. Despite the fact that it was Sunday, because October is the harvest season, most of the villagers were working in the fields. Proudly showing us a shoe factory and a lumber mill, two of the village's some twenty cooperative industries, Chang explained that along with the privately owned businesses like raising pigs and poultry, these industries accounted for the major share of the village income.

For me the most picturesque sight was the old village houses, with their low thatched roofs and well-tended front yards planted with bamboo. We were shown through the interior of a large home. The central living area had an earthen floor, a kitchen on one side, and a pigsty leading off from another side. The floors of the *two bedrooms were cement, and the largest contained a beautiful old Chinese red-lacquered canopy bed with a television set next to it. It was another striking example of the old and the new China existing side by side.*

In the kitchen the grandmother was tending a pot of soup simmering on the large, wood-fueled, black iron-top stove, and looking after her grandchild while the parents were away in the fields. Chickens and pigs ran freely throughout the house, and though the stench was overpowering, the ambiance was pleasantly homey.

In a Chinese Village

My family has lived in this village for many generations. Now we have 2,000 people living here, but before liberation there were only 800, and we were very poor. We have more than 2,000 acres of land, but it was all owned by only ten landlords and the peasants worked for them. Each family was allowed to farm a small portion, and they could keep only one-third of the harvest for themselves; two-thirds went to the landlord.

I was born in 1944, so I was only six years old when the liberation came, and the local government divided the land among the peasants. Before the communes were organized in 1958, each peasant owned a piece of land, and they formed groups to help each other.

The commune system brought collective ownership. All the land belonged to the commune as a whole, and the peasants were organized into production brigades. Before that, production was very good, but the party insisted that the people organize into communes. Maybe they wanted to learn from the Russians, but if they did not take that road, I think our agriculture would have developed faster. The commune system was not good for our country.

A few years ago, the new government made another reform called the production responsibility system. They contract land to each household, so we farm our own plots again. We have increased production, and the income of the peasants has gone

Chang Yu Xheng, administrative leader,
in the Wu Guei village lumber mill, one of the new
sideline businesses operated by peasants

up, too. They also allow us to have industries that belong to the township or the village under collective ownership, and many households have their own private sideline businesses.

Rice and wheat are the major crops. We must sell a certain portion to the government, and we can keep the rest to use or sell on the free market. But we can do as we wish with the production from the pigs, ducks, and other sideline business.

There were two reasons for the food shortage of 1960 and 1961. One was the policy of organizing the communes too fast, and another was climate conditions; there was a great drought.

In 1979, when the government of Sichuan province made the new reforms, the communes became townships again and the brigades became villages. Before that the brigade leaders were in charge of everything, but now we have divided those responsibilities between two committees. One is in charge of administration and the other of production. I was selected by the people to head the administration committee for this village, and a man is head of the production. Wu Guei is considered a medium-size village. We have only about 2,000 people, and the largest in this township has more than 3,000.

In our country many women have become leaders. For example, in Tian Yuan township we have fourteen villages, and among them we have four women leaders. So it is not unusual to have a woman leader. There has been a big change for women peasants since the liberation. Before we had no economic, political, or social position, but now we can take part in making decisions in all activities. We enjoy equal rights with men. And in each family men and women share the housework because the women also do the farm work.

The mothers look after the infants, and the grandparents help. When the children are three years old, they can go to the village kindergarten, and later they go to the primary school. I'm married and we have two children, twelve and fourteen, but since the government is now trying to control our population, the families in this township are complying with the one-child-to-a-family request.

Family planning works well in this village. Many people of my age have two or more children, but when the one-child limit was put into effect in 1979, the people cooperated and now more than 100 couples out of 514 have only one child.

In our village if you have a baby girl, you enjoy more benefits than if you have a boy. For instance, if one of the cooperative industries needs more workers, the leaders will give priority to a couple that has only a girl, and that increases the family income.

You can make more money from the industries than from farming. We are short of farm machinery. We could increase our production and our income with modern machinery. Right now we have only three automatic planting machines and none for harvesting the crops, so most of the work is done by hand.

We now have twenty different kinds of industries, but they are small. For instance, we have construction teams that build our houses, we have a furniture factory, we have a shoe factory, and many others. So if we mechanize the farming, we can always expand the other industries. But we can never increase our land holdings because with our large population, there is a land shortage in China.

I have no special skills, but I am young and well educated. I graduated from senior middle school, and I have a talent for organization. As the administrative leader, one of my duties is to settle the problems that come up among families and neighbors. Sometimes people quarrel about who is right or wrong about something, and sometimes a daughter-in-law and mother-in-law do not get along. There are also quarrels between the younger and older generations, and I help mediate them.

If peasant children can pass the examination, they can go to college. If not, they stay in the village. This year two of our students passed the university examinations, and after they graduate, they will be assigned to jobs by the government. But most of our children want to stay in the village because with our sideline production, our income is even higher than in the cities.

In recent years, three women and four men passed the college entrance examinations. Also, 40 percent of our youngsters go to senior middle school, and about 50 percent of those are women. I think women are as intelligent as men, but when the women get married, they have housework and other things to do, so they have less energy. Generally speaking, men and women share the household chores, but women still do more. And when peasant women give birth, they nurse their children longer than city women, so that makes them tired.

We have a medical care station for peasants who have minor kinds of illnesses, but if they have something serious, they go to the county hospital. We also try to teach people how to prevent diseases, and in the spring and autumn we give them preventive treatment like injections and herbal medicine.

YEE ZHENYING

Qian Zhou Township

Known as the land of fish and water because of its many lakes, canals, and fisheries, Jiangsu province lies in the center of China's eastern coast. A heavy rice- and wheat-producing area, it is densely populated with over 50 million people, most of whom are peasants. As we drove to Qian Zhou township from the city of Wuxi one morning, the fog was so thick we literally could not see the narrow road ahead, so we were forced to move very slowly. We arrived late for our appointment, but just as we drove through the township gates, the sun broke through, lighting the green rice fields and making the dewdrops gleam like diamonds.

Qian Zhou township, composed of twenty-one villages, has a population of 37,000, almost the same as Tian Yuan township, but it is much smaller in area. Waiting to greet us at the community meeting house were the deputy leader and secretary [both males], and Yee Zhenying, the representative from the women's federation. She had been delegated to act as spokesperson.

Though smaller than Wu Guei, the village we saw in Qian Zhou seemed more prosperous. One huge factory was producing highly sophisticated textile-dyeing machinery for city mills, and again we found that the people now make more money from their cooperatively owned industries and private sideline businesses than from farming. After they pay the national government 15 percent of the profits for taxes and the township a small percentage for

common expenses, the villagers divide the balance among them-
selves. By Chinese standards, they are becoming rich.

We saw a number of new homes similar to American town-
house condominiums. One large two-story building was divided
into twenty-six units with common walls separating them, and
the unit we toured was very spacious. The ground level included
a kitchen, living room, dining room, and a lovely glass-enclosed
atrium containing a fishpond and plants. On the second level
were three good-size bedrooms as well as a cement sundeck. The
unit also had a yard area where the family raised vegetables and
chickens. Some they consumed themselves; the rest they sold on
the free market.

The furnishings, all new, included a color television set and
an expensive-looking stereo unit with a tapedeck. Next year, the
wife said, they plan to buy a refrigerator and a washing ma-
chine. The home cost the family 5,000 yuan, which they were
able to accumulate in only three years.

Few Women Leaders, But
"It Doesn't Matter"

There are twenty township industries and ninety-nine village industries in Qian Zhou township, and our population is more
than 37,000. We have 37,100 mu [about 6,000 acres] of cultivated land. There are 10,008 households divided into 21 villages and although our population is large, we have sufficient
land. Last year, the average yield per mu was 1,235 chin [a chin
is 1.333 pounds]. The total grain output of the township in 1982
reached 14 million chin, a very high yield.

Our township is located on low-lying land all surrounded by
dikes. Before we built irrigation, the grain output was very low,
only about 400 chin per mu. After liberation, it was raised to
over 700 chin, but since 1970, after we built irrigation and
drainage, the output increased even more. We have invested 15
million yuan in farming during the past thirteen years, mainly
for irrigation and drainage projects like bridges, canals, dikes,
and channels.

The largest village consists of 3,400 people, and the smallest only 960. When the township was made into a commune in 1958, the brigades were formed on the basis of the village boundaries that existed before the liberation. Then, when the new government abolished the communes a few years ago and we again became a township, the village boundaries remained the same.

Of the twenty-one villages, there is only one woman leader, but although the township leader is a man, one of the two deputy leaders is a woman. We planned to ask her to receive you, but it's a pity; two days ago she gave birth to a baby. She got married late and she is now thirty-eight years old. The men leaders take the women's problems into consideration. They care about their well-being, so it doesn't matter that we have so few women leaders.

Our national constitution stipulates that men and women are equal, so now in every family, the husband and wife share the housework. You can not judge equality only from numbers of men and women leaders, because the men care for the interests and welfare of the women and children and the work of the nurseries and kindergartens. You can judge from the number of workers in the factories. Sixty percent of them are women and in the fields it's usually half-and-half. But during the busy farming season, 60 to 70 percent of the field workers are women. They account for 49.7 percent of the population of this township.

On an average, women farmers receive a salary of sixty to eighty yuan a month. The policy in China now is that women get equal pay for equal work. Those who work more get more, and those who work less get less. Those who don't work get nothing. We don't use work points any longer. The township fixes the output quota on a household basis, so now it doesn't matter if the work is done by a man or a woman. Payment is made to the household. In the factories, we use the piecework system, so payment depends on how many pieces each worker puts out.

In the past, women were suppressed by what we call the four mountains—the husband, the son, the mother-in-law, and religion. But now, in almost every household, the wife makes the financial decisions. For instance, my husband is an accountant for one village, but when he receives his salary, he gives it all to me and I buy things for the family. Men are not as good as women at managing money. Women are more cautious.

Every village has its own kindergarten for the education of preschool children, and when a child reaches the age of four, he or she may attend. From the age of seven, they go to the village primary school, but because of the Cultural Revolution, we do not have enough teachers who have graduated from normal university [a university that trains teachers], so we must use teachers with only an upper middle school education. Each factory in the township also has its own nursery. For the farmers, the custom is that the grandfather or grandmother will look after the babies, but the factory workers have infant nurseries. This township also protects women farmers during pregnancy by giving them lighter work to do. And when a woman is menstruating, the leaders do not allow her to work in the water because it's not healthy.

After a woman gives birth to her first child, she can enjoy ninety days off from her work with pay. She is also given lighter work to do during the breastfeeding period, and a half-hour break each morning and afternoon. She is taught how to take care of her health during that time, too.

But if a woman has more than one child, she will not be treated as well as a woman who has only one. Nearly 99 percent of the newly married couples have received their one-child certificates [pledges that they will have only one child], so there are very few newly married couples who have more than one child. The current law allows only those couples who have a defective child to have another. If they have one healthy child and then another, they cannot enjoy those benefits. We must control the population.

In 1983 the industrial output of this one village alone reached over 8.5 million yuan, far beyond the agricultural income. But during the height of the farming season, the factory workers must go to the fields, so the factories are not in full operation. A woman factory worker can earn between 130 and 150 yuan a month, and a man can make between 150 and 160.

The men do heavier labor than the women, so they earn more. We have one factory where they make textile-dyeing machinery. It's owned by the township, and the earnings from that factory alone will reach 11.5 million yuan this year. The people of this township enjoy much larger incomes now because we have the opportunity to engage in cooperative industry and sideline businesses. Almost 85 percent of the township families have built new houses with the profits from their own labor.

LIU QIQI

San Yuan Li Township

The following is a continuation of the interviews I conducted at San Yuan Li township, just outside Canton. In the "Health Revolution" chapter, two of the township's barefoot doctors, Ni and Liang, discussed health. Here, Liu Qiqi, a local representative from the women's federation, talks about life in the township in general.

One of the major industries of San Yuan Li township is construction. In fact, the evening before the interview we attended a symphony concert at one of Canton's large concert halls. Later, I discovered that the hall had been designed and built by the construction company from San Yuan Li, which has a team of 900 workers.

After my interviews with the barefoot doctors, we toured one of the township villages, including the new home of barefoot doctor Ni and her husband, who have three children. The husband, an architect for the township construction industry, designed their spacious three-bedroom house, and it was even more attractive than the one at Qian Zhou. Ni's was larger and had all the modern conveniences—a refrigerator, a stereo, a television set, and a washing machine.

Liu Qiqi and I talked in the village meeting hall.

Industry On the Farm

There are quite a lot of factories here, both on the township and the village levels, but the main industry is architecture and construction. We constructed this big meeting hall ourselves. It took 900 workers to design and build. We also design and build offices and homes in this township, as well as some buildings in Canton.

The second-largest industry is our clothing factory. Men and women workers make clothes for people in the township, and we sell them to city people as well. We also have a car maintenance and repair shop for our own automobiles and trucks, a chemical fertilizer plant, and a factory where we make small agricultural equipment. Last year our industries made a profit of 10 million yuan, and after we gave the national government 400,000 yuan, we divided the rest among the workers and peasants. So our large industries are collective, not private, and some of the profit goes to the government like a tax. But now each person in this township makes more money, and our standard of living increases every year.

We grow mainly green vegetables, rice, peanuts, and sesame seeds that we process at our sesame oil factory. We have 37,000 mu [more than 6,000 acres] of land for about 11,000 families, and our agricultural income is still a little more than our industrial. Last year the income from our crops was 40 million yuan and from the industries it was 38 million.

Each family also has a little sideline business like raising pigs or chickens. Some, like Liang [one of the barefoot doctors], raise cows. Her family has four milk cows, so their agricultural income is less than the milk income. Last year she made 10,000 yuan from the cows, so they are quite rich. The family still farms some land, but the less work they do in the fields, the less income they get from farming. Most of their income is from the cows. Liang herself does mainly barefoot-doctor work; her husband and son do the field work and take care of the cows.

Because she does no field work, she has no land, but her husband and son were assigned a small space. Now we have a production policy called the responsibility system. When a space is assigned to you, you are responsible for it. For example, Liang's husband and son put all their energy into their land, and in her spare time, after she does her barefoot-doctor work, Liang cuts grass for the cows. So even though the cows bring in more income than the agricultural production, that doesn't mean her family does less farm labor.

CHAPTER

10

SOCIALISM CHINESE-STYLE

*We know that some people . . . believe
that China is turning from the
socialist road. These include confirmed
anti-socialists who would like to see
China edging into their camp, and
friends of socialism who are worried.
The former are doomed to disappointment.
The latter will, we hope, be able to
understand China's situation and the
need for reform more clearly in the
years to come. China . . . will not
abandon socialism, but she will, after
thorough testing and thought, build a
Chinese-style socialism that conforms
to her own realities and the interests
of her people.*

China Reconstructs
Editorial, August 1984

My two months in China came at an exciting time. Articles were beginning to appear in the press designed to prepare the nation for what the preceding editorial calls Chinese-style socialism.

A more appropriate name for the series of reforms being instituted in all areas of the Chinese economy might be "Deng Xiaoping–style socialism" or the "whatever works" policy, the term often applied to the 81-year-old leader's philosophy of governing. In addition to the sweeping changes in the nation's agricultural system, extensive reforms are emerging in China's industrial sector as illustrated by the story of Bu Xinsheng, manager of the Haiyan Shirt Factory.

Located in the southeastern coastal province of Zhejiang, Bu's enterprise was originally a general clothing factory, founded by the government in 1956, with thirty workers. For the next twenty years the factory never even made enough to provide pensions for its retired workers, and when Bu took charge in 1976, it was on the verge of bankruptcy.

By 1983, after a series of dramatic reforms, the original factory with its outdated equipment had been replaced by a large modern plant. Sales totaled over $5 million, and the number of employees had risen to almost 1,000. With bonuses, salaries had doubled to an average of $40 a month, and most workers now enjoy such benefits as free medical and child care, better housing, retirement pensions, and factory-sponsored cultural and sports activities.

Bu had to move slowly at first, but despite threats and angry charges that he was a capitalist dictator, he attacked the most serious problem faced by Chinese industry: shockingly low productivity. He tightened discipline, abolished eating and sleeping during work hours, and began paying workers on a piece-rate basis. He discontinued the production of a wide range of un-stylish and unpopular clothing and specialized in practical and appealing shirts and blouses. With a government loan, he ren-ovated the plant and organized a research department to do market analysis and develop designs that would be more attractive to the public.

When Deng Xiaoping took power in 1978 and dramatically revised government industrial policies, Bu was able to move much more quickly. One of his boldest reforms was to abolish the old "iron rice bowl" policy that guaranteed workers their jobs for life no matter how they performed. The policy, which also included a rigid system of promotion, had seriously blocked industrial de-velopment by discouraging efficiency. Everyone received the same pay regardless of ability, work habits, or productivity.

Until 1984 the Deng faction, which includes Communist Party General Secretary Hu Yaobang and Premier Zhao Zi-yang, had to move slowly in implementing new ideas that were opposed by a large segment of die-hard Maoists. But the gradual purge of this leftist group from party membership and govern-ment leadership positions evidently gave the Deng followers confidence in their strength. At the 1984 session of the National People's Congress, Premier Zhao outlined a series of radical policy changes.

To encourage competition in industry and eliminate mo-nopolies, he announced, managers of China's 400,000 indus-trial enterprises would be given more authority to take risks, to sell their products on the open market, to set their own produc-tion quotas, to reinvest profits for expansion and development, to choose their own suppliers, to start joint ventures, to appoint their own assistants, to award bonuses on the basis of outstand-ing performance, and to fire incompetent employees.

He also replaced the old practice of turning all profits over to the state. Industries, he said, would pay income, sales, and payroll taxes that would allow efficient firms to retain their prof-its. On the other hand, he would end state subsidies to those who couldn't make the grade. The state would no longer allo-cate funds for major industrial projects. They must be financed instead by bank loans to be repaid with interest, a change that should force managers to evaluate their projects' economic viability. Also, major public works construction contracts would be awarded on the basis of open bidding, and workers for those projects would be hired for individual jobs, not for life.

Most shocking of all to China's workers was Zhao's announcement that the nation's "iron rice bowl" policy was abolished. There would be no more lifetime jobs regardless of performance. He also encouraged workers to buy their own houses or apartments, as farmers now do, in order to end the practice of low-cost government-subsidized housing. Furthermore, in the cities, small state-owned businesses like restaurants, clothing stores, and shoe-repair shops would be leased to individuals or small groups of workers.

If this is socialism Chinese-style, how does it differ from capitalism? The official Chinese answer is that the socialist system will be maintained through government- or collectively owned means of production, and state control of overall economic planning. The goal, they say, is to remove obstacles to effective management and to increase competition.

The new policies have already resulted in higher production, more consumer goods on the market, and an increase in the ability of the Chinese to buy them.

We saw examples of the new economic policies in cities where a few individually or collectively owned businesses were already operating. In Shanghai we had lunch at a neighborhood restaurant that could seat about sixty people. A group of unemployed youngsters had opened it with a $5,000 loan from their neighborhood committee, which they were able to repay within six months. Specializing in Western food, a cuisine taught to them by retired chefs who worked for foreigners living in Shanghai before the Communist takeover, the youngsters were doing a brisk business. They had already accumulated enough capital to open another restaurant. Cooperatively owned, the group elects the manager, and each person receives a salary based on his or her work contribution as well as a share of the annual profits.

We found the food good, the atmosphere pleasant, and the premises much cleaner than most of the government-owned restaurants in which we had eaten. The accountant, a young woman, sat with us during our meal urging us constantly to criticize the food and service so they "could make improvements."

In addition to alleviating the unemployment rate, the small independently owned businesses increase work incentive, eliminate the bureaucracy inherent in most government-run enterprises, and provide badly needed services like shoe repairing, dry cleaning, and tailoring that were virtually eliminated during the Cultural Revolution.

Though a few large industries had been reorganized under the new liberal policies while I was in China, the changes were still not extensive, and many women I interviewed were not aware of them.

DAI SUI SHENG

Director, Peking Woolen
Research Institute

An expert at textile-machinery design and director of one of China's largest woolen mills, Dai Sui Sheng insisted that our meeting take place at the Guangming Daily *offices. I was disappointed as I was also interested in seeing the woolen mill. When she extended her left hand in greeting, I was surprised, but I later discovered that half of her right hand had been severed in an industrial accident. Now, after a series of operations, she can use it, but is embarrassed about exposing it to strangers. At the beginning of our conversation, she was very reserved and careful, but after a few minutes, when she apparently decided I was not there to paint a black picture of China, she relaxed and in the end, invited me to visit her at the woolen mill later that same day.*

Located on the outskirts of Peking, the Woolen Research Institute consists of a large compound of buildings and employs some 2,500 workers. It produces fine woolen fabrics, half of which are exported to England, West Germany, Hong Kong, Canada, and the United States, with the balance used domestically. A textile

*expert, Dai, in her early fifties, is also vice chairman of the Pe-
king Science Institute. She spent a year in England and Russia,
studying their woolen industries, and also taught herself to read
English, Japanese, and Russian.*

*During our tour of the workshops we met two very pretty
university graduates who had majored in textiles, serving a stint
as apprentice technicians at the mill. Dressed in blue work clothes,
the young women were sitting on the cement floor oiling machine
parts. Though the factory was not modern, it was spotlessly clean
and all the workers seemed busy.*

*We also visited the mill's clinic, which was fairly well equipped
to handle routine medical problems. It had X-ray, surgery, and
ear, nose, and throat departments, and a pharmacy that dis-
pensed both herbal and Western medications. Workers and their
families receive free medical care, though those with more than
one child must pay half the cost for the second child [part of China's one-child incentive policy]. The factory grounds also included boarding and day-care nursery and kindergarten facilities, as well as a basketball court and a small theater where
employees could see stage and film productions.*

From Worker to Leader

I majored in textiles at Bei Yang University in Tianjin and graduated in 1950, one year after the liberation. It was unusual for
women to go to university in those days, so I was one of only
six women out of nearly 1,000 students. It was not easy for me
to go because my family was not rich. But our financial situation was better when I started college because my eldest sister
had already graduated from normal school, so she helped a lot,
and my other sisters had graduated from middle school.

After I finished university, I became a technician at this
woolen mill. Later I was put in charge of a workshop, and eventually I was made director of the whole factory. Then I was given
the title of engineer expert for all woolen mills in Peking.

I found it quite easy to be promoted because, since the People's Republic of China was established in 1949, the government policy has been to reward individual efforts regardless of sex. And I worked very hard. It was not easy to graduate from the university, and because the government had given me an opportunity to work as a technician, I felt a great responsibility to do something for my country.

I was married in 1952, just three years after liberation. My husband is an engineer in charge of electronic techniques, and right now he is working with chemical fibers. We live in Ching Heh, a suburb near this factory, but when we were first married, my husband was a teacher at the Navigation Institute in northeastern China for twenty years. It was quite far from Peking, so we were separated for a long time. We saw each other only on holidays.

Our own children are grown up now, but in 1979 I adopted a baby girl who is now five years old. She was left alone after her parents died, so I felt a responsibility to take her and my husband agreed. She now goes to boarding kindergarten, and we have her home on Sundays. Home life is not difficult for me because my husband eats at his workplace, and my sister helps me with the housework.

Before liberation, women were looked down upon in China, but since then, by law, we are emancipated. Actually, however, we do have some equality problems. For instance, though our child-care system has developed much further than in other countries, we still do not have enough facilities. You need a good system for taking care of children before you can emancipate women. We are also trying to make household chores a joint husband-and-wife responsibility, but that is still not happening enough. Most women still give a great deal of time to house tasks and children, while their husbands just naturally neglect those things. And that is quite bad for women's emancipation.

Jobs are assigned by the government, and they also set wages. So men and women have the same job opportunities if they have the ability to do the work. But there are some jobs women are not physically suited for, such as heavy work in the iron and steel mills. Women are not strong enough. We do have women truck drivers and army air force pilots, but on our commercial airline, CAAC, they can only be stewardesses because they do not meet the physical standards for pilots.

I would like my daughter to be an artist because she loves to paint. I've also noticed that she likes to learn foreign languages very much, but because she is still so young, it's too early to tell. If she has the ability, the government will select her to be educated in the career of her choice, and I would like her to do whatever makes her happy.

In a few years I will retire, but socialist countries take care of retired people. Our system provides that if you have worked a certain number of years, you can have a pension up to 100 percent of your salary. Almost every work unit has an association for retired workers. They organize trips to other cities, study courses, and entertainment, so their lives are quite full.

ZHAO YOU-YI AND LI CHUN GHU

Director and Trade Union Chairperson,
Wuhan Cotton Mill Number One

Wuhan, with its crowded streets and European-style buildings, still retains a Western atmosphere left behind by the foreign merchants and industrialists who invaded the city during the 1920s and 1930s.

A huge complex of buildings, located on the outskirts of the city, the Wuhan Cotton Mill looks very much like the Peking Woolen Research Institute. We met with mill director Zhao and trade union chairperson Li in a large second-floor reception room furnished with a long center table and the usual 1930s-style sofas and lounge chairs. The walls at either end of the room were lined with glass-fronted cases displaying samples of the various types of cotton fabrics woven at the mill.

Zhao, a pleasant-faced, rather stout woman of fifty-one, and Li, slim, attractive, and in her late thirties, were dressed similarly in simple tailored cotton slacks and jackets. Both were very friendly and eager to cooperate, and our conversation provided interesting information on trade unions in China.

Following the interview, we toured the factory and saw the entire milling process, from bales of raw cotton to finished bolts of cloth ready for shipment to dyeing plants. Most workers at the machines were women. In some areas there was a great deal of cotton dust in the air and a deafening noise level.

As we walked, I asked Zhao what was done to protect the workers from lung diseases and loss of hearing. She assured me that they were provided with earplugs and that their diets were supplemented with black fungus, a substance that grows on tree bark. Commonly used in Chinese cooking, the fungus is said to cure respiratory ailments. As we continued on the tour, I checked carefully but did not notice any workers wearing earplugs.

Non-Striking Unions

ZHAO: More than 70 percent of the textile workers in China are women, and about 50 percent of the mill directors are also women. Traditionally, textile work has been considered women's work. This mill employs more than 6,700 workers, and while the men do maintenance and repair jobs, the women operate all the machines.

LI: The union tries to improve the workers' welfare. For the women we have arranged what we call a five-period protection plan. The first is the wedding period. When a worker marries, we provide a wedding party, and she gets a holiday. Then, during her pregnancy period, she enjoys special protection at work. For instance, if she has a heavy job, she can change to lighter work, and after the birth of the baby she receives maternity leave. It used to be fifty-six days, but now it's ninety. There is also the menstruation period. If a woman is ill during that period, she can have a few days off, but only if she is in pain. Women with babies under eight months old can have one hour off every day to bathe their babies, and we also provide child-care facilities. We have two kinds at this factory; when an infant is fifty-six days old, he can be cared for in the nursery center, and then, from

Zhao You-yi, director of Wuhan Cotton Mill Number One

the age of a year and a half to six years, he can go to the factory kindergarten.

ZHAO: Those benefits are all national policy. But we have eight union officials at this mill, five women and three men, and they are elected by the workers.

LI: Wages and working hours are set by the state, but we can negotiate with the director on worker welfare benefits. For example, in the past we had three shifts in this factory, and now we have four. Since the shift system changed, workers can have two days off after working six days, and they can also change from the morning to the afternoon or the night shift every two days. That was something the workers requested.

Every year we have two workers' conferences, where they elect union representatives who present the workers' opinions and demands to the factory director. We negotiate with her and, generally, we reach an agreement. Throughout the history of this factory, a strike has never happened.

ZHAO: Generally their demands or requirements are reasonable. When workers give me their opinions about production, protection measures, and other benefits, usually we try to satisfy them and solve their problems. The workers here are very happy and have good things to say about the factory. So generally the union and management are not in an adversary position; their purpose is to increase communication between management and the workers.

You see, the director of the factory is also a worker. The only difference is that we have different kinds of jobs.

Some jobs are physically more suitable for women. For instance, at our mill, in the shops where we work with cotton, you have to work very carefully, and because women's hands are smaller and softer than men's, women can do the work better and faster. When Chairman Mao said women can do anything men can do, I think he only wanted to encourage women and build their self-confidence. Of course, most of the great artists are men and in our machinery building, though most of the workers are men, there are also five women. So perhaps it's really tradition that keeps men and women in certain jobs.

As director of a textile mill, I want to stress the changes in my industry. Now we have women directors, women engineers, women accountants, and women technicians. Compared to preliberation days, those are big changes, and though we still have a long way to go, I think there will be further improvements in the future.

PAN HUIPING

Housekeeper, Jinling Hotel

Most tourists who visit China have one major complaint: the lack of attractive, clean hotels. By the time we arrived in Nanking, we had stayed in five hotels, all supposedly first class. Though some were better than others, in comparison to American and European hotels they were dark and dingy. Strange insects roamed freely through the rooms, and although linens were changed and carpets vacuumed daily, they were usually stained, and it seemed that the practice of washing bathroom floors was unheard of.

I had been reading reports in the newspapers of government efforts to upgrade hotels and establish management schools in order to increase the already lucrative tourist trade, but I had seen little evidence of results until we arrived at the Jinling Hotel.

Designed much like the beautiful Regent hotels, which are strung throughout Asia and the South Pacific, the Jinling is very elegant indeed. Built with Hong Kong and Chinese joint-venture funds, it was only a year old when we were there and has an international flavor. Off the lovely and spacious lobby, its handsome furniture and marble floors covered with handwoven contemporary rugs, were a number of restaurants serving both Chinese and Western foods. A plain ham sandwich for lunch that afternoon was a welcome relief from a solid month of Chinese cuisine, even though it was the best I had ever eaten.

In Canton we had the pleasure of staying at the new White Swan Hotel, which was, without exception, the most beautiful I had ever seen. I heard reports that many more of similar quality

*are opening throughout China. Like everything else in the coun-
try, it seems that the hotel business is undergoing startling changes.*

*Pan Huiping, assistant executive housekeeper at the 800-room
Jinling, is a slim, shy, and soft-spoken woman, then in her mid
thirties.*

Learning International Standards

I studied at the Nanking Foreign Languages School, which is a
senior middle school. First I studied German and then, in 1973,
I began studying English. Before I came to the Jinling Hotel, I
was a middle school teacher, and later I worked as a secretary at
the same school.

I always liked foreign languages, and I felt that if I worked
at a hotel, especially an international hotel, I would have a better chance to learn English. About 2,000 men and women took
the examination for this job, but because I had the highest mark,
I was selected.

First I was sent to the Mandarin Hotel in Hong Kong for
training. I was there for forty days and worked as a room maid,
learning how to make beds, clean the rooms and bathrooms, and
do all the things a maid should do. At first it was very difficult,
but it was also interesting because they use scientific methods.

Americans, especially, like a room very, very clean, but I
found that all Westerners have a much higher standard of
cleanliness than the Chinese. When I returned from Hong Kong,
I began work at the Jinling. The executive housekeeper is a man
and a very hard taskmaster. He was trained in America for three
months, and then he was manager of another hotel in Nanking,
but it does not have the same high standards as the Jinling.

I'm responsible for the cleanliness of the rooms on all the
floors. I see that everything is kept in correct order, that the linens and towels are changed every day, and the carpets and upholstery are shampooed and repaired regularly. This hotel has
almost 800 rooms, and we have one maid for every 12. As each
floor has 24 rooms, there are two room maids on every floor. I

do only spot checks, but we have floor supervisors who check each room. There are ninety-two employees on my staff.

Every night I read all the forms that are sent to me by the front desk, so I can know all the guest information—the current guests, the arrivals and departures, and the reservations. Then I assign jobs to the maids, and if a room will be unoccupied for a while, I assign someone to steam-clean the carpets and the upholstery.

Each room maid has a work sheet. When she cleans a room, she will ticket it, and then the floor supervisor checks it and makes a note on a supervisor sheet. Every supervisor is in charge of three floors, or seventy-two rooms, and they watch carefully to see that each maid is doing her job. If a maid is not doing her work well, it's recorded, and I will have a talk with her.

Every morning I visit the floors and check to see that everyone is working, especially the new staff people. They have to be taught.

If someone is doing her work well for a period of time, we have a meeting. We praise her in front of everyone, and we ask the others to learn from her. She will also receive a bonus, and that is a very important incentive.

When I returned from Hong Kong, I trained all the room maids and floor supervisors. None had ever done that kind of work before, so I was able to train them in the methods I had learned rather than those used by other hotels in China. We must establish scientific hotel management. Last month I went to America and visited many hotels. Some were very old, but they were still very clean and fresh. In China we need much better management to keep up the standards. For example, there should be a schedule for when to change the upholstery, shampoo the carpets, and do all the other things that are necessary to keep a hotel fresh and clean. Here in Jiangsu province, we plan to establish a school to train people in hotel management. It will be a traveling school, and the teachers will be Chinese who have already studied hotel management abroad—the United States, Japan, Hong Kong, Switzerland—countries all over the world.

The entire staff is selected according to their marks on an examination, and of my ninety-two staff members, only twenty-four are men. Everyone on my staff must speak English, and females seem to learn languages better than males.

There are very good opportunities for women at this hotel if they work hard. We have a woman deputy manager in sales and another in engineering who is in charge of all hotel construction. But still, all of us are assistants to men; there are no women at the very top in management. I think that will happen one day.

I work about sixteen hours a day, six days a week. I start work at 8 in the morning and I usually sleep here at night because I'm on night duty, too. I go off duty about 10 in the evening. So it's a hard job, and I see my husband and child only when I go home for supper and on my day off. My husband is an engineer who works at a radio factory in Nanking, and my son is five years old. He goes to a day kindergarten and lives with my husband's parents. But my husband is very supportive of my work, and to give me more time to do my job, he does most of the household chores. Sometimes I miss my child, and I want to play with him more, but I think my job is very important. The Jinling opened very recently, so we all have to spend more time here because we have to train the staff. In the future I think that will not be necessary, and we will have more time off.

Right now China feels it's important to raise hotel standards, and I feel proud to be helping.

SAI WEI

Saleswoman

The Chinese word guanxi *means "connections" or "relationships." In China, using* guanxi, *or "the back door," is a useful and commonly accepted means of circumventing bureaucratic channels to get things done or to obtain merchandise that is in short supply.*

Sai Wei, a slim, sweet-faced woman of thirty-five, is a salesperson in one of Chongqing's largest department stores. When I

*interviewed her in my hotel room, she spoke frankly about the
practice of guanxi in the department store where she worked, and
I was surprised at her openness.*

*Her eager-to-please attitude explained why she has won so
many awards. She is the perfect salesperson.*

The Little Expert

After I graduated from middle school, I worked for an agricultural production brigade in Hunan province. It was during the
Cultural Revolution, and all the youngsters who graduated at
that time were sent to the countryside to do farm work.

I was there eight years and though I learned a lot about
farming, I feel I still don't know enough. I enjoyed farming and
was very happy until I became ill because I was not used to the
climate. Every year they had big monsoons, and sometimes it
rained for three months continuously. So I was given permission to come back to the city, where I worked in a neighborhood committee health clinic. Then they built a big department
store in Chongqing and they needed help, so with my father's
influence, I got a job there. My mother, who was also a salesperson, taught me how to count money and wait on customers,
and I was also sent to a special school for three months to learn
how to use an abacus.

The department store is one of the ten biggest in China, and
I sell mainly glassware. I've learned a great deal about the qual-
ity of glass since I've worked there, and I've won many honors.
I'm a representative to the Provincial Conference, a Model
Worker of Chongqing, and they also gave me the special title of
Little Expert in the Commercial Field. [The Chinese govern-
ment has made it a practice to confer titles and organization
memberships, usually in lieu of salary increases or cash awards.
The Provincial Conference is a local consulting organization with
no real power.]

In a socialist country, people always want to do a good job,
so we don't use the word *competition* because it would mean

that one person is jealous of the other. I was chosen because I was outstanding, and my co-workers had no complaints because I was qualified to have those titles.

There are two ways to be selected for those honors. One is by the staff members of the store. Every year they vote for who they think is the best worker. Another way is by the customers. They vote on who they feel is the best salesperson, so if you serve them patiently, quickly, and always with a smile, and if you make no mistakes, you get more votes.

There is more merchandise available in our store now, and I find that men usually want to buy electronic products and women want things like sewing machines and refrigerators. But if they don't have enough money for a refrigerator, they buy beautiful clothes. During the Cultural Revolution, women dared not wear bright colors, only blue or black, because they were afraid people would call them capitalists. But now everyone wears brighter colors. Over the past few years, I've seen women's clothing change a lot in color and design, and there is also more and more variety. And with the prices coming down, people can buy more.

I love my job very much, and I feel all the workers in new China should love the jobs they are assigned to. If the government asks me to do something else, I would be happy to make the change, but if not, I will keep this job all my life.

I stand all day long, so it's natural that my feet should feel tired. But in my heart, I'm always happy because I'm in direct contact with the common people. To serve the people is my happiness, so I don't find that being tired is a big problem.

When there was a shortage of goods, some customers could buy things through the back door. We couldn't satisfy everyone, so if a customer had a good relationship with a salesperson, he was given priority. Of course, that's not a good thing, and it's unlawful, but people did it. I think that gradually, when we have produced more and more goods and have better quality and variety in our production, that kind of practice will disappear.

Most people thought the back door policy was wrong, and I never did it myself. In fact, that's one of the reasons I won awards. When I saw that kind of thing, I tried to persuade my colleagues not to do it anymore, but I did not report it to the boss, because if I did, it would harm my relationship with my co-workers. But if the salesperson continued doing it with bad results, like causing the store to lose money or arousing anger in customers, I reported it.

After the twelfth Conference of the Party Central Committee, the government launched a campaign to clear up back door corruption, and things have changed greatly. It has almost stopped. But it's hard to say it will not happen again.

ELLEN LIU

Construction Company Executive

Soon after I returned to Los Angeles, I interviewed Ellen Liu (a pseudonym), an executive with a large Southern California company that was constructing large hotels in China under its new foreign joint-venture policy.

A short, plump woman in her early fifties, Liu preferred to remain anonymous because her company does business in China. We met in her rather posh company office. Friendly and warm, she proved to be a woman of very strong opinions—which were mainly negative when she discussed life in her native country since the Communist takeover in 1949. Of all of the Chinese women expatriates I interviewed for this book, she was perhaps the most vociferous in expressing her disapproval of government policies as well as the attitudes of the people.

Moral and Intellectual Deterioration

My father was manager of a British-owned shipping company, and although my mother had a college education, she did not work. We were considered part of the upper class in China. My father was the eldest of seven brothers who all had university degrees, and I attended a very famous middle school in Tianjin that was run by Christians. Later I went to a university in the same city and graduated in 1953. I was an only child, which was unusual in those days, but my parents were very unusual. They didn't want a large family, and I know my mother had two abortions.

During the Chiang Kai-shek era, we saw a lot of corruption and inflation. Everything was very bad, so we didn't like the Nationalist government. Just after liberation, because everything seemed lively and nice, we were happy. But gradually the Communists took our property, and they forced my father to retire. By that time he held a very high position in the company, but when the government took over, all the high-ranking officials had the choice of going abroad or staying in China on a retirement pension. My father chose the latter. He owned two houses, and prices were so low that many things he loved, like fine fresh fish, were easy to buy, and he preferred to stay.

But that situation lasted only one or two years. Then the Communists forced him to buy government bonds, and they took his houses away. Of course, they discriminated against everyone from the upper class. After the liberation everyone was assigned to a job. Because I had been a swimmer and skater, I was given a job as a coordinator at the Physical Culture and Sports Institute in Peking, where I worked for twenty-six years. But I was sent to the countryside for a year in 1958, even before the Cultural Revolution. I was twenty-eight and married by then, and I had just given birth to my son.

My husband was a gymnast and also a graduate of the Tianjin University Engineering Department. His job was in Tianjin and I was in Peking, so every week our small salaries would go for train tickets. In 1956 he was able to get a transfer to Peking, but he had to give up engineering and become a physical culture teacher at a university.

When I was a university student, I tried to join the Communist Party, but they wouldn't allow it because of my family background. But at that time I was not so politically aware. During the Cultural Revolution, I was dispatched to the countryside again for two and a half years, and before that I was imprisoned for five months at my work unit. I didn't know what had happened to my family, and I tried to commit suicide twice.

By then I felt there was no meaning to life. After it was all over and I had returned to my original job, I found that my parents had both died of cancer. My husband was kept prisoner at his work unit for only three months, and his mother took care of our children. I returned to Peking in 1972 and continued working hard. In 1979 someone recommended me to a corporation that had been one of the biggest capitalist companies in China before the revolution, and I was hired to set up their ledgers.

Then some relatives on my father's side, who had moved to America before liberation, came to China on a visit. My daughter had just graduated from a foreign-language college, and because we were thinking about her future, I asked if they would sponsor her and my husband to come to the United States, and they agreed. It would have been impossible for all of us to go together. Then my husband's brother sponsored me, so I came out six months later. My son was a middle-school graduate and he had already passed the university examination, so he didn't want to come out then. But he did last August [1983] and now my whole family is together again.

When I left China, I had a refrigerator, a color television, and a tape recorder, so my living standard was high and my life was good. I had a fine job and I was able to travel at government expense about four months out of each year for national and international athletic events. But there were many things I disliked. For example, everyone was supposed to improve their appearance, but clothes were not supposed to look too luxurious. The women all wear those cotton shoes with flat heels, and I could hardly walk in them.

They also say everyone should have more knowledge, but the younger generation doesn't want to learn; they just accept the party line and never think for themselves. They believe everything they read in the newspapers, and everybody just lives like a machine. Also, before liberation, when you went into a department store they had lots of merchandise. But afterward there was very little, and people just accepted it; they didn't even ask for more.

People also have very low standards. For instance, when a girl looks for a husband, I think she should consider his cultural and educational level and his work attitude. But the younger generation just doesn't care about that. If a boy makes forty dollars a month, the girl says okay, even though he should make at least seventy dollars, which is an average income. And they don't teach their children to be polite. If a child grabs something that belongs to others, they just let it go. The morality is getting lower and lower, and I don't like it.

I saw those changes take place after liberation, and I believe it's because of the system that says that young kids with no knowledge are better than professors who have a great deal of knowledge. And because those kids make as much money as professors, they don't care to make an effort to learn. During the Cultural Revolution it was even worse, but that attitude was there from the very beginning.

You know that every ministry in the central government has a leader, and every department has a director. Most of them came from the army, which was made up of peasants. After liberation, those were the people who became department or section leaders, and because they were uneducated, they didn't know anything. They made many wrong decisions, but everyone had to listen to them, so the social, cultural, and technical development of the country went downhill. Those old leaders also tried to suppress the intellectuals, and finally, in 1957, after the Antirightist Campaign that followed the Hundred Flowers Campaign, the intellectuals were quiet. [In 1956 Mao called upon intellectuals to voice their criticisms of the regime. In a speech he said, "Let a hundred flowers blossom," but when artists, writers, and scientists responded, they were persecuted in the Antirightist Campaign of 1957.]

After liberation more women went to work, but their moral standards became very low; they care only about themselves. And the government only *said* women were equal. For example, when they elect ministers, they choose only one or two token women. The woman who is now minister for water resources and power [Qian Zhenying] is very good, but the others are just wives of high-ranking officials. They have no real power, yet they think everybody should listen to them.

Women now have equal rights legally but not actually, and

they already had those freedoms. Even before liberation if a woman wanted a divorce, she could get it. The society was like Taiwan is now. Most Taiwanese girls try to rely on a wealthy man if they want to move up. In China everybody just tries to get a job in the city. I suppose in that respect China is better than Taiwan, and Chinese women also try to go to school so they can be more independent and rely less on men. That's also an improvement.

People don't pay attention to whether or not a woman marries, but I've found that almost everyone does marry sooner or later, although it's very difficult to meet a potential mate now. They don't have parties anymore, so they usually meet through a friend's introduction or at work. But everyone works six days a week, eight hours a day, and there are very few chances to date. When I was at university, we had parties three times a week and on holidays. We also had nightclubs, bands, and dancing groups, and there were all kinds of activities like skating and swimming, where people could meet. But now they don't allow university students to date, although I've heard that in 1980 they began setting up matchmaking organizations.

There's a well-known story about the problem of privacy. During the Cultural Revolution, a young couple was sitting in Tiananmen square and a policeman asked what they were doing there. The girl said, "We are dating. We want to talk to each other, and there's no place to go. We can't go to the park because there are many young rascals there who pretend they are policemen and rob people. The cinema has no tickets, there are no coffee shops where you can sit, and in every restaurant, somebody is waiting for your seat. So we came here just to talk. We won't do anything bad." But still the policeman told them to leave. So there is really no place to go.

And though people say there is very little sex before marriage in China, what I heard was different. The leader of a junior middle school once estimated that of twenty-three girls in one class, only one or two were still virgins. And these were only thirteen- or fourteen-year-olds.

One day, when my daughter was riding to school on her bicycle, several girls forced her to get off, and they beat her up.

When I reported it, her teacher told me that the ringleader had been in trouble before. She was raped by her stepfather, and after that she just slept with anybody. When the teacher had a talk with her, the girl was defiant. Then the police went to her house, and they saw her go inside with two boys. They were there a long time, so the police knocked at the door and asked her to come out. When she refused, they broke the door down and found her in bed with the boys.

They arrested this girl and kept her in jail for about a week, but I'm sure she did it again. The problem is that most of the high-ranking officials do the same. At the beginning of the Cultural Revolution, they had lots of big-character posters telling people things, like the illegitimate child of a certain person in a certain department is residing in such and such a place. Also, that a certain woman had been raped by so-and-so. Now they say that sort of behavior is due to Western influences, but it's not. It's true that in capitalist countries you can do as you please if you have the money, but in China, you can also do whatever you please if you have the power.

During the Cultural Revolution, when all of the middle-school graduates had to go to the countryside for reeducation, some were dispatched to northeast China, and a whole army platoon was sent there to police them. The head of that platoon bought houses for six girls, and he raped every one of them. They had to become his concubines because they needed his approval if they wanted to come back to the city. After the Cultural Revolution he was shot, but it shows that people with rank can get anything.

In the cities the job opportunities are limited, and all the good ones are occupied by the children or grandchildren of high-ranking officials. That's why the people lost confidence in the party.

Whoever comes out of China becomes somebody, and whoever stays in becomes nobody. I don't feel I'm stupid, and I want to have a good life. I don't mean material things; I want freedom and the opportunity to do what I want. As I said, after I graduated from university and was assigned to a job, five years later I had to go to the countryside. Then, when I was sent away again during the Cultural Revolution, my home and personal things were taken away by the Red Guards. They shouted names at us, and some people even died. Of course, the Cultural Revolution was exceptional, but even in normal times both my husband and I worked very hard, and we got nothing, although we were highly respected. Both of us were invited to Tiananmen Square during the October 1 ceremonies [National Day, an annual holiday celebrating the date the People's Republic of China was established], and that is a very high political honor.

American women are very fortunate; their lives are easy in every way. In China, when you become pregnant, although you get free medical care you have to worry about finding a good doctor. If you get someone who graduated from medical school just after the Cultural Revolution you could have trouble because education was terrible during that time. Then, after the baby is born, you have to look for nutritious foods for the mother and child. Even ordering milk is difficult, because you need a hospital certificate, and even then they give you only twenty-five bottles a month. After that you have to find a babysitter you can trust, because the sitter may steal all the special food you bought. Then, when the baby is older, you have to find a good nursery. Most nurseries will take only fifty children, and usually there are 400 people who want to get their babies in. So, because of the shortages, everything is difficult.

When the child is ready for primary school, you have to find a good one, because that can affect his whole life; he may not get into university. My son passed the examination for a very good primary school that admitted only 200 out of 7,000 who applied. Then, when the child gets into primary school, you have to begin worrying about the next school level. Clothing is also difficult. You can't buy readymade children's clothing, so you have to go to a tailor, and if you don't order a winter coat in the summer, the child will have no coat to wear when it gets cold. Life in China is just too hard.

But American women have a very easy life. They can choose their work, and if they are not happy with their jobs, they can change. With their long fingernails, they may look like what the Communists call revisionists, but they are very efficient because they have incentive. They work hard, and they have very good attitudes. Really, they are the greatest.

I'm very happy to be living here, especially because my boss trusts me 100 percent. I'm not watched every minute, and my knowledge is fully used. My husband sells restaurant equipment, and he is also very trusted; they let him run the whole factory. I think our work attitude is good, and though that may be due to the education we had under the Communists, the Chinese should learn work ethics and efficiency from the West.

But there is something here I don't like. The moral attitude of the youngsters is very bad. All they care about is their own enjoyment.

CHAPTER

THE
EXPATRIATES

I was aware of China's policy of importing "foreign experts" to assist in modernization efforts. They include teachers, architects, doctors, scientists, engineers, and other professionals, usually hired on one-year contracts, who are willing to work for very low wages and live under comparatively primitive conditions in exchange for a China adventure. I ran into a number of them while I was there.

But I was surprised to learn of the small group of Westerners, about two dozen, who have devoted almost their entire lives to China. Most arrived prior to the Communist revolution and have lived there from thirty-five to sixty years.

I became intrigued. Who are they? What prompted them to go? Why had they given up the physical comforts of the West to live under difficult conditions (at best) in a nation in constant political turmoil? And why do they stay, even after the disillusioning years of the Cultural Revolution?

One of these devotees of China's socialism is Sidney Rittenberg, who helped to arrange my invitation to the People's Republic and is now writing his own memoirs. Born in Charleston, he graduated from the University of South Carolina. While serving in the United States Army during World War II, because of his fluency in Chinese, he was sent to China as an interpreter in 1945, and became enamored with Chinese Communist ideology. After being discharged from the army, he decided to stay. Eventually Rittenberg married a Chinese. They had four children, and for many years he worked as an adviser to the Mao government on Western political events.

During the Cultural Revolution, however, he aligned himself with a faction that fell into disfavor with the power structure. In 1968 he was arrested and confined for ten years in Qin Cheng Prison, the top-security stronghold where political prisoners like Jiang Qing, Mao's widow and leader of the Gang of

Four, are held today. Yet, Rittenberg, like the other foreign ex-patriates, is still devoted to China.

I requested interviews with Western women who were long-time China residents and was able to meet with three of them. I also interviewed a Los Angeles woman who had been working in Peking as a foreign-language expert for only a few months when I arrived. Her story is quite different from the others.

TALITHA GERLACH

At eighty-seven, Talitha Gerlach was still alert and vigorous when I visited her at home in Shanghai. Born in Pittsburgh and raised in Indianapolis, she had been living in China for fifty-seven years. Gerlach's home is Western in style, attractive and comfortably furnished. Books, artworks, and photographs, collected over the years, are everywhere, and her front garden was blooming with chrysanthemums when we arrived.

I noticed that Yaqing, my interpreter, and Cui Jing Tai, our Shanghai guide, appeared reverent when we were all introduced. Later they told me that she is considered something of a legend because she has devoted so much of her life to the Chinese. They also interrupted the interview occasionally to inquire after her health, which annoyed Gerlach. She was delighted to have American visitors and kept urging us to stay even longer.

When we were settled in the living room, her longtime Chinese housekeeper served coffee, cookies, and a delicious hot fruit compote made with lichees. The two women showed a great deal of affection for each other.

Gerlach told me that only eleven of the Western women who are longtime residents are still alive. Although most of them live far from each other, they are a closely knit group and keep in touch through letters or phone calls.

The Shanghai Connection

I graduated from high school in Indianapolis, intending to enter college in the fall and become a teacher. But I wanted to do something that summer and my high school botany teacher recommended me for a job in the State Board of Health's bacterial laboratory, so I began learning about germs. One day the head of the laboratory told me that Indiana University, which was based in Bloomington, was setting up some courses in Indianapolis, and I could begin acquiring college credits. So I registered for a course in medical social service. In those days there were only two places in the country that were training medical social workers. One was Massachusetts General Hospital and the other was ours. And that's how I met Ida Pruitt.

Ida was working for the Rockefeller Hospital in Peking [now Capital Hospital] and she was organizing a medical social service department there. After a visit to Massachusetts General, she came to Indianapolis to see how we operated, and began going with me on visits to some of my cases. One day, while we were out in the country, she asked if I would like to come to Peking and help her set up the social service department. By then I was in my early twenties and had a number of years experience, but I refused Ida's invitation for two reasons. The first was the Rockefeller Foundation. I had grown up in an atmosphere of distrust for people and organizations that had a lot of money. The other was that I had become interested in the YWCA programs.

I was the daughter of a Methodist minister, and in those early years, the churches collected money to send missionaries to different countries. Our church supported several in China, and when they came home on furlough, they would often visit the parishes that supported them. I recall several staying with us and telling stories about China. That opened a whole new area of interest to me, but early on I decided I didn't want to be a missionary. I knew that when people were sick the missionaries would visit and preach to them, and I didn't approve of that. But I was interested in China and when I was thirty I finally went with the YWCA. I was recruited by the foreign division of their national board to work with the China YWCA, but those of us who were foreigners were completely under the direction of the Chinese leadership once we were there.

My parents never pressured me to marry. In fact, there were

Talitha Gerlach in Shanghai
(from her private collection)

six or seven children in my mother's family, and two of the girls never married, so there already was something of a tradition in my family for the women not to marry.

The Chinese YWCA had requested some experienced foreign secretaries to help with their programs. One of their major ones was education, because in those early days, only women from wealthy families could go to school, so our program was very important. The YWCA here in Shanghai developed a most positive and worthwhile program of classes for women factory workers. Part of my training was to visit the factories and workers' housing. I learned that countless young girls were brought in from the countryside to work in the textile mills, and they lived in these fragile little shacks. They were required to work sixteen hours a day, and their working conditions were really terrible.

One of my early experiences was a visit to a silk factory. I was taken into a little room where there were large vats of boiling-hot water. In front of each was a little girl, perhaps eight or ten years old, and her job was to keep tapping the silk cocoons so they wouldn't go under water. Eventually an end would come loose, and the child would fasten it to a gadget that would unwind the silk thread. But the children's fingers were red and swollen, and some were even bleeding. This was in the dead of winter, and I still remember that the room was like a steam bath. The girls wore only one thin layer of underwear, and when they left the factory at night, they went right out into the cold with no other garments to put on. They were soaking wet, and their little fingers were badly puckered. I'll never forget those terrible working conditions.

At the time the mills were owned mainly by Japanese, and to some extent, Germans. There were very few British and American owners, although they controlled that part of Shanghai politically, and they were all exploiting the Chinese workers.

I lived in the industrial area because the Chinese staff felt we should live with the workers. Their living conditions were deplorable. One building I visited had a platform built on the second-floor landing, and there were girls sleeping on it. There wasn't even enough room for them to stand up, and the building itself was so flimsy there could have been serious accidents.

The Chiang Kai-shek government was in power then, and with the political situation, the YWCA program was really quite pathetic. The secret police were always coming around and trying to block it. When the Chinese staff rented an apartment in the industrial area, they always wanted a foreigner living with them because the local authorities wouldn't be as likely to cause trouble.

The only power the YWCA had was its membership, and I don't know whether you could call that power. They solicited women members from all areas of the society—wives of factory owners, lawyers, and others who had money and could bring pressure on their husbands. One time a YWCA secretary was arrested when she was attending a discussion of the National Salvation Association. But a Chinese member who was married to an attorney got her husband interested, and he was able to have the girl released, although she had to report to the local police station once a week after that.

The YWCA had contacts from the lowest level of women workers through the students and on up to the women who had education, money, and high positions. I think the foreign staff was quite instrumental in educating the women on the board about the conditions of the workers. Some of them really changed their attitudes and began to exert some influence.

I arrived in 1926 and spent my first year in Peking studying the Chinese language. My first work assignment was in Chengdu for three years, and then I was transferred to the national headquarters in Shanghai and lived here from then on. On July 7, 1937, the Japanese launched an all-out attack, and we knew they would keep pushing south and eventually take possession of Shanghai. So countless people who had been bombed out of their homes or who did not want to live under Japanese rule fled to the interior, and there was a great need for refugee relief funds. Sun Yat-sen's widow, Soong Ching-ling, was in Hong Kong and receiving reports about the refugee conditions. With the cooperation of some British, American, and Chinese friends, she set up the China Defense League to solicit help from abroad. They needed money for medicine, food and clothing and they also wanted to let the world know about the actual situation in China. Israel Epstein, who is now editor of *China Reconstructs,* was in Hong Kong at the time, and he helped publish a newsletter that told the world Chiang Kai-shek was launching military attacks on the Chinese Communist armies when he should have been fighting the Japanese. Then, when the Japanese were approaching Hong Kong, Soong moved her organization to Chongqing, the Nationalist capital, and operated out of there until World War II ended.

Meanwhile, I returned to the United States. The YWCA allowed its foreign workers to go home on a six-month furlough every two years, but by the end of 1940, I felt I was getting older, my hair was turning gray, and this was the *Young* Women's Christian Association, so I moved to New York City, where I continued to work with the YWCA's national division.

Then, when the war was over, I received a letter from the China YWCA asking me to come back and work with them. They were organizing a special training course for new staff people and wanted me to help. So in 1946 I found myself working in Peking. Soong Ching-ling had moved her organization there, and it didn't take long before we got together. I began working with the China Defense League as well as the YWCA, and by the time I went back to the United States again in 1948, Soong and I were so close she saw me off at the airport. Just before I boarded the plane, she asked me to stay and work only with her. I said I would love to, but I was getting on in years. I felt I should maintain my connection with the YWCA until I reached the official retirement age of sixty so I could be sure of having my pension. She agreed with that logic and kept in touch with me. Meanwhile, her organization, which by then had become the China Welfare Institute, developed very rapidly. When I got back to the United States, I began making speeches all over America about conditions in China.

On the whole, the audiences would hang on every word, but my friend, Welthy Fisher, who was a missionary in China for many years, had some very hostile reactions when she came back to America and spoke about the revolutionary movement in China. Once, when she was speaking to a group, before she could get started, a few people in the audience kept firing hostile questions at her. They were obviously trying to label her a Communist, and finally, after several interruptions, she just looked at one heckler and said, "I've come here to tell you about conditions in China, not about Welthy Fisher," and that silenced them.

But as a result of my speeches, the YWCA national board refused to renew my contract. This was during the McCarthy years, and I was fired by not being rehired. Some of the dear ladies on the national board had engineered the whole thing by assigning my responsibilities to other departments and leaving me with nothing to do. That was the reason they gave me for not renewing, but a very good friend of mine who had also worked for the China YWCA told me the reason that my contract was not renewed was the speeches I was making about the revolution in China. The dear board ladies did not like the word *revolution*. I was also active with a very progressive union that was negotiating a contract with the YWCA board, and the dear ladies didn't like that either.

When the word about my being fired got to China, I received a cablegram from Soong Ching-ling reminding me that I was coming to work with her, so I went back to China.

I was fifty-seven by then, and I wrote a letter to the national board pointing out that I had been employed by them for twenty-five years, that there had never been any question about the quality of my work, and yet they were cutting me off without my full retirement benefits. So the dear ladies had to reconsider the issue. They decided to guarantee my annuity payments because the funds had accumulated for over twenty-five years. But in those years the United States didn't permit American money to be sent to China, so even though the pension payments were being deposited in an account at Chase Manhattan Bank in New York, I couldn't touch a penny of that money. It just accumulated and accumulated.

I have a very capable lawyer in New York, and I once wrote and asked him to get a release of some of my funds so I could buy some books. He wrote back that the United States Treasury

Department wanted to know the titles of the books, and I felt it was such a stupid question I dropped the matter. Some years later I heard that my Aunt Martha, who was then ninety, was living in a private nursing home, and her nieces and nephews were paying for her care. I felt I should make a contribution, so I asked my lawyer to try and get some of my money released for that purpose, and the Treasury Department agreed.

Finally, in 1979, when the United States resumed diplomatic relations with China, my funds were released, and believe it or not, I can now write checks on my account in New York.

When I came back the last time, I became an adviser to the institute and I still am. The China Welfare Institute has never even hinted that I retire. I try to stay up-to-date on the program developments in Shanghai—the nursery school, the kindergarten, the Children's Palace [where they have various activities for children], the children's theater, the children's magazine, and our maternity and children's hospital, which has over 300 beds. But since the doors of China opened to the outside world, a great deal of my time has been taken by foreign visitors who request interviews.

For several years before that I visited the programs daily and made suggestions and criticisms to the staff. I still go to the Children's Theater every time a new play is in rehearsal. They have performances for a small group, so we can give our criticisms. The children's magazine is printed only in Chinese, and I keep urging them to put out an English-language edition because so many foreign visitors are interested in it. Now the staff is giving that serious consideration. Our hospital has supported population control since 1970, when the movement started, and a great deal of educational work had to be done. At first the government limited families to two children, and now it's only one. We have classes on birth control for the women who come to the hospital and outpatient clinic, and their husbands are also encouraged to attend. Our hospital is internationally recognized for its fine work on population control.

I also work with our magazine, *China Reconstructs*. For a long time I read every issue from cover to cover and wrote critical reports. But that took a lot of time and energy, and now I don't have that much. But I still read every issue even though I don't get my ideas down on paper. I've known Israel Epstein and his wife, Elsie Cholmeley, for many years, and we have a good working relationship.

The twenty-four hours in a day are not enough. My health is still very good, though once in a while I have pain in my knees. Two years ago my knees felt so painful I began getting acupuncture treatments and hot compresses every morning and evening at our clinic. The pain was lessening and then, one day, I looked the doctor straight in the eyes and asked, "How do you diagnose this? Is it arthritis?" He smiled and said, "Maybe for aged people, but not for you." I have very little pain now, so maybe you could call it a fleeting case of arthritis.

When the Cultural Revolution first broke loose here in Shanghai, the streets were filled with young people marching up and down, and they were very orderly. But the staff at the institute told me not to come to the office because they just didn't know what those young people would do. So I stayed home for two solid weeks, and then a worker came and said things had eased up a bit and they would send a car to bring me to and from the office. They also made a car available for my shopping expeditions, and they've never changed that practice.

Jerry Tannenbaum, another American on the staff, and I attended the criticism meetings at first. Then word came from Peking that foreigners could not attend those meetings, and we were advised by our Chinese co-workers to just keep a low profile. We did attend some of the mass meetings in Shanghai, but we never sat down in front.

The Children's Palace had to close, and while the nursery school and kindergarten were allowed to continue, it was on a limited scale. We couldn't accept as many children as we formerly did, so we stopped publicizing the program. The Children's Theater couldn't put on performances and, though the hospital continued to function, it, too, was very limited. Often we couldn't get medicines, and many of the doctors were persecuted.

I know that a number of Western people living in China were imprisoned—people like Sidney Rittenberg—but because Jerry and I were practically the only Westerners in Shanghai at that time and we had our own private homes, we weren't very visible. There were also some American women here, who had married Chinese, but they were classified as Chinese. Jerry was married to a Chinese actress, and he was ready to fight anyone who tried to molest her. He's very tall and strong.

Women here are still not completely free, mainly because of the old feudal ideas that still dominate many areas of Chinese life. It's mainly husbands and people of the older generation who still try to practice the old restrictions. They are still conditioned by the feudal ideology, so it's really a question of re-education. Soong Ching-ling made one of her most important contributions in that area. As long as she lived she constantly emphasized the rights of women and children.

I would like to see total compliance with the law that says women have freedom to choose their marriage partners. The newspapers are constantly reporting cases of forced marriages, mainly in the rural areas, but the country people are moving to the cities and they bring those ideas with them. When the People's Republic of China was established in 1949, the Marriage Law was the first one they passed, yet it's still not totally observed.

China has an excellent record on health care and education for both men and women, but it still has a way to go in matters like arranged marriages and equal pay for equal work. I'm really shocked when I read articles about how some work units still prefer hiring men because they feel women, even though they are equally qualified, will take more time off for pregnancies and child problems. But now there can be only one child, and the husband should share the responsibility. Progress is being made, but there's still a long way to go.

Even after living here so many years, I don't think I've even begun to have as thorough an understanding of China as I would like to have. But my Chinese co-workers and associates are very generous in their attitudes. They don't expect very much.

JOAN HINTON

Joan Hinton and her husband, Sid Engst, have lived in China for more than thirty-five years. In 1979 Hinton accompanied her husband to the United States, where Engst entered Boston General Hospital for open-heart surgery, a procedure not being performed in China at the time. Unaware of the high cost of medical care in America, they brought $5,000 with them, thinking that sum would surely be enough.

When Engst was ready to leave the hospital, he was presented with a bill for $17,000. Desperate, Hinton phoned the Chinese Embassy in Washington, describing their plight. An attaché immediately cabled Peking and within twenty-four hours the government cabled back, authorizing the immediate issue of $12,000.

The attaché was my interpreter, Zhao Yaqing, who was stationed in Washington at the time. She told me of the incident.

Joan Hinton is regarded as one of China's great heroines. A physicist, she worked on the development of the atomic bomb with such world-renowned figures as Enrico Fermi and Robert Oppenheimer. After the bombing of Hiroshima, Hinton was among the group of scientists who petitioned the United States government to prevent military control of nuclear energy. When they failed, Hinton went to China in 1947 to join Engst and her brother, William. Former roommates at the Cornell University School of Agriculture, both men had gone to China soon after World War II ended and were working on farms in the Communist-held territories. After returning to the United States in the 1950s, William Hinton wrote Fanshen, *a book about his experience with land reform in Long Bow Village. [He revisited the village in the early 1970s and wrote a sequel,* Shenfan.*]*

Joan Hinton and Engst remained in China. Over the years they have lived on a number of experimental farms, developing dairy machinery and breeding new strains of milk cows. When I asked the young reporter from Guangming Daily *to arrange an interview with Hinton, he hesitated because the dairy farm on which she was living was in a restricted military zone about forty*

*miles from Peking. Within a couple of days, however, he was
successful in obtaining official passes for us.*

*When we arrived at the farm late one afternoon, we found
Hinton and Engst examining some two dozen healthy-looking new
calves, the offspring of cows they had bred by artificial insemi-
nation with sperm imported from Canada. Until recently, cow's
milk was rarely consumed in China. Now, though still scarce,
it's very popular. During our trip we saw people queued in front
of a store only once, and our guide told us they were waiting to
buy milk.*

*Hinton is still overflowing with enthusiasm about "building
a great society." Dressed in baggy blue cotton work pants and
jacket, with her blond hair carelessly arranged under a Mao-style
cap, her face is constantly alive with excitement when she speaks
about her life in China. Before starting the interview, she insisted on showing us the entire farm—the grain fields, the live-
stock, the barns containing new milking machinery—everything.*

*Though spacious, the Hinton-Engst home is definitely no-frills.
The cement-block house, with its gray cement floors and walls,
is unadorned by carpets, photographs, or art. Containing a
hodgepodge of furniture, it is obviously only a place to eat, sleep,
and work. A large drafting table, where Engst draws plans for
new farm machinery, dominates one section of the living room,
and an old coal-burning stove in the center is the source of heat.*

From Atom Bombs to Baby Cows

My mother was an educator. She taught first through third grades
at Shady Hill, a well-known progressive school in Cambridge,
Massachusetts. When Jean, Bill, and I finished primary school,
she started a high school in Putney, Vermont, because she wanted
us to continue our progressive education. She called it the Putney School and it was founded in 1934, just in time for me to
enter the first freshman class. I think it was one of the first coed
boarding high schools in the country.

The school was on a farm, and she believed in learning by
doing, so we went to school in the morning and did farm work

*Joan Hinton and her husband, Sid Engst,
with the new strain of calves they are breeding
on an experimental farm near Peking*

in the afternoon. But she didn't believe in homework. Instead she planned all kinds of activities, such as art and music, for the evenings, and we could choose what we wanted. The first graduating class did very well on the college board exams, and many went on to Ivy League schools like Harvard and Yale. Over the years they always chose Putney graduates, even though her education ideas were different.

Having her for a mother was a very exciting experience. She always took us somewhere in the summer, because she believed that if you're going to be strong and stick up for your principles, you must also be strong in body and be able to take hardships. One summer, when I was four, she took us to Mexico and we rode into the hot desert areas on donkeys. When I was six, we went to Glacier National Park and hiked all summer, carrying backpacks. She also got a job with an organization called Experiment in International Living. One summer she took a group to Germany. We lived with a German family and rode bicycles through Austria. Being allowed to take her three children along was her salary. We got to see different parts of the world, and she considered that part of our education.

After graduating from Putney, I went to Bennington College in Vermont, which is also a progressive school, and that's when I got interested in physics. While I was there, Pearl Harbor was bombed, and we went to war. Bennington had a work-study system where you worked in the field every winter for six weeks, and I worked with the cyclotron crew at Cornell. The field of nuclear physics was just opening up then, and I was reading all the journals. But then it began sort of petering out, and when I asked my physics teacher about it, he hinted that it was becoming classified. That was the first inkling I had that anything was going on other than pure science.

After finishing at Bennington, I became a teaching assistant in the University of Wisconsin physics department. They had two big Van de Graaff accelerators in the cellar of the physics building, and one day they just cut a hole in the wall and took them away, along with the people who had worked with them. I still didn't know what was going on, but later I received a letter from the people I'd worked with at Cornell asking if I would like to work with them in New Mexico. Of course, by then I knew it had something to do with the war, but I didn't know exactly what.

So I went to Los Alamos, and all the top physicists of the Western world were there—Teller, Oppenheimer, Fermi, whom I'd worked with at Cornell, and the whole Cornell cyclotron crew.

When you entered Los Alamos, they took your handprints, and from then on, you couldn't leave. We could go anywhere in the area, but not into any cities. It was all very top secret. The scientists insisted that they should be able to talk to each other, and at first there was a big fight with the army over that, but we won out. Our letters were censored, and when my mother and sister visited, they stayed at Oppenheimer's cabin, which was quite a way from Los Alamos. They couldn't come to the site, but I was allowed to visit them. That was in the summer of 1945, just before the test bomb went off in the desert at Alamogordo. I was there when it happened.

It's interesting because up until then we just worked very hard because we didn't want the Germans to get it first, so we just thought of it as part of the war effort. But when it went off, and we saw that light and heard that noise, it was like nothing we ever imagined.

It was very early morning, still dark, and we were sitting on a little knoll. When the bomb exploded, we felt as if we were standing naked in front of the world; suddenly there was no secrecy anymore. It was all in the open and we knew it worked. We'd made an atom bomb! But the worst was Hiroshima. We were on a bus when we saw the newspaper headlines, and that really affected us. One scientist immediately called a meeting, and we formed the Association of Los Alamos Scientists. First we went to the Alamogordo site, got some of the radioactive pieces of melted sand and had them embedded in clear plastic. We sent them to every mayor of every city in the United States with a letter saying, "Do you want your city to look like this? Fight for civilian control of atomic energy."

We also lobbied in Washington. I recall going to the office of one senator and telling his secretary I wanted to talk to him about atomic energy. She asked, "Does this have something to do with your school work?" And I was an atomic scientist in my twenties by then!

For a while we thought we had won the battle, so a lot of us who hadn't finished went back to school. I got a fellowship to study at the University of Chicago Institute of Nuclear Studies, but it was the beginning of the McCarthy period. The nuclear science field was always very secret, and it got even worse. You could just feel this whole witch hunt coming down. Then I learned that the fellowship had come from the Navy, and I was shocked. I finally realized that the military had the nuclear field completely tied up, and there was no way to change it.

My brother Bill had gone to China by then. He was a conscientious objector at first, but then, when he became convinced that he had to fight the Fascists, he tried to join the army but couldn't pass the physical. So he joined the Office of War Information, and they sent him to Nationalist China close to the end of the war. He worked with Jerry Tannenbaum and they went to Chongqing when Chou En-lai and Mao Tse-tung were there. Bill asked for an interview, and when Mao found out that he had worked with American farmers, he interviewed Bill instead. Bill told me that the longer their talk went on, the smaller he felt because Mao was so well informed. It was a turning point in his life because he got very interested in what was going on in China. But he had to come back to the United States to resign from the OWI.

Meanwhile, Sid, who was my brother's roommate at Cornell, had become a dairy farmer in upstate New York. Then he decided there was more to life than farming, so he auctioned off his animals, got a job with a United Nations agricultural team as a dairy specialist, and went to China with them. The cows never arrived, so the team went on a famine survey instead. Sid stayed in China, and then Bill went back again in 1947.

Because of Bill, I was also very interested in China by then, and nuclear physics looked like a dead-end street for me. But I was torn because I was working with Fermi, and I enjoyed it very much. He had an evening group that I was lucky to be in. There were only five of us, and two were Nobel Prize winners, so it was quite special. On the other hand, I knew it couldn't last forever, and I wanted so much to find out about China, so I decided to just go and have a look.

It wasn't so easy to get there, because in 1947 the war between the Communists and the Kuomintang had started in earnest. My brother and Sid went just before that. Finally, I managed to get a job with Soong Ching-ling's China Welfare Institute in Shanghai. She sent me a letter of hire, which I sent to the State Department with a request for a passport, and they issued it. After I left they found out I'd worked at Los Alamos, and they didn't like it one bit.

They really had nothing to worry about. I arrived in 1947, but it took me a year to get through the Kuomintang lines to the liberated area, and I found nothing there when I arrived. Even if I'd wanted to work on a bomb, there were no facilities. It was all such nonsense. While I was waiting to get there, I worked with a very interesting program Soong had going. They would get a few children from the slum area and teach them ten Chinese characters. Then each child would go back and teach them to ten other children, and they would teach them to ten others. It was called the Little Teacher Program, and it promoted literacy. I taught English, music, and art to the slum children.

In those days there were two Chinas. Shanghai was a mess. Beggars were all over the place, and people had no place to live or sleep. Even women and children were lying in the streets. But that wasn't liberated China; it was Kuomintang China. The Communists were trying to change all that, and who couldn't support them? Sid told me that when he was in Changsha in 1946, every morning they came with trucks and picked up the bodies of about 200 people who had starved to death on the streets. When you see things like that, you support anyone who is trying to make changes, and I wanted to meet those people.

Soong had connections with the underground, operating to help intellectuals get into the liberated area, but since we were "long noses," as the Chinese say, it was hard to send us through. I tried many ways. Bertha, my brother's first wife, was with me, and she was able to cross at a point where people from the Friends

Service Committee were operating on both sides of the lines; she just walked across with them. But I got sick with malaria and had to go back to Shanghai.

Then I tried to go through with Sidney Shapiro and his wife. Because she's Chinese, she posed as a peasant and I posed as Sid's wife. We flew to Peking and met some underground people who tried to get us through on a truck that was headed for Tsinan, which was in the liberated area. We were supposedly going there on business, but the Kuomintang soldier at the checkpoint didn't believe us, and we had to go back. Finally, we were liberated along with the rest of the city when the People's Liberation Army took Peking. Sid and Bill were in Yenan, and I found some people who were taking a truckload of equipment there. I was allowed to go along, and I rode for two weeks on bombed-out roads. Sid was working in a factory that was a two-day walk from Yenan, but he came back and we were married, and I went to work in the factory with him. This factory actually consisted of about twenty caves with about forty workers who were making plows, cooking pots, and other things that were needed. We'd get some coal and scrap iron from the hills— bombs, old truck wheels and other articles left over from the war—and melt everything down in a mud furnace. First we soaked the bombs in water for a while and then broke them up with a sledge hammer. Mostly we made woks and other cooking utensils, and we were also part of a little group that was experimenting with making farm tools. Sid made a four-wheel cart, and I made a windmill. We had no equipment, nothing but our hands, and, coming from Los Alamos, it was quite a change. But the spirit was wonderful. These people had so little and they knew so much. As soon as I got there, I felt as if I'd come home.

Later, we went into Inner Mongolia. There was a plan to improve the sheep and cattle in Shanxi province, which borders Inner Mongolia, so we went up there. We set up this farm in a big, dirt-walled fort built by Belgian Catholics. Inside there was a Catholic church, the local Mongolian government office, and our farm. We had about twelve fine merino sheep, captured from the Japanese.

Sid had gone to Cornell Agricultural School, and I had been farming all through high school. So I was a farmer first, then a physicist, and then a farmer again. You see, my mother taught me that the world is yours; you can do whatever you want and there's no limit. Actually, what I've been doing with farm machinery is very similar to what I did as a nuclear physicist.

We had about twenty people working on this farm, and it was very far from everything. It took two weeks to walk to Yenan, and there were no radios and no electricity. On October 1, 1949, when Mao Tse-tung announced the establishment of the People's Republic of China, we knew nothing about it until October 20, because it took twenty days for a donkey to bring a newspaper up there. We were really cut off.

But that was China in those days; there were many places like that. When we first got there, the People's Liberation Army was still trying to liberate the rest of China, and all the local warlord armies had joined them. They were more or less bandits to begin with. But after the main armies had moved south, the local army in our area suddenly became bandits again, and we were in enemy territory. We had only three units—the Belgian priests, our farmers, and the local government—and we had to prepare for an assault. They assigned me and a seventeen-year-old kid to a slit in the rampart, gave us a baseball bat and a pile of bricks, and we were supposed to hit them with the bat and throw bricks down on their heads when they attacked the fort. But by then we had become friendly with the local people, and one evening, just at sunset, one of the bandit scouts went to a Mongolian house that had a view of the fort, and he saw animals galloping about, raising a lot of dust. He thought it was the PLA cavalry, and when he asked the Mongolians, they assured him it was. When he went back and reported, the bandits went tearing north. Actually, he had seen our milk cows. They'd been penned in for a week and when we opened the gate, they went rushing out, raising a lot of dust.

I never really made a decision to live in China. I just kept staying on because it was so interesting. At first the United States government was after me. I hadn't done anything but go to a place where there was nothing except your own hands and some animals. But according to the United States, I was an atomic spy giving secrets to China, and if I'd gone back, I'm sure they would have invented something to use against me, especially during the McCarthy period. After all, the Rosenbergs were executed, and they didn't know as much as I did. They really didn't know anything. But I probably would have stayed in any case, because there wasn't all that much for me back there.

My brother moved back to the United States in 1953 after living in China six years. He wrote a book on land reform, and later he wrote a second one about the same village.

We have three children, and they're all in the United States now. They went back when they were in their twenties. But they were born in China, and none of them knew any English. It's like the first generation born to immigrants in the United States. The kids often don't know the language of the parents.

We always had a Chinese woman to care for our children. Under Chinese living conditions, child care and housework are a full-time job, so any working mother must have her own mother or a maid living with her. Our maids spoke only Chinese, and if we tried to speak English to the children, the maid felt left out. So we spoke Chinese to them and English to each other. The children heard English all the time, but couldn't speak it.

It was hard for these blue-eyed, blond-haired kids in China because they were different. It's like being black in the United States, and if blacks spoke a different language, it would be even worse. But our children went right through school with the local Chinese children.

We wanted them to go to the United States. We think people should get to know different cultures, all kinds of people, and we felt they should see what the United States is like. But it was up to them. We would have been just as happy whether they chose to go or stay. After all, the world is made up of the human race; we're all one big family.

Our two youngest, a son and a daughter, twenty-six and twenty-seven, went to a farm during the Cultural Revolution. They spent four years in the countryside, and it was very exciting for them. We actually had to fight to get them to allow our kids to go, whereas everybody else had to fight to keep them home. We're always on the other side of the fence.

Then my daughter went to Peking University and majored in biochemistry and went to the United States after that. She was in the Yale University biology department, but she didn't realize she had to know English. On her first exam she only got a twenty because she couldn't understand the questions or write English. Now she's studying English and has applied to some graduate schools.

Her brother came down with a heart disorder, and his older brother who was already in the States invited him to visit while he was recuperating. When he got better, he began taking courses at Temple University in physics, electrical engineering, and computer science. After he graduated, he became a research assistant at the University of Illinois.

All the children have to earn their own living, so he scrubbed floors all those years he was in school. Now he doesn't have to do that anymore; he's really liberated. His wife, a Chinese girl he met on the farm, had to work in a Chinese restaurant in Philadelphia while she was in school, so they had quite a time. The first year they had only $200 a month to live on, but two kids brought up in China know how to do that.

And our eldest son is great. He worked on my brother's farm for a while until he learned some English. Then he went to Philadelphia and got a job as an electrician at a big steel works through an ad in the newspaper. When they asked him if he had any experience, he said, "Four years in China." They tested him and he passed. He's also studying economics at Temple, so they all have their wings now.

Women of old China were really chattels. I knew of women who were sold for a bag of grain. The Mongolian women are different from the Han women [the majority nationality in China]. Mongolian women do all the work, and the Mongolian men don't do any. In those days, they only smoked opium and did the trading. In 1949 a Mongolian woman told me, "Huh, it costs $600 to buy one of us, and it costs only $200 for a Han woman." Marriages were always arranged, and because it was a border area, the two nationalities were mixed. But if a Han married a Mongolian, the children were considered Mongolian. Of all the mixed marriages we saw, the ones that worked best were Han men married to Mongolian women. If it was the other way around, they starved because Han women of northern China didn't do field work; they just stayed in the home. And Mongolian men just smoked and rode horses.

In the beginning all marriages in China were parent decisions. There was no freedom of choice; women were just sold. I don't know if anyone else agrees with me, but I recently made a discovery. You know, Chinese women don't change their surname when they get married as Western women do. And it has nothing to do with freedom. It's an old feudal custom, and I've decided it was because of the child-brides. A family would take a baby girl into their home to eventually become the wife of their son. But she had to keep her own surname because if the boy had sisters, they wouldn't know which one was the intended bride.

Women are still not equal in China. But there's been such an improvement over what it was, the fact that they're not doesn't occur to them. But I notice it all the time. People always put Sid first and me second. In America we don't do that; we're much more equal there. In China women are just not equal, and it's very obvious.

People sometimes ask if I miss the conveniences and luxuries I had in the United States, but I think once you've had those things you don't crave them. For example, in the United States, if you go into a poor neighborhood, you find they are the people driving the big limousines and overdressing. When you come from a family like mine, an Anglo-Saxon and well-established old Mayflower family, you've already had the material possessions, and you know that's not the answer. But if you've never had them, that's what you work for.

With my background, the hardest thing was not having a stimulating life. For me it's the enjoyment of creating that's important, not the level of living. It's such fun here. Everybody is working together to build a whole new society, so you're part of something huge.

ELSIE FAIRFAX CHOLMELEY
AND ISRAEL EPSTEIN

I interviewed Elsie Fairfax Cholmeley in the foreign wing of Peking's Capital Hospital, where she was being treated for a heart condition. As is the custom in Chinese hospitals, her adopted Chinese son and daughter were taking turns sleeping in her room each night, so she could have constant attention. Ai Songping, her handsome twenty-eight-year-old son, was present during my visit but spoke no English.

At seventy-eight Cholmeley was alert, good-humored, and happy to speak with me despite a number of interruptions by her husband, Israel Epstein. Concerned that she was tiring herself, he kept urging her to hurry along, but she was having fun reminiscing and kept waving him away. Finally, in an effort to bring the interview to a conclusion more quickly, he also took part.

Epstein is editor in chief of China Reconstructs, *a monthly publication of the China Welfare Institute, founded by Soong Ching-ling. Mailed to subscribers throughout the world, the magazine's purpose is to build good will by publishing articles about China in the best possible light. Printed in seven languages—English, Spanish, French, Arabic, German, Portuguese, and Chinese—it was one of the publications I subscribed to myself before going to China. And, though it should be read with a grain of salt, it's a good source of information.*

Born in Poland in 1915, Epstein came to China with his parents when he was two. At fifteen, he started writing for an English-language newspaper in Tianjin and became a free-lance correspondent for American newspapers during the Sino-Japanese War. In 1938 he wrote a newsletter for Soong's China Defense League, which later evolved into the China Welfare Institute.

Just before I left for China, an issue of Time *magazine carried a cover story by Theodore White that expressed his views on the Mao Tse-tung era. The issue was banned in China because White, in explaining Mao's mistakes during his last years, especially the Cultural Revolution, speculated that Mao was a victim of Alzheimer's disease (hardening of the arteries leading to the brain). When I asked Epstein his opinion on the story, I was surprised by his anger, especially in view of White's earlier writings.* Thunder Out of China, *written with journalist Annalee Jacoby just after they returned to America after covering the Sino-Japanese War, was very favorable in its treatment of the Communists, as was White's later book* In Search of History. *In fact, his reporting during those early years led to a clash with his boss,* Time *publisher Henry Luce, a staunch supporter of Chiang Kai-shek, and to the loss of White's job. Yet Epstein, despite the fact that he and his wife had been imprisoned for five years during the Cultural Revolution, would not forgive White for that one article.*

Elsie Cholmeley

My papa was a squire. He owned about a thousand acres in Yorkshire, but we were really not financially well off; we weren't poor, but we weren't rich either. I guess you might call us land poor.

At that time boys got all the encouragement. Both my brothers went to Eton and then to Cambridge. I went to Reading Agricultural College because I wanted to farm, and it was unusual for a girl to go to school at all. They generally stayed home with governesses. Reading was the best agricultural college in England, and I studied dairy farming there for two years. Then I took over the family farm for quite a long time, but the soil was so heavy it didn't produce very much.

In 1927 there was a worldwide depression. Things got so bad I finally decided there was no reason to stay on the farm, because all we did was lose money. So I went to London and enrolled in a secretarial college, where I learned typing and shorthand.

I had various jobs, but none was very satisfactory. In fact, I got the sack once because I put letters in the wrong envelopes. I didn't tell my parents because they would have thought that was the limit, so I just went around London thinking about far-

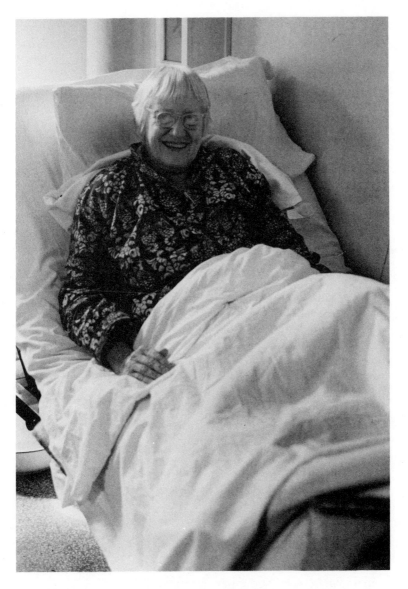

Elsie Fairfax Cholmeley in Capital Hospital, Peking

off places like New York or Moscow. The reason I considered Moscow was I felt that Russia was a place where women had equal opportunities.

Then a friend told me about an American named Carter who was looking for a secretary to go around the world with him. He was secretary-general of the Institute of Pacific Relations, an organization concerned with the economics of countries in the Pacific. I went to see him, and he hired me, but it was a strange deal. There was no salary, and I had to pay half the price of the voyage, but I wanted so much to go, I agreed. There were five of us, three secretaries and Mr. and Mrs. Carter, and we went to Hong Kong, Shanghai, Nanking, and Peking. That was in 1935, and it was my first time in China.

When our steamer docked in Shanghai, my first impression was of coolies sweating away with these great loads they were hauling. They had terrible sores all over their bodies, and I thought, "What a frightful place." But the houses looked decent, and of course we attended huge banquets that were really excessive. I was living in luxury and surrounded by poverty. I saw the same thing in Nanking, but I felt better there because they were doing quite a bit of scientific work on crops. Peking was much the same as it is now.

We were in China five weeks, and then we traveled all around the Pacific—Japan, Honolulu, New Zealand, Australia. Then we went to the United States for a conference that was held at Yosemite National Park. Later I became a member of the permanent staff in New York and worked with people like Owen Lattimore, the editor of *Pacific Affairs*. In 1939 I requested a grant to do a research project on Chinese agricultural implements, and they gave it to me, so I went off to China.

I lived with some German friends in Hong Kong, but because the Sino-Japanese War had been going on for two years by then, I couldn't do the research project. Instead I did publicity for the Chinese Industrial Cooperatives, which had been organized to help the war effort. So many refugees had come in from Japanese-occupied cities, and they had nothing to do. So they started some small industries to employ them and also to provide commodities that were scarce because of the occupation. Soong Ching-ling and her organization, the China Defense League, were in Hong Kong by then, and I also worked with her. Then, when the Japanese dropped bombs on Pearl Harbor in December 1941, and it looked as if they would soon be occupying Hong Kong, as many important Chinese as possible were loaded on airplanes and taken to Canton. I was supposed to go too, but I missed the last plane so I stayed in Hong Kong.

I could have been evacuated to England, but I couldn't think of anything worse than that. I liked my work and the Chinese people, and I had many good friends by then. But I didn't think I was going to stay forever, and I didn't become a Communist. I was more like Agnes Smedley, who believed in the Chinese people and hated the cruelty that was inflicted on them. I knew Agnes, Anna Louise Strong, and all the YWCA people, though most of them had gone to mainland China by then.

Soon after Pearl Harbor, the Japanese put me into Stanley Internment Camp, and in March five of us, including Eppie [Epstein], escaped in a boat we found on the beach. That's when I really got to know him. We thought we could get to the Communist guerrilla area north of Hong Kong, but instead, we were swept south, so we just went with the tide. We would sail at night and put into land in the morning absolutely exhausted. We slept on the sand. One time some villagers came out and asked what we were doing there. When we told them we'd escaped from Hong Kong, they urged us to go into the hills because the Japanese were on the other side of the island, and their planes might spot us. They're marvelous, the Chinese. They took us into the hills and put us into some caves. They were so poor themselves, all they had to eat was sweet potatoes and sugar, yet they shared with us. Some of us spoke Mandarin, but they spoke Cantonese. We managed to make ourselves understood, however. They kept us there overnight, and the next day we went to another island, where a man took us to a village and put us on a boat to Macao.

Maybe you can help me now, Eppie.

Israel Epstein

We had to go through Japanese lines to get into unoccupied China territory, and we went to Guilin, which is now a very scenic spot for travelers. Elsie stayed there, and the rest of us walked to Chongqing. At that time, walking was the only way you could travel. We would set out at four or five in the morning and walk until evening. We usually covered about thirty miles a day.

Elsie remained in Guilin and worked with the industrial co-operatives there, while I worked as a newspaper correspondent in Chongqing. She joined me in 1943 and we were married. In fact, we were the first couple to get married under the new laws that allowed foreigners to marry without going through their embassies. Before that they had separate laws for foreigners, but when the Japanese came, they did whatever they damned well pleased.

After our marriage I went to Yenan, the Communist area in the north, and Elsie stayed in Chongqing. The Nationalists wouldn't let her go because they were afraid if we both went, we might not come back. So she was a hostage. We made quite a row about it. I was the first writer for the Foreign Correspondents Association to go to Yenan, but they said the trip was too hard for a woman.

Then, in 1944, we decided to go to England and the States. We had to go with a convoy because of the war. We lived in New York, and I worked for the same news agency I'd worked for in China. I also worked at the Office of War Information, and I did various odd jobs. We stayed in the States until 1951, and then we returned to China. By then the liberation had taken place, and we didn't like the United States policy of supporting Chiang Kai-shek. We were quite vocal about it, too.

Soong Ching-ling invited us back to set up *China Reconstructs*. The purpose of the magazine was to tell the outside world the truth about what was going on in China. Soong had great prestige all over the world, and nothing was coming from China except broadcasts and piecemeal news that never got through to the foreign press. And what did get in was so distorted it was as if someone in Hong Kong was looking through the wrong end of a telescope. Our magazine came directly from China. At that time Americans had to go to the post office and fill out a declaration stating they wanted to receive the magazine. Otherwise the post office burned it. Elsie and I moved to Peking, and we worked on the editing and production of the magazine.

We had one of those courtyard houses, which was very comfortable, and later we adopted two Chinese children, one in 1952 and another in 1955. The girl was ten months old, and the boy was only ten days old. The girl's mother had died when she was born, and her father already had five or six children, so he couldn't manage another. It was difficult to adopt a child because they were very careful. Before the liberation children had been treated badly, so the father had to be very clear about wanting his child adopted, and it was the same with our boy.

Our children never learned much English because we were both very, very busy, and they were in school. We left the house at eight in the morning and came back home long after they were asleep. Our housekeeper, who was a very wonderful woman, actually brought them up.

We were arrested during the Cultural Revolution and sent to separate prisons for nearly five years. Our children were sent to farms, and they both learned to drive tractors. They didn't have too bad a time. And I knew it would come out right because I knew the Chinese revolutionaries and the Chinese people. I not only had faith, I was certain.

I think the reason it all happened was that, basically, there was a great desire on the part of many people to push the revolution forward very, very fast. In a revolution sometimes it's disastrous to be too slow, and sometimes it's disastrous to go too fast. Timing is very important. If you have a situation where you can take hold and you don't, that's a very great crime because you've moved too slowly. On the other hand, when you have great responsibility for everything, and sometimes you try to push forward too fast, you make an awful mess. I think that, essentially, is one reason. Another was the terrific development of factionalism, in which factions became sort of ends in themselves instead of keeping to the principle. Both were sure that they were completely correct, and they were also being manipulated at the top by people like the Gang of Four. It was a very bad business.

During the late 1950s, I think Mao had a terrific grasp of the realities of China and the whole revolutionary process—the military, the political, and the social performance. But I think after the 1950s he got a little isolated and wanted to go fast. That was not always the case, because sometimes he went very carefully and slowly, like with the stages of land reform.

He did some marvelous things, and he'll go down in history like George Washington and others. Of course, he was ill during the last ten years of his life.

I think Teddy White's *Time* magazine piece stinks, absolutely stinks. The charge that Mao was insane is nonsense. I know it's not true. At the end of his life he was quite enfeebled and could work only a couple of hours a day. He used to be able to go out and check for himself, but in his last years, he could only attend to what was put in front of him. So who put it in front of him and what was put there is very, very important. Teddy White wrote a thoroughly corrupt book. We knew him in Chongqing when he was working with Anna Jacoby. They wrote *Thunder Out of China* and it was a good book. But if you read *In Search of History*, you will see Teddy in that. He's a terrific climber; he can't stop climbing even when he's on top, and he is pretty well on top. When I say he's corrupt, it's not in the ordinary sense of money because he's got plenty. But he will do anything for a phrase, and he has crazy phrases in there [*Time* article] like saying that China has little history. China has a hell of a lot of history. And saying Mao was insane is incorrect.

He even referred to us as the people who spent four or five years in solitary. Of course, what he didn't say is that people like us feel that the Chinese revolution has been a rather positive thing. It zigzags in various areas as things do in the States, so if he says one thing, he should give the other side. That's just as important—even more important. You could go around Los Angeles or anywhere and make it anything you like, from a glorious place to a sink of crime.

The big problems here now are the results of tremendous problems that evolved for centuries. For example, you solve the problem of mass starvation, so you double your population, and then you have another problem, a very serious one. We also have the problem of balancing light and heavy industry. Before 1949 China had virtually no heavy industry, so of course they didn't have that problem. But the development of heavy industry was a tremendous step forward for one-fourth of the people of the world. Of course, a lot of grinding gears go with it, and that's why we do as we do.

Some of the young Chinese say, "Well, what the hell. Look at Japan, look at the States. Why are we so slow getting there?" They wonder why the Japanese income is seven or ten times higher than the basic Chinese income. But the Chinese income includes a lot of invisible items like very low rent. And now there's a revolution of rising expectations. First everyone wanted a bike and a wristwatch; now everyone wants a television and a washing machine. But the baseline in China is one billion, which means one of those things for every five or six people. That takes time.

Actually, socialism is materialistic, but if you pursue the materialistic without the spiritual, you are not going forward.

CHOLMELEY: I don't think women here fight hard enough for equality.

EPSTEIN: The basic thing is that women were in a very subdued position. They had no property, but since land reform, women got a piece of land like everyone else. In other words, each woman has an independent economic base. Whether she uses it or not is a different matter. It's a little different here from the women's lib movement in the United States. The problems are different. For instance, there's equal pay for equal work, but what is equal work? In the countryside, pushing a plow is very physically taxing. But transplanting rice is physically taxing in another way, though it doesn't require much strength. Are we going to grade those things equally or not? If you tell a man at the plow to go and transplant rice, he'll say, "That's hard."

CHOLMELEY: Heavy work is better paid than light work, but what is light and what is heavy? I think it's quite light work to drive a horse and cart with a load of vegetables, but that's considered heavy physical work. And I think planting rice with your body bent double is heavy physical work. In fact, it's been proven that men can't do it. But still it's considered light physical work and the pay is lower, so women lose out.

(Elsie Fairfax Cholmeley died in Peking on September 24, 1984.)

BEVERLY POLOKOFF

I met Beverly Polokoff in Los Angeles when I was making my China connections. A petite blond woman in her early fifties, she had just signed a contract with the Chinese government to work for a year as an English language polisher (a person who edits the English written by Chinese staff people) for Radio Peking, and was to leave in six weeks.

Polokoff describes herself as a loner, "never afraid to pick up and do things on my own." She attended the University of Missouri for two-and-a-half years as a sociology major, dropping out when she became engaged to marry a fellow student. Though the engagement was broken, she never went back. Instead she began doing public relations for political campaigns and nonprofit organizations.

In 1960 she moved to Los Angeles, was married for a short time, and continued working as a media buyer and publicist for liberal political candidates and organizations such as Alternative Energy, a group opposed to the construction of nuclear power plants. She was also development director for KPFK, a noncommercial radio station in Los Angeles, a member of the city's Commission on the Status of Women, and on the paid staff of the U.S.-China People's Friendship Association (USCPFA).

Polokoff and I got together again in my hotel room soon after I arrived in Peking. She had been in China only two months.

An Exciting Life

I began doing some volunteer work for the U.S.-China People's Friendship Association in the early 1970s. I was dating someone who was active with them, and that's an embarrassing admission. Becoming involved with something because of a man you're dating is not exactly what we feminists usually do. But prior to that I really didn't know very much about the People's Republic of China because our country had been cut off from them for so many years. It was almost as if one quarter of the world's population didn't exist.

Then in 1974 Han Suyin attended the USCPFA convention in Los Angeles, and I arranged a press conference for her. But, though many media people attended, none of them reported on it. I was also shocked by the behavior of the reporters who were there. They were very cynical. Even though Han Suyin is a respected writer and had gone back to China many times after the liberation, they said she was brainwashed, that she hadn't really seen the things she talked about. They would not admit that anything positive was happening in China. That piqued my interest, but still I didn't become active with USCPFA until 1977.

I'd arranged a number of press conferences by then, and they wanted to repay me by giving me an opportunity to go to China. I was to pay my own way, but their tour was inexpensive and about the only way anyone could go at the time.

There was a long delay in getting a passport, and it was also difficult to get an entry visa from the Chinese government. In 1972, after Nixon visited and the Shanghai Communiqué was signed, we had a relationship with China, so I don't think there was any way our government could prohibit an American citizen from going.

At any rate, I went. China was such an unknown to me, I didn't know what to expect as far as hotels, food, sanitary conditions, anything. There were twenty-four people on that trip, all members of USCPFA, but I hadn't met any of them before because I was the only one from the Los Angeles chapter. It was a very intensive tour. They had scheduled things to do morning, noon, and night, but we had a good leader.

We visited a May 7 Cadre School, which few foreigners ever saw. Supposedly the people were there for re-education. Actually they'd been sent to the countryside to farm during the Cultural Revolution. Even though the Gang of Four had been smashed by then, those schools were still operating. We were shown the whole place—the dormitory, the dining room, how they lived and worked—and they said that people really looked forward to going there because they wanted to be close to the peasants who were producing the food. We had no reason not to believe them because we couldn't talk to anyone there; they didn't speak English. We saw them playing basketball and it looked like a summer camp. Now I find that many of the people working at Radio Beijing [Peking] were sent to those schools, and, of course, they were not what we'd been told.

When I came back to the United States, I was offered a job with USCPFA as assistant director of tours in charge of public relations and advertising, so I went to work for them.

I fell in love with something in China, but didn't know exactly what. I guess it was really the people. They looked so relaxed and healthy, and it seemed they had a purpose, a contentment. China appealed to my political and humanist ideas. Here was a country with a billion people trying to equalize living standards. It was a very poor living standard, but it was the same for everyone. I think what impressed me most was that people were not exploited; everyone was committed to helping everyone else. I know I was terribly naive, but I didn't see any warts. I thought everything was wonderful and beautiful, a perfect society. They were providing medical care, housing, clothing, and education for a billion people, most of whom had been in very dire circumstances before liberation.

We would sit there and cry with them. Some had been beggars whose children, sisters, and brothers had starved to death. And there they were with an apartment—tiny, but they had a place to live, food, and clothing. So I saw only the wonderful things, and I wasn't looking for anything wrong. Actually, I still feel that way, and I'm probably still naive, even though I know now what happened to people during the Cultural Revolution. It was pretty terrible for them, especially for the intellectuals, yet they're not bitter. They don't want to talk about how bad it was; they just don't want it to happen again. Their attitude is, it's over, and we're moving forward.

But China lost a great deal during those ten years, a whole generation of technological and scientific advancement, and it's hard to catch up because the other countries are moving ahead so fast. The Chinese were so closed off from the world I don't think they realized how far behind they were getting. Of course, even if they had, I don't think it would have made a difference.

I visited again in 1979, 1980, and 1981, and on those trips I was tour leader for groups of journalists hosted by *Xinhua*, the Chinese news service. Finally I began to realize that China was becoming very important to me—that one reason I was working was to support my trips. And by then I had a couple of friends who had gone there to work as foreign experts. So I put the word out that I was interested in doing the same thing, and I found out that *Women of China*, the magazine published by the All China Women's Federation, needed a language polisher. I wrote and applied, but they had already hired someone else. I was devastated. Then some good friends in China took my resumé around. One was a reporter for the *People's Daily* who had been stationed in the United States for two years, and he thought I'd be great. When he found that Radio Beijing needed another English polisher, he contacted me immediately. They inquired into my background and offered me the job.

It was funny because they sent me a letter in March 1983, which I never received, and a telegram in April: "Please respond to our March letter regarding your availability for one to two years." I didn't know if they'd offered me a job or just wanted to know if I was available. So I called a friend at the Chinese Consulate, and she told me to just wire, "Gladly accept job, pending receipt of details," which I did. One night I got a phone call from someone at Foreign Languages Press, who told me that Radio Beijing just wanted me to know that things were moving along and not to worry. Then I received a call from the Chinese Consulate in San Francisco. They had a two-page message out- lining the details of the job, and wanted to know whether I agreed to all the conditions. I agreed to everything. I couldn't think of anything they would ask that I wouldn't agree to.

They just stated the working hours, the salary, my duties, and that they would provide me with a ticket. At the end of the year, if both parties agreed to continue the arrangement, they would pay my expenses home for a one-month leave. They also wanted a doctor's certificate confirming that I was in good health and had no communicable diseases, and I had to send four pictures of myself. Then things happened very rapidly.

Actually, I was fortunate because they gave me three months' notice, and often they give only a month. I had to sell my car, lease my condominium, find a home for my dog, and get all my furniture into storage. My life was in a turmoil for the next three months.

Most of my friends and relatives were quite surprised and kept asking why I wanted to live in China. My family knew by then that I was quite attached to China, but, of course, they had some anxiety about what my life there would be like and whether I'd be happy. Once I made up my mind, I knew it was right; I had no feelings of uncertainty. But I didn't cut my ties. I'm only committed for one year, and by then I should know whether I want to spend the rest of my life in China.

Although my living quarters here are certainly not as luxurious, the people I'm surrounded by are incredible. They come from every country in the world, and they're very friendly. And everyone I work with speaks English, so it's not as if I'm in the countryside, where I can't communicate.

I live in the Foreign Experts Building, which is right on the grounds of the Ministry of Radio and Television, my employer. My division is called Radio Beijing, but some of the foreign experts work for Central Television and other communications offices. We are isolated to the extent that no Chinese live in our building. However, right next to us are some Chinese who also work for the same ministry. As a matter of fact, the building has a wing at each end, one for foreigners and one for Chinese, and though there are no connecting doors, we're not shut off. When I come home each evening, I usually stop for a few minutes and play with the Chinese children who live in that wing. So I don't feel segregated. Of course, you can't just go out and find an apartment building where Chinese live. What would you do when you got there?

I really don't feel isolated. I shop at the friendship stores [open only to foreigners] and Chinese stores. When I go out, I take my little dictionary and point to the word I need in Chinese, but mostly I just make gestures like I'm doing a little charade. And I often find someone who speaks English. Many Chinese are learning that language now, and they love to practice. So I feel as if I'm with the Chinese a lot.

They seem to charge a little more at the friendship stores, but it's difficult to compare because they don't have the same brands. It's not very much more, and my salary is very high by Chinese standards. Foreign experts make an incredible salary compared to the Chinese. Where I work the starting salary for the Chinese is about one-tenth of what they pay me, but they live very comfortably. Some of my Chinese co-workers have invited me to their homes, and most of them have television sets. Some even have refrigerators and washing machines. Their rent is very low, and usually several family members are working. Their only big expense is food, so they can even save money.

I've noticed only two things that must be very hard for the Chinese. One is the tiny living quarters, where a family of three or four lives in one room and shares the kitchen and bathroom with another family. The other is queuing up every day at the food stores. They can't just go into a supermarket and buy fish, meat, eggs, and produce. They have to queue up for everything. At the friendship stores, we can just go to the grocery section and buy everything in that one department, and it's never crowded. So life is much easier for foreigners. The Chinese spend a great deal of their time shopping, cooking, and cleaning, and they also work long hours.

I get up at 6:30 A.M., and right now I eat in the building dining room because I don't have cooking facilities yet. As soon as my hotplate and refrigerator arrive, I'll be able to cook in my rooms. I'm supposed to work from 8 to 11:30, but from 11:30 until noon I usually coach one of the Chinese radio announcers in English. Then I'm home for lunch from noon to 2, and I'm also supposed to rest, but I'm usually busy doing things. I haven't gotten into that napping routine yet.

In the afternoon my hours are from 2 to 5:30, but I also polish the evening news, so sometimes I'm there until 6:30 or 7. Then I go back to my building and eat in the dining room, and there's so much to do in the evening I never seem to have time to finish everything. I have many friends in the building, so we visit or I do some reading. I usually listen to the news broadcast to hear how it sounds and find out if I can do a better job the next time. And there are always clothes to wash and things to dust or sew. I also work Saturdays from 8 to noon.

Most Chinese I work with are there all day Saturday, but foreigners are supposed to work only half a day; I'm the only one who comes back. I work about ten to fifteen hours a week more than I have to. In fact, when I asked to be evaluated on how I was doing, they kept repeating, "Everyone thinks you are working too hard." But I enjoy it. Polishing includes correcting the grammar and the style; taking out what they call Chinglish and making it sound the way it would in an English-speaking country. For example, a term like *rectification campaign* would be meaningless to foreigners, so we put in a little explanation. My job is catching those things and making the news easier to listen to.

I'm also finding out how little Americans know about international relations. Working here, I've discovered countries I never even knew existed, countries like Gabon in Africa. The Chinese I work with know them all. I don't know if that's because Americans are complacent, or because we don't think very much in terms of government-to-government or people-to-people relations. The Chinese have differences with governments, but not with people. They feel that people throughout the world are their friends.

The most shocking thing is not having a telephone. And I'm disappointed in myself for not having learned more Chinese. I thought once I got here that it would just sort of happen by osmosis, but I know very few more words now than when I arrived two months ago. It's a very difficult language for me to learn; totally different from French, Spanish, or any of the Romance languages. I do know the street names, so I can get off the bus when my street is called. I haven't been lost once. I depend on buses because I can't balance a bicycle, and though cabs are inexpensive, you can't just go out on the street and hail one. You have to go to a hotel where you know there's a cab stand, or to a friendship store. But the bus transportation is good. Buses are very crowded, so you have to shove your way on and off, but people are constantly trying to give me their seat, even people older than I am, because I'm a foreign friend.

My housing is a bit disappointing, but I didn't expect anything as luxurious as I had in the United States. And I didn't anticipate a food problem. Our dining room does not have good food, but there's a hotel nearby where they have very good Chinese and Western restaurants, so I eat there sometimes. Having come from California, I'm also not used to the cold winters. Neither my office nor my apartment is heated properly, so probably the cold will bother me more than I anticipated. And they don't have air-conditioning, so I think I'll take my home leave in the summer.

But I'm really very happy. My life is exciting, and I think working in the newsroom makes it even more exciting.

(Polokoff did return to Los Angles for a month in July 1984. We had dinner together, and I found that after living in China for a year, she had not lost her enthusiasm but was still not committing herself to spending the rest of her life there. She also told me that things were changing very rapidly in Peking, especially the appearance of the women. She was noticing many more women who had their hair curled and were wearing makeup and brighter colors, and skirts instead of pants.)

REFLECTIONS

After almost two years, my mind is still filled with them—the women of China. I know what Beverly Polokoff meant when she said, "I fell in love with something . . . I guess it was really the people."

Though I traveled through a considerable part of China and interviewed many women representing a wide variety of backgrounds and interests, I'm still far from being an expert. I did, however, have an experience available to few Americans, and I want to share some observations about China and Chinese women.

No American woman who reads this book could fail to identify closely with the women of China. Life in the People's Republic is very different from life in the United States, but in many ways the problems for women in both countries are similar. The stereotypes still exist in both societies, "the old feudal ideas," as the Chinese say.

Some years ago I was hired as a writer by a large organization. At the time I was divorced and supporting two children. Four years later, when I resigned, I discovered that a man who had been hired on the same day for the same work had received a starting salary of $1,000 a year more than mine. When I confronted my employer, a man of strong social conscience, he explained that my male counterpart had a wife and child to support. He admitted he had operated on the premise that I would surely marry again and have a husband to support me.

American women now have recourse through the Equal Pay Act of 1963 and Title VII of the Civil Rights Act of 1964, which established commissions to investigate complaints of discrimination in the area of employment. But we are still confronted with the problem. Statistics show that women and minorities are the last to be hired and the first to be fired. Fear of retribution, as well as the lengthy and cumbersome legal process, make them reluctant to file complaints.

There are also employers, both male and female, who hire women in preference to men. This may seem a positive action, but in many cases it's yet another form of exploitation. Women have fewer employment opportunities, hence they will often work for less money.

A *Los Angeles Times* poll, published in September 1984, revealed that 54 percent of the women in the United States now hold full-time jobs, yet they earn only fifty-nine cents for every dollar earned by men.

Chinese women also face job discrimination. Men are hired in preference to women, a practice based on the premise that women will take more time off for child and household responsibilities. The *Times* poll showed that in the United States the premise is very real, that women "feel to some extent that they must try to balance their responsibilities on the job with their duties at home," and that "women are more likely than men to take time off for child rearing—bearing out the beliefs of some employers that women are less committed to their careers, a notion that slows women's advancement."

But one of the greatest problems for Chinese women is the still-prevalent perception that certain jobs are suitable for males or females on the basis of mental aptitude or physical strength.

For the great mass of workers, salaries are set by the government, using the guideline of heavy or light physical labor. But as Elsie Cholmeley asked, "What is light and what is heavy work?" Is planting a rice field, primarily women's work in China—and, incidentally, brutal backbreaking labor—less physically taxing than driving a horse cart filled with produce, generally a job category filled by men? The female director of a textile mill believes that, because their hands are smaller, women can do delicate work better than men. A farm leader said that the women in their factories earn less than men because women do lighter work. The head of the preschool education department at a large university said that women are better suited than men for teaching young children. Perhaps most shocking of all was the woman from Wuhan University's foreign office, who firmly believes that men are *inherently* more capable than women in the sciences. I don't know why I was so shocked: I've heard American women make similar remarks.

In the area of job penetration, Americans have probably advanced further than the Chinese. Many new fields of endeavor have been opened to American women in recent years—police work, fire fighting, aeronautics, space travel, and other jobs formerly limited to men. This happened largely as a result of intense lobbying and legal actions brought by privately supported women's rights groups, such as the National Organization for Women, founded in 1966—a force that does not exist in China.

Early on the Communists recognized that true equality for women had to begin with economic equality. In principle—and often in deed—the Chinese government supports equal education and job opportunities, socialization of housework, and child-care facilities. To implement those goals, the All China Women's Federation was established. But, although the federation has in many ways been an effective instrument, it is under government control and thus conforms to the vagaries of government policy. Under China's system, women do not have the right to organize private groups, to petition their government, or bring legal actions. The practice of bringing pressure to bear on the government itself, common in the United States, is difficult, if not impossible, question in the People's Republic.

Chinese women have made greater strides toward equality during their thirty-five years under Communism than ever before in the history of that ancient nation. But as women's federation leader Lei Jieqiong pointed out in 1983, although women have come a long way, they occupy only 2 percent of the nation's top leadership positions. American women are essentially in the same boat. According to the United States Census Bureau, by 1980 women held 30.5 percent of the middle-management positions, as compared to 18.5 percent in 1970, but like their Chinese sisters they were still a small minority in the top power circles. Only one of the 500 largest corporations in the United States was run by a woman, and the United States Congress included only 4.5 percent women.

For both American and Chinese women the greatest obstacle is the old stereotypes—how large segments of the society view women and, equally important, how they view themselves. It is Phyllis Schlafly's large and highly vocal women's organization, Stop ERA, that has so far been successful in blocking the Equal Rights Amendment to the United States Constitution. Also, according to the *Los Angeles Times* poll, women by an overwhelming majority still prefer to work for men rather than women. The reasons: They believe women managers tend to push women around—that they are less effective supervisors and are also less fair than men. Thus women are often their own worst enemies, providing ammunition to males already reluctant to promote women.

This fact was further demonstrated during the 1984 national election campaigns. In an historic first, the Democratic Party nominated a woman, United States Congresswoman Geraldine Ferraro, as the party's vice presidential candidate. The event was hailed by women activists as a major breakthrough for women in politics with predictions that the Ferraro candidacy would spawn enthusiasm among women voters and help elect a large number of female candidates that year. But polls over the next few months revealed that the majority of female voters did not approve of a woman vice president and election results showed that most women candidates got disappointingly weak support from female voters.

Los Angeles Times political writer Sara Fritz reported that many female candidates complained of obstacles like "intense scrutiny of family finances, fierce opposition from antiabortion groups, and bias in the news media, obstacles encountered to a much lesser extent by male candidates . . . 'At this rate,' said Stephanie Solien, executive director of the Women's Campaign Fund, 'it's going to take 410 years for women to achieve equal representation with men.' "

It's difficult for a visiting American to understand or accept the unrelenting presence of government and government policy that colors every aspect of the China experience—the restrictions on basic human freedoms such as the right to choose one's job or place of residence, the right to travel, the right to speak freely, the right to assemble—in fact, all the freedoms guaranteed in a democratic society. Tien Fan said that the Chinese are not ready for democracy, that freedom would mean chaos. With more than a billion people, most of them living under crowded, uncomfortable conditions, perhaps these restrictions are necessary, as necessary as the one-child-per-family rule. Perhaps Tien is right. Perhaps China, in this period of her history, could not solve her enormous problems under a democratic system of government. But what a price to pay! Freedom is the one sacrifice I would find most difficult to make.

How many Chinese hunger for freedom, I don't know and they can't say. The chasm between my political experience and theirs is so deep that I find it impossible to put myself in their place, to see the world as they see it, to dream their dreams. But what a wonderful people they are! And what a wonderful experience to be a "foreign friend."

BIBLIOGRAPHY

Bernstein, Richard. *From the Center of the Earth*. Boston: Little, Brown, 1982.

Bonavia, David. *The Chinese*. New York: Penguin Books Ltd., 1980.

Butterfield, Fox. *China: Alive in the Bitter Sea*. New York: Times Books, 1982.

Croll, Elisabeth. *Feminism and Socialism in China*. London: Routledge and Kegan Paul Ltd., 1978.

Eunson, Roby. *Mao Tse-tung*. New York: Franklin Watts, Inc., 1973.

Eunson, Roby. *The Soong Sisters*. New York: Franklin Watts, Inc., 1975.

Garside, Roger. *Coming Alive: China After Mao*. New York: McGraw Hill, 1982.

Kingston, Maxine Hong. *The Woman Warrior*. New York: Alfred A. Knopf, 1976.

——————. *China Men*. New York: Ballantine Books, 1981.

Lord, Bette Bao. *Spring Moon*. New York: Harper and Row, 1981.

Mathews, Jay and Linda. *One Billion: A China Chronicle*. New York: Random House, 1983.

Moseley, George. *China Since 1911*. New York: Harper and Row, Inc., 1970.

Mosher, Steven W. *Broken Earth: the Rural Chinese*. New York-London: The Free Press, a division of Macmillan, 1983.

Seidel, Ruth. *Women and Child Care in China*. New York: Penguin Books, 1973.

Suyin, Han. *My House Has Two Doors*. New York: Putnam, 1980.

White, Theodore. *In Search of History*. New York: Harper and Row, Inc., 1978.

Witke, Roxane and Margery Wolf, editors. *Women in Chinese Society*. California: Stanford University Press, 1975.

BOOKS PUBLISHED
IN CHINA

Gu Hua. *A Small Town Called Hibiscus*. Beijing: Panda Books, 1983.

Liu Xinwu, Wang Meng & others. *Prize-Winning Stories From China*. Beijing: Foreign Languages Press, 1978–1979.

Pa Chin. Translated by Sidney Shapiro. *The Family*. Beijing: Foreign Languages Press, 1978.

Shapiro, Sidney, *An American in China*. Beijing: New World Press, 1979.

Su Wenming, ed. *Life at the Grassroots*. Beijing: Beijing Review, 1981.

——————. *From Youth to Retirement*. Beijing: Beijing Review, 1982.

Twenty Authors From Abroad, Living in China. Beijing: New World Press, 1979.

INDEX